THE TANDOOR MURDER

Maxwell Pereira is one of India's best-known (retired) cops, winner of gallantry awards, and with a reputation for honesty and courage. He is now a familiar face on television debates.

Praise for *The Tandoor Murder*

'*The Tandoor Murder* puts back the spunk into publishing's favourite cliché: page-turner. The pace of Pereira's story-telling, his reconstruction of the crime scene and the recounting of the progress of the investigation will keep the reader breathless.'
Mint Lounge

'[A] nail-biting read—as intriguing as novels by Stephen King and Agatha Christie—mainly because of the hair-raising series of events that are unveiled for the readers. ... Pereira has carefully delineated nuggets of information as he lets us witness how the policing and political systems work in our country.'
Business Standard

'[A] vivid, detailed, racy memoir of the "tandoor murder" that shook the conscience of the nation in 1995. ... The book offers a ringside view of the grisly Naina Sahini case. ... But, it is not voyeuristic. It is gentle—candid and empathetic.'
The Week

'For those who did not follow the case closely or those who were too young to, at the time, *The Tandoor Murder* is a nail-biting thriller. For those who followed the case, it helps bust a few myths and provides perspective on why getting justice, in what could be called an open-and-shut case, sometimes takes years.'
The Indian Express

THE TANDOOR MURDER

THE CRIME THAT SHOOK THE NATION AND BROUGHT A GOVERNMENT TO ITS KNEES

Maxwell Pereira

First published in hardback by Context, an imprint of Westland Publications Private Limited, in 2018

Published in paperback by Westland Books, a division of Nasadiya Technologies Private Limited, in 2023

No. 269/2B, First Floor, 'Irai Arul', Vimalraj Street, Nethaji Nagar, Allappakkam Main Road, Maduravoyal, Chennai 600095

Westland and the Westland logo are the trademarks of Nasadiya Technologies Private Limited, or its affiliates.

Copyright © Maxwell Periera, 2018

Maxwell Periera asserts the moral right to be identified as the author of this work.

ISBN: 9789395767828

10 9 8 7 6 5 4 3 2 1

The views and opinions expressed in this work are the author's own and the facts are as reported by him, and the publisher is in no way liable for the same.

All rights reserved

Typeset by Jojy Philip
Printed at Gopsons Paper Pvt. Ltd, Noida

No part of this book may be reproduced, or stored in a retrieval system, or transmitted in any form or by any means, electronic, mechanical, photocopying, recording, or otherwise, without express written permission of the publisher.

To law enforcement officers across the world,
whose mistakes get highlighted while their untiring
work rarely gets recognition or appreciation.

Contents

1.	Tandoori Night	1
2.	Kunju's Discovery	11
3.	Twenty-four Hours	21
4.	The Crime Scene	34
5.	Family Trouble	45
6.	Murder Most Foul	50
7.	The Earth Shakes	57
8.	Getaway	67
9.	Medical Complications	79
10.	Opening Gambit	92
11.	The Noose Draws Tight	103
12.	The Circus Comes to Town	123
13.	Contrition and Recriminations	138
14.	Corpus of Evidence	154
15.	Ravi Naina Sahni	167
16.	Hanging the Man	177
17.	Let the Games Begin	195
18.	Trials and Intrigues	209

19.	Wheels of Justice	227
20.	On With the Motley	234
21.	Judgement	248
22.	Aftermath	268
	Endnotes	276
	Acknowledgements	290

1

Tandoori Night

It was a steamy Sunday night. Summer and monsoon were locked in their yearly contest for the city, and most people had retreated to the comfort of fans, desert air coolers and air conditioners. Delhi was as quiet as it could get, given the incessant growl of traffic that lulls you to sleep if you've lived here long enough. After three decades in the city, I could sleep through pretty much anything. Except the shrill ring of the telephone – a flattish, cherry-red instrument which sat malevolently by my bedside, threatening to disrupt my sleep most nights.[1] This night was no exception. The phone screeched in my ear, jerking me awake.

The life of a policeman revolves around the telephone. You cannot afford to ignore it, regardless of where you are – at the office, in your car, in the loo, at a party or even a PTA meeting – and whatever you are doing – necking, showering, crapping, sweating in a sauna or sitting atop the Qutb Minar. Somebody, somewhere in his misbegotten wisdom decided a cop in India should never be off duty. Must have been a bureaucrat.

Why is it that Indians have a fetish for adding home telephone numbers to their business cards? The more the merrier, as if a string of numbers adds up to an elevated social status. Nowhere else in the world is Joe Public or Aam Ram encouraged to call a … well, public servant, at home. Here, it's his god- or government-given right to expect a police officer to be available round the clock. It was now past

1 a.m. Fighting the urge to stifle the annoying ring with a pillow, I picked up the receiver.

'Hello …?'

'Sorry to disturb you, sir. But there is something that needs to be in your knowledge.'

It was Deputy Commissioner of Police (DCP)[2] New Delhi, Aditya Arya. As fine a cop as anyone could wish for, but not someone I wanted to chat idly with at 1 a.m. Surely he knew better than to wake me up for a minor traffic violation.

'What's happened?' I snapped.

'There's been an attempt to burn a body in a tandoor,'[3] he replied instantly.

It took a couple of seconds for me to digest this. The man, I realised, was out of his mind and I told him so.

'What? Are you crazy? What body? Whose body? And where? Where are you?'

'I'm at Yatri Niwas, sir. There's a restaurant here, the Bagiya. It's outside the main hotel building, in the garden area. I am speaking to you from the spot. Perhaps you'd like to come right away, sir.'

Right away, my boy. You can bet your epaulettes I'll be there right away. Yatri Niwas was just 500 yards down the road from where I lived on Ashoka Road. 'Uh-huh,' I grunted.

Trying to make sense of what Aditya had just told me, I rolled off the bed and into my trousers with the kind of practised, gymnastic motion that comes from years of being dragged out of bed at odd hours by odd people, whose usual idea of a good time is hurting others – especially police officers.

Before I'd finished buttoning my shirt, the doorbell rang. My official Ambassador car, its engine revving, was at the gate. Trying to prove himself the kind of pro he was, Aditya must have got someone to inform my driver even before he called me.

Something between a curse and a resigned sigh escaped my lips, even as I was on my way.

Constable Abdul Nazeer Kunju of Connaught Place police station, Delhi, was a long way from home. A soft-spoken, intense young man in his late twenties, Kunju walked a beat some 2,000 km from his home state, Kerala, which flanks the southernmost west coast of peninsular India. His home state is a lush, fecund land, bordered by the Arabian Sea and boasting an intellectual heritage as rich as its trading and agriculture. Kerala's yield of proud, adaptable people has ventured forth from the comfort of 'God's own country', as it is popularly known in India, to every corner of the subcontinent. Indeed, Keralites can be found plying their trade from the Middle East to Middle America, and everywhere in between.

Delhi Police has always endeavoured to see that people from different parts of the country are represented in its ranks, and Malayalis are part of its diverse, talented force. I have often pondered, though, the factors that brought Constable Abdul Nazeer Kunju, a man did his work without fear or favour – and one eminently capable of rising to a challenge – to the overnight Western Court–Janpath beat on Sunday, 2 July 1995.

There was, as is so often the case with significant events, at least one quirk of fate on the night in question: the ill health of Kunju's colleague, and a change in roster to compensate for it. Kunju had started his working day at 4 a.m. by attending a demolition at the Western Courts. He expected to spend the evening with his wife and three-day-old baby daughter, but at the end of a gruelling patrol, he was told his counterpart for the next shift had reported sick. Kunju would have to handle the overnight beat from 11 p.m. to 5 a.m. He wouldn't be making it back home that night.

Being assigned extra shifts at short notice, like callouts in the middle of the night, is an unavoidable facet of a policeman's life. Keeping the peace and criminals in check cannot wait as other work may. Kunju didn't complain. He attended his evening briefing and met Home Guard Chander Pal, a decent, dependable local who would be his partner for the beat.

Delhi Home Guards were brought into the force in the early

1960s to compensate for a lack of police manpower in the city and to provide employment for local youth. Ostensibly volunteers, these home guards assist in keeping the peace, fire-fighting, bringing relief in disasters and civic emergencies and helping traffic regulation and law enforcement agencies.

In practice, this mostly means being an adjunct to a Delhi Police constable on patrols; a home guard is, for all intents and purposes, a junior constable with limited authority. And for all the high-minded sentiment of 'volunteer' duty, home guards like Chander Pal were dependent on a meagre daily stipend for their livelihood. Most were aspiring constables, serving in the Delhi Home Guards only because it was more accessible than the capital's police force.

This is not to say that a police constable's job is in any way enviable. Far from it. Too seldom do we spare a thought for honest, diligent beat officers like Constable Kunju and Home Guard Chander Pal, and if we did, it would be hard for us not to sympathise. Most middle-class Indians would consider a police constable's job thankless, dangerous and woefully underpaid, given the exigencies of the work and the hardships of patrolling.

A constable's salary is less than that of a base-level bank clerk, but unlike a clerk, who is permanently ensconced in a safe, air-conditioned office, a constable beats the pavement in all kinds of weather and puts himself in harm's way on a regular basis. And while a bank clerk's duties can be clearly delineated in the neat black-and-white confines of a duty statement, the true demands of a constable's job defy codification and, at times, reasonableness.

A beat constable, like other members of the force, is expected to be part lawyer, part mediator, part social worker, and a full-fledged law enforcer. He is expected to be conversant with the nuances of criminal law and apply the powers of arrest with due discretion and tact. Despite his formidable everyday workload, he is routinely called upon to settle all kinds of local disputes, in addition to his regular work. In a country of manifold beliefs and countless ethnicities, this means the constable has to rely more heavily on the power of persuasion than the threat of force – even when force may be warranted.

Kunju and Chander Pal were to spend six hours patrolling the Western Court–Janpath beat together on that fateful Sunday evening/Monday morning. The beat was bounded by Ashoka Road, starting from the roundabout of Ashoka Road, past the Windsor Place roundabout and Janpath, which divides Eastern Court and Western Court, up to the traffic light adjacent to Imperial Hotel. It follows Jantar Mantar Road, including the area encompassing Janpath Hotel, Imperial Hotel, Kanishka Hotel, Ashok Yatri Niwas and other buildings, as well as some servants' quarters, two or three guesthouses, small shops and a kiosk. Close to the corridors of power, it is usually a fairly quiet beat, and Sunday nights, the end of India's day of rest, are usually uneventful.

Constable Abdul Nazeer Kunju and Home Guard Chander Pal set off at 11 p.m., on 2 July 1995, from the Connaught Place police station, which was at the time temporarily accommodated in the Public Works Department hutments near Hanuman Mandir on Bhagwan Das Marg. The pair wore summer khaki uniforms: trousers with short-sleeved shirts and berets. Aside from his 'DHG' shoulder badges and the absence of a lathi, the home guard was virtually indistinguishable from his constable colleague at a distance.

It would astonish many a beat policeman elsewhere in the world, who is usually girded with a hefty duty belt carrying a radio, a truncheon, a set of handcuffs, a service revolver or an automatic pistol and ammunition – these days, even a taser or pepper spray – to know how lightly equipped Kunju and Chander Pal were for their patrol. As Kunju had mistakenly left his wireless set behind at the police post in Janpath that morning, the pair was armed with just one lathi – and a notebook and a pen.

Firearms are not a prominent feature of law enforcement in India; they are carried only by officers of the ranks of assistant sub-inspector and above. I am happy to say I never carried a firearm in my thirty-five years in the force: my 'gun man' carried my weapon for me. One can only hope that the system remains effective without the regular use of firearms. The events that transpired on the Western Court–Janpath beat on the evening of 2 July 1995 would suggest that an able, determined law-enforcement officer can, except in the most extreme situations, fulfil his duty to the Indian public and the force without resorting to guns.

Around 11.25 p.m., Kunju and Chander Pal were patrolling on Ashoka Road. As they approached Ashok Yatri Niwas, Kunju spotted tongues of fire leaping above some adjacent buildings and into the night sky. Worried that this could be the start of a major fire, the pair hastened to investigate. Kunju strode towards the main entry gate of Yatri Niwas, heading to the front of the Bagiya Barbeque restaurant on the left, just inside the main entry gate of the hotel. He could see the flames were coming from the rear kitchen area of the Bagiya. At the entrance, a uniformed security guard stopped him and explained that the fire, he had already been informed, was caused by some waste paper and cardboard that had been set ablaze near the outdoor tandoor. There was nothing to worry about, the guard assured him – all was under control. Satisfied, Constable Kunju and Home Guard Chander Pal walked away towards Janpath Lane.

As they started, Anaro Devi, a middle-aged vegetable vendor who usually displayed her produce beside the Mother Dairy milk booth at the entrance to the lane from Ashoka Road, came scurrying to them.

'*Hotel mein aag lag gayi, aag lag gayi!* (There is a fire in the hotel!),' Anaro said, her voice quivering with fear. She had already caught the attention of a couple of men nearby, and they were also raising the alarm.

For Kunju, the seriousness of the situation was now as apparent as the size of the fire. Clearly visible from the lane, the blaze seemed to be out of hand, its intensity quite beyond any simple burning of rubbish. Reaching some thirty or thirty-five feet, high above the outer wall of the Bagiya on the Janpath Lane side, the angry flames were sending thick plumes of white smoke into the Delhi sky. Kunju and Chander strode back to the entrance of the closed restaurant.

Kunju was cursing quietly. 'These idiots are trying to burn the whole bloody hotel down.'

This time, Kunju proceeded past the hotel entrance and to the canvas screen in front of the Bagiya Barbeque. As he peeled back the screen and peered into the darkened restaurant, he was met by a thin man, perhaps in his late twenties or early thirties, around 5'10" in height and dressed in a white kurta.

'*Purana poster jala rahe hain* (just burning some old posters),' he told Kunju casually. The fire, he said, was under control. Adequate precautionary steps were being taken, there was no cause for concern.

Constable Kunju was anything but convinced. Leaving Chander Pal near the hotel, he hurried to the nearby PCO[4] to raise an alarm. Finding it closed, he jogged to the police picket at the rear of the Western Court[5] complex, a couple of hundred metres away. There, he flashed an urgent wireless report of the fire to the Connaught Place Police Station and telephoned the Police Control Room (PCR) and the fire brigade, asking for immediate assistance.

Kunju then hurried back to the hotel. To his dismay, he saw that the blaze had intensified in his absence and smoke was billowing high above the hotel complex. He stormed to the entrance of the restaurant with Chander in tow and bluntly demanded admission to enter and inspect the fire.

Again, the men at the restaurant barred his entry. But this time, he would not be deterred. After feigning retreat from the Bagiya, Kunju and Chander Pal shared some furtive words as they walked away together from the front of the hotel.

'*Lagta hai ye paagal log aag se khel rahe hain* (Seems like these bloody fools are playing with fire),' Kunju muttered agitatedly to Chander Pal.

'*Chalo, doosra rasta dhoond lete hain* (Okay, let's find another way)!'

The pair dashed along Janpath Lane and without pause clambered over the seven-foot-high wall at the rear of the restaurant. Pushing aside the bamboo-screen fencing, Kunju gained access to the canopied rear of the garden restaurant. Then they made a beeline for the fire.

The fire was utterly incongruous and quite out of proportion in the kitchen. Fuelled by wooden logs, planks and other material that was piled atop the tandoor, it raged furiously. A slim man, the one who had earlier fobbed off Kunju as he peered past the screen at the front of the Bagiya, was stoking the flames with the help of wooden beams and bamboo poles. Another man, wearing a blue printed shirt, and a well-built youngster stood nearby. Further away, next to the canvas screen at the entrance of the hotel, stood another, solidly built man in white kurta pyjama. The men seemed quite oblivious to the foul odour emanating from the flames.

'Don't you know your playing with fire could burn the whole hotel down?' Kunju yelled at the man stoking the blaze.

At this, the firebug told the constable that he was a Congress party worker and was simply burning old posters, banners and waste paper. Unfazed by this mention of the governing party, Kunju quickly cast around for a bucket. Perhaps here the young constable began to distinguish himself in earnest. Many lesser men would have wilted at the mere allusion of a political connection, especially to the mighty Congress party, and sidled away after issuing a gentle caution about fire safety. Kunju, however, was undeterred, and alarmed at the veritable bonfire he was faced with. He and Chander Pal grabbed whatever buckets and vessels they could find, filled them from a kitchen tap and began dousing the flames.

Sub-inspector Rajesh Kumar, PCR Head Constable Majid Khan and Constable Rajbir Singh arrived on the scene just as Kunju and Chander Pal were working to subdue the fire. Evidently, no one had the audacity to send a sub-inspector on his way as they had tried to do with a constable a little while ago. Two security guards from the main hotel accompanied Rajesh and his two constables into the restaurant. They all joined Kunju in quelling the blaze. Within minutes, it was extinguished.

The soaring flames had already set some plastic-coated overhead cables alight, however. Taking the cause of this mischief with them – or, at least, the man who appeared to be the cause – Kunju, Sub-inspector Rajesh Kumar and the guards from the main hotel went to investigate the extent of damage to the cables, and to ascertain if the fire had spread to the first floor of the building. They proceeded to the main lobby of Yatri Niwas leading towards the Coconut Grove restaurant. They went up two flights of stairs and onto the lower split-level first-floor terrace overlooking the Bagiya complex.

Looking for the wires that had caught fire, Constable Kunju peered over the edge of the mezzanine roof, only to be met with a blast of scorched air and fetid smoke rising from below. To his astonishment, he saw that the fire above the tandoor, which they had extinguished minutes earlier, was once again ablaze. One of the men he had seen in the Bagiya, the stout man wearing a white kurta pyjama, was now stoking the flames. It beggared logic. Kunju's alarm gave way to exasperation at these men's cavalier disregard for safety. They had to be stopped.

Rushing to the rear edge of the roof, with little thought for the sheer drop below, he leapt down, his uniform shoes impacting hard on the paved rear courtyard of the restaurant. Making his way to the fire, he flattened the wicket fence that blocked his path and reached the tandoor from the rear.

By the time he reached the kitchen area, the man wearing the kurta pyjama was gone, as were his two companions, but the fire was still roaring. It was now that Kunju's nostrils twitched. Along with a pungent, rank smell, a strange waft of roasted meat permeated the air. It was the unmistakable odour of burning flesh.

Wondering what was being cooked at this time of night – the restaurant was closed, and none of the staff were present – the constable turned to the tandoor. Almost by reflex, his mind transferring its agitation to his limbs, he seized a bucket and began feverishly dousing the fire again.

With the flames somewhat subdued, Kunju peered into the blackened mess steaming over the mouth of the tandoor. Seizing a pole that had moments earlier been used to stoke the blaze, he probed the burning logs and ash. To his horror, he could vaguely discern the charred contours of a human form, crouched in a foetal position amidst the logs, sticks and other blackened material. He hastily quelled the remaining flames.

As he probed further, Kunju's grisly discovery became more recognizable. This strange bonfire atop the Bagiya Barbeque tandoor was a ghastly, makeshift funeral pyre for an unknown woman, whose hair had somehow endured the flames. Whoever this woman was in life and whatever the manner of her passing, in death she had been disposed of in a heartless manner, along with posters and banners from some forgotten political campaign.

An out-of-control fire in a restaurant kitchen had suddenly metamorphosed into a murder investigation. All eyes – and the firm grip of a constable – were now on the slim man whom Kunju had seen stoking the fire: Keshav Kumar, the manager of the Bagiya Barbeque restaurant.

2

Kunju's Discovery

The Central Police Command and Control for Delhi is commonly referred to as the Police Control Room or PCR. It responds to distress calls from citizens, dialled on the number 100. The nomenclature PCR was also extended to its emergency response vehicles – why the vehicles were deemed 'rooms' I cannot fathom[6] – which numbered perhaps 300 in 1995, spread across the city as flying squads to reach a trouble spot in the quickest possible time in response to 'distress calls' or information received. Delhi Police, it must be said, boasts one of the best response times in emergency assistance around the world.

On receiving Constable Kunju's message, the PCR lost no time in alerting the Connaught Place Police Station and the fire brigade.[7] Before Kunju's shocking revelation of a charred body on a tandoor at the Bagiya Barbeque restaurant, the report simply concerned a fire in the vicinity of the hotel on Ashoka Road. This itself was no small matter. Sobered by the loss of thirty-seven lives in the Siddharth Continental Hotel fire of January 1986, Delhi's authorities ensured that emergency services were vigilant and prompt in their responses to reports of fire.

Following Sub-inspector Rajesh Kumar, PCR Head Constable Majid Khan, Constable Rajbir Singh and Sub-inspector Jawahar Singh rushed to the scene. Another posse, consisting of Sub-inspector

Jagat Singh, Assistant Sub-inspector Dayanand, Head Constable Shahbuddin and Constables Jaichand, Rashid and Ramkaran, led by the Connaught Place SHO (Station House Officer) Inspector Niranjan Singh, was not far behind.

I had known Niranjan since the early 1970s, when he was still a sub-inspector and I was the chief of the Parliament Street Sub-division. He had been part of my team when I was the Delhi Traffic Police chief some years later, and I had always been impressed by his efficiency.

Niranjan Singh was a man with a perennially calm demeanour – no one ever saw him flustered, let alone losing his temper. He sported a light, carefully trimmed moustache, and a receding hairline accentuated his genial, rounded features. Though he stood no more than 5' 8" tall, and was in Punjabi parlance quite 'healthy', he exuded a quiet toughness that only a foolhardy offender would overlook. At this time, Niranjan was a veteran policeman with an illustrious track record.

Constable Kunju, holding on to Keshav all the while, briefed his SHO about his gruesome find.

On the inspector's briefing, other senior officers reached Yatri Niwas: Assistant Commissioner of Police (ACP) Nuzat Hassan, whose turn it was to be the 'night patrolling officer' of the district; also ACP (Connaught Place) Alok Kumar and DCP Aditya Arya.

Inspector Niranjan took in hand the inspection-of-scene-of-crime operations that were already in place by this time, and the attempts at reconstructing what had transpired. The gravity of it was just beginning to sink in. For most, the revulsion evoked by initial accounts of the sequence of events was overwhelming. So many aspects of the crime seemed grotesque, offensive on a visceral level. Burning a corpse in a restaurant – what is more, the corpse of an obviously murdered woman on a tandoor – defied credulity.

The cultural context of the crime magnified its iniquity, if that was possible. The act of burning a corpse is, in itself, not offensive. Indeed, in India it is the most common means of disposing of a body. Cremation is a sacred rite, an obligation for Hindus to consign the mortal remains to ashes amidst prayers and tears – that the soul may be free to continue its journey. This perverted cremation, where a murdered woman's corpse was burned in the middle of the night in secret, devoid of love and ceremony, was thus especially odious. Rather than liberating the departed soul, the fire lit by the miscreants was meant to obliterate the hapless woman's very existence.

Perhaps this goes some way towards explaining why the scene that greeted me at the Bagiya became etched in my memory forever; deeper, perhaps, than any other event of my thirty-five-year-old policing career.

As my Ambassador was waved into Yatri Niwas just after 1 a.m. on 3 July 1995, everything appeared normal, apart from the few police vehicles in the car park. Delhi was still in the grip of a hot spell, and all was quiet. When I entered the Bagiya, it was a different matter altogether. The crime scene was teeming with police personnel of various ranks, all engrossed in different duties.

Inspector Niranjan Singh had assigned the duty of drawing site plans to some officers and deputed others to question the staff and security personnel at the hotel. This was the first step in the process of compiling the panchnama.[8]

The mood was sombre; I would quickly number among the many there who could barely contain their disgust.

Aditya greeted me, accompanied by Niranjan. He motioned towards the restaurant kitchen. 'It's a grim sight, sir.' His jaw set and his eyes darkened, as if to emphasise the point.

The pair gave me a guided inspection of the crime scene and explained the sequence of events of the evening. Upon Niranjan's instruction, the photographers had already taken some perfunctory shots which, given the equipment of the day, could convey little more than crude, grim outlines. The makeshift pyre had been removed by the investigating team from the top of the tandoor, and the whole gruesome mess, complete with the semi-cremated remains within, was placed on a tarpaulin sheet on the Bagiya's kitchen floor and covered by a sheet.

Niranjan informed me that along with the body, an assortment of flammable objects had been burning atop the tandoor, as a substitute for regular firewood. Broken boards, old crates and bamboo poles, cloth banners, posters and buntings had all been piled amidst logs of wood, on top of the tandoor and around the body. Everything was burnt or partially burnt.

The size of the fire was evident from a sooty halo on the side wall of the kitchen above the tandoor. The intensity of its heat had caused a whole section of tiles to fall inside it. The tandoor, inside a rectangular masonry exterior standing some three feet high, was itself covered with the same cream-coloured faux-brick tiles that decorated the walls. It was built into the raised area next to the barbecue, along the side of the kitchen.

The bundle on the kitchen floor that was the pyre was uncovered before me as Aditya and Niranjan stood by.

The corpse was a horrifying sight. The limbs were charred, the abdominal wall had ruptured in the heat, and the intestines and their contents spilled out from the torso. The teeth were exposed, as the lips and the flesh above them had been roasted taut; what was left of the face wore a blank, horrific grin. One leg had burned as far as the knee; the other, only up to the ankle. The lower part of one of the arms was detached from the body; the other, still entire with the torso, was burnt to the elbow, and the remaining bones, including the distal phalanges (bones of the fingertips), had been retrieved from the ashes within the tandoor.

The condition of the corpse would surely challenge any forensic pathologist. But while the outer crust of the body had been incinerated beyond casual recognition, it was unquestionably that of a woman. Niranjan surmised that the body belonged to a woman between twenty-five and thirty years of age. Some hair on the scalp, tied in a bun, along with the clip that held it together, had somehow survived the fire. There were scraps of partially burnt clothing amidst the ashes, too. It was as if the last vestiges of this woman's femininity had persisted to thwart her murderer's intent.

The contents of the tandoor had been emptied and sifted through to reveal more charred remains. There were pieces of broken bones that appeared to be missing parts from the limbs, and two damaged silver anklets of the kind often worn by Indian women.

There was some doubt regarding the victim's ethnicity, though. During closer examination of the body, someone suggested the possibility of it being Caucasian, going by a few patches of white skin that had survived the blaze. Another officer speculated, in view of the burnt bones recovered from inside the tandoor, that the woman had been cut up during the commission of the murder; or perhaps the limbs had been chopped off post-mortem and then burnt.

A black polythene sheet, like a tarpaulin, had been left on one side of the tandoor. Careful examination revealed spots of blood at various places on this sheet. Bloodstains were detected, too, near an iron storage shelf, where restaurant equipment was stored and, most notably, on Keshav Kumar's clothes.

Niranjan pointed to the worried-looking Keshav, who was trying to avoid engaging with the head constable talking with him. The hand of another constable lay heavy on his shoulder. 'This is one of the suspects. Keshav Kumar, the restaurant manager.'

'Is he talking?' I asked.

'Plenty about his work at the restaurant, but nothing useful, sir,' Niranjan replied.

'He seems to be covering for his boss, Sushil Sharma. We can't work out if he is loyal or just scared. Sharma is a well-connected political type in the Congress party,' Aditya added.

'He is the former president of the Delhi Pradesh Youth Congress, and an up-and-coming political heavyweight. They say he knows how to use a bit of muscle too,' said Niranjan.

I looked over at our first suspect. The young head constable was coaxing Keshav to reveal his role in the crime, but the restaurant manager was silent. His face wore a downcast look and he remained subdued, his demeanour that of a man coming to terms with his self-ruination.

The procedure for handling a suspect in India differs from that of most Western countries. The most obvious difference that evening was the absence of handcuffs. In a 1980 landmark Supreme Court ruling in *Prem Shankar Shukla vs Delhi Administration*, the legendary Justice V.R. Krishna Iyer held that 'to manacle man is more than to mortify him;[9] it is to dehumanise him', effectively proscribing regular handcuffing of prisoners. It would have been quite unnecessary anyway, with the constable's hand firm on Keshav's shoulder. There was also a massive police presence at the Bagiya.

Another practice, perhaps rare in Western jurisdictions, is that of holding the suspect at the crime scene. This had as much to do with manpower issues as anything else, but it must have had some effect on Keshav. Within the confines of the restaurant premises, he could not escape his terrible handiwork; he could see the police methodically combing the crime scene, and his life unravelling. The pressure on him must have been harrowing.

Though I spoke a few words with him, Keshav betrayed little of what was going on in his mind. A tallish, skinny man whose clothes seemed to hang on his spare frame, Keshav had the appearance of a man who had no choice but to work for his living. While his dark, clouded eyes showed he was haunted by the enormity of the situation, he did not strike me as one who had just crossed a moral Rubicon. He was simply anxious about his fate, which could only have seemed dire in those early hours of 3 July 1995.

All the officers present were convinced that Keshav harboured full knowledge of the crime. In view of the nature and seriousness of the offences, the investigating team would almost certainly be granted police custody of the suspect by the Judicial Magistrate's Court, for interrogation and to prevent collusion with the prime suspect who was yet to be identified.

In the absence of Keshav's confession, police personnel continued to note everything at the crime scene. As with all investigations, they tried to fit each piece of information into the emerging jigsaw puzzle that was taking shape before them. There was a great deal of follow-up and verification to be done to recreate the sequence of events. The investigators were, however, unanimous in their conclusion that the murder had been committed elsewhere, and the body transported to the Bagiya for disposal.

By the time I arrived, K.K. Tuli, the general manager of Yatri Niwas, had been summoned, as I had been, from his slumber. In his presence, the police questioned the hotel's guards, Mahesh Prasad and Sultan Singh, and the security supervisor, Rajiv Thakur. Everyone in the vicinity, mostly hotel staff, was questioned. No one seemed overly uncomfortable with being questioned, or showed any sign of masking complicity in the crime. Mahesh told Niranjan that at around 10.15 p.m., the owner of the restaurant, Sushil Sharma, had arrived in his white Maruti car, registration number DL-2CA-1872. He also revealed that a large bundle was brought into the Bagiya Barbeque from the dickey of this same white Maruti car.

This was a critical breakthrough. Eyewitness accounts were corroborated by an entry in the security register maintained by the guards at the hotel gate. The arrival was recorded at 10.15 p.m. After parking his car, Sushil had entered the restaurant, then stood near the canvas screen at the front of the restaurant, not permitting the security staff or the police access to the place.

After further enquiries, investigators learned that Sushil was one of the partners in the consortium that had contracted with India Tourism Development Corporation (ITDC)[10] to run the Bagiya Barbeque restaurant. Sushil Sharma was a very well-known figure – something of a Delhi celebrity– and he was recognised locally as the managing owner of the Bagiya.

For a forensic inspection of the crime scene, the police called a team of experts from the Central Forensic Science Laboratory (CFSL)[11], in addition to the Delhi Police crime team, to thoroughly examine the entire topography for clues. Under Inspector Niranjan Singh's supervision, the police seized many crucial items as evidence and lifted samples. The kanaat (canvas screen) that was used to block entry into the garden restaurant was taken into possession, as was the black polythene sheet stained with blood. Items retrieved from the tandoor – silver anklets, bones, remains of burnt clothes and ash – were all sealed in separate exhibit parcels and logged as evidence, as were charred tiles, a wooden pole with one end burnt and the other end partially burnt. Upon Keshav's arrest, the bloodstained kurta he was wearing was also taken as evidence.

Inspector Niranjan Singh recorded Kunju's statement and without loss of time endorsed it in the form of a ruqqa[12] to the Connaught Place police station. Under the provisions of section 154 of the Criminal Procedure Code, First Information Report (FIR)[13] no. 486/95 was registered, under Indian Penal Code sections 302 and 201, for destroying material evidence. Keshav Kumar was formally arrested.

On the same night, the inspector initiated proceedings under Section 174 of the Criminal Procedure Code for an inquest in respect of the corpse discovered at the restaurant. He started with a sketch plan of the crime scene and recorded a brief chronological report of the case. He then ordered that the charred body be despatched to the forensic facility at Ram Manohar Lohia Hospital, some two kilometres away, for a post-mortem. In accordance with police protocol, an autopsy can be conducted only after formal identification of the dead body. Because the body had not yet been identified, hospital authorities were requested to preserve it in their morgue for at least seventy-two hours, giving the police adequate time – so they believed – to identify the victim.

The inquest and post-mortem documents, along with the panchnama, would need to be part of the supporting material for the charge sheet[14], when the case was finally prosecuted. But that was a long way off. The main suspect was yet to be found, the identity of the victim had not been established, and the motive for the murder was yet to be ascertained.

Having established that Sushil Sharma had brought the body there, the police pressed forward. And their questioning revealed further details: On Sushil's arrival at the Bagiya in his white Maruti, Keshav hastened to the car and sat talking with him for some ten minutes. Sushil, it seemed, told Keshav to close the restaurant for the evening. Keshav then went back into the restaurant and, after declaring the place closed, hurriedly showed patrons the door. All the staff were dismissed for the day and handed grub-money for their evening meal, ₹25 each, in lieu of the privilege of eating at the restaurant.

Once the restaurant had been cleared of guests and staff, Sushil reversed his car to the steps of the Bagiya Barbeque, and Keshav and he picked up the human bundle they had wrapped in a black plastic sheet. The pair then hastily built an improvised pyre on top of the tandoor with waste material – mostly party propaganda material and scrap wood that was lying around in the lawns. The body was placed within this makeshift funeral pyre, the limbs compressed roughly in a foetal position, and the pyre set alight.

Every connoisseur of fine food knows of the reliance on ghee in much of Indian cuisine. And every Hindu knows the importance of ghee, or clarified butter, in religious ceremonies and in a cremation. It is a strange and fitting coincidence then, that the Bagiya, a tandoori restaurant, had insufficient ghee that night. Inexplicably, the restaurant was short of butter too.

Sushil then despatched Keshav to buy some butter. In the absence of ghee, it was perhaps the only readily available accelerant which would not attract attention with an unpleasant smell. Not that this would be of any great consequence given the stench of the fire itself and the manner in which events would unfold. Keshav returned a little later with four packets of Amul butter, which was all he could find at that hour. This was fed into the pyre. It was the sudden leaping of butter-fuelled flames that attracted the attention of people outside, including Anaro Devi and Constable Kunju, at around 11.25 p.m.

Enquiries also established that Sushil was present throughout the attempt to burn the body and had later managed to slip away immediately before Constable Kunju's discovery of the burning corpse. Kunju's police supervisors, including me, considered this most unfortunate.

While Keshav had been apprehended on the spot for clear complicity and participation in destroying material evidence in a murder case, and a few others were being questioned, the motive and identity of the actual killers and the identity of the victim – as well as several other angles in the case – still eluded the police. There was, at this early stage of the investigation, no particular clue with which the identity of the deceased could be determined. And there was no evidence or indication as to where the murder had taken place.

Police were keen to interrogate Keshav, as only he seemed to hold the key to these mysteries. Until now, though, he had parried most questions. When asked about his relationship with Sushil Sharma – whom the police had, by then, deemed to be the primary suspect for the murder – Keshav merely said, '*Un ke mujh par kaafi ehsaan hain* (I am highly indebted to him).'

3
Twenty-four Hours

Force of habit akin to addiction makes me a limp vegetable on a day without my morning walk. Nothing, not even spending the better part of the night and the hours before daybreak at a crime scene can deter me from taking a brisk walk up to Rashtrapati Bhavan, along Rajpath, India Gate and back. I have trodden the same route over many years, and I never tire of it. If there were a Guinness World Record for the number of times one has touched the exquisite wrought-iron gates of Rashtrapati Bhavan, I would probably be the winner.

Perhaps the ordered beauty of the avenue and its environs gives me perspective for the challenges of the day ahead. Lutyens' sublime architecture, connected by a glorious avenue with its manicured landscape, stood in stark relief to the ugliness of humankind that I encountered in the course of my work. That day was no different.

Rambo, my trusty, affectionate German Shepherd, was waiting for me at the gate, and he greeted me enthusiastically when I returned home from the Bagiya Barbeque around 5 a.m. It was still dark as I changed from my formal trousers and shirt to shorts, T-shirt and track shoes for my walk. My arrival had roused my nephew Rohan from his sleep. Rohan, a medical student studying in New York at the time, was in India for an internship at the All India Institute of Medical Sciences (AIIMS) and was staying with me for the duration of his placement. When I told him I had been at a crime scene overnight, he couldn't believe that he had slept through it all. He had not heard the telephone ring or my slipping out of the house in the early hours. He now decided to accompany me and Rambo on our walk.

During the walk I narrated the happenings of the night before to my horrified nephew. As we got to Ashoka Road from India Gate for the return lap, I felt I should take a detour to check on the progress at the crime scene, and I let Rohan tag along.

We left Rambo with a constable in the garden and stepped inside the restaurant. Investigators were still mopping up at the tandoor. The body had long been removed, but the grim atmosphere persisted. The officers were going about their duties quietly, as if in respect for the departed.

Even without the sickening physical evidence, the ghastliness of it all had a palpable effect on Rohan. He was rendered speechless by his tour of the Bagiya and remained so on our walk of two blocks, back to the house. A medical student becomes inured to blood and guts quite early in medical school. But the mere mention of the crime was nauseating for virtually everyone, and it remains so more than two decades later. Many in the nation's capital and beyond swore off their beloved tandoori food for months after the murder.

By the time we returned from our ten-kilometre jaunt with Rambo, it was time for me to shower, change into my uniform and head to the office. The first order of the day was my morning report – a daily ritual for all police officers, especially those with a field charge (a position involving direct duty/contact with the public).

My superior officer was Nikhil Kumar, the commissioner of police, a man with a dignified bearing and impressive political lineage. He was a hard taskmaster and satisfying him was not always easy – especially during the morning report. However well-prepared one was, Nikhil had an uncanny knack of piercing one's ego with a few crisp sentences. When a subordinate faced this lion in his den, he was bound to be met with some query that would have him murmuring, 'I'll check further and get back to you, sir'. I suspect the man truly believed that unnerving juniors with pointed questions was among his more effective managerial techniques. Most officers in the force were wary of this strategy; they were convinced he did it simply to overwhelm them.

I enjoyed working with Commissioner Nikhil Kumar. It may have been challenging, but I was comfortable with his demand for the highest standards of efficiency and, more importantly, I was confident he knew who could deliver. His assiduity kept the force in fighting form.

At around 7 a.m., I gave my morning report by telephone from home. I carefully recounted the events of the previous night, right from Kunju noticing the flames at the rear of the Bagiya as he and Chander Pal patrolled on Ashoka Road. Nikhil did not seem to like anything he was hearing. He was livid on learning that one of the suspects, by all accounts the main culprit, had made good his escape.

'Why was the accused not arrested on the spot? Place him under suspension,' he barked, referring to Constable Kunju.

The situation was far from catastrophic, but I found this difficult to convey to my superior without resorting to blunt language. It would have been no small injustice to Kunju had he been suspended, so I took a deep breath and proceeded in my most diplomatic tone.

What had been achieved, I told the commissioner, was essentially because of the efforts of a lone beat constable. That he had uncovered a burning torso atop a tandoor and managed to nab one of those actively involved in the crime was laudable. Such exemplary initiative was rarely witnessed in the normal scheme of things. It would have been wonderful if the police had been able to catch all the perpetrators at once. But such luck does not always come our way.

Without giving the least indication that he had been swayed by my advocacy, Nikhil Kumar continued, 'Do you know who Sushil is?'

'He is a political personality – a prominent youth leader, sir. With plenty of nuisance value!' was the most fitting reply I could muster.

'He belongs to the ruling party, and I believe he enjoys quite a lot of clout'. Nikhil's question was for my benefit: coming from a powerful Congress family, he would surely have known of Sushil Sharma.

'Are you sure of your facts? You'll need to tread carefully and verify every single thing twice over.'

I assured my superior that things were under control, that I had taken pains to verify each fact before reporting the matter to him. Then I requested him to visit the scene of the crime, knowing full well he would do it even without my asking. Such a sensational case, apparently involving an absconding political figure, surely warranted the commissioner's personal attention. He said he had an inspection scheduled that day at the Paharganj police station and promised to drop by at the Bagiya en route.

In the meantime, the commissioner's instructions were clear: Get Sushil quickly – without fail and without loss of time.

The police force never sleeps. Inspector Niranjan Singh and his team were hard at work that morning while I spoke to the commissioner, and they hadn't slowed their investigation or their pursuit of the main suspect overnight. During his initial questioning at the Bagiya, Keshav Kumar had told the police that Sushil was probably at his parents' house in Pitampura. With this first clue, a police team rushed to north-west Delhi in the early hours and raided his family home in the Maurya Enclave of Pitampura.

There was no sign of Sushil, and no indication he had been there recently. His parents, a devout Brahmin couple, were woken from their sleep and seemed genuinely surprised and deeply troubled by the raid. They informed the police that Sushil had been away in Chandigarh the last two days. Whether this information was a red herring or an alibi, one could not say, but it was definitely not to be taken at face value, at least at this stage. The team then verified with neighbours that Sushil had not been at his family home.

Raids at other likely places and possible hideouts followed, as bits and pieces of information slowly emerged from Keshav's interrogation and from questioning the restaurant's employees and associates. A lookout notice was flashed for the vehicle in which Sushil was last seen: the white Maruti, registration number DL-2CA-1872 – the car used to transport the woman's body to Ashok Yatri Niwas.

Niranjan's team probed Sharma's business affairs to see what leads they could turn up. They took documents from the hotel management relating to the business structure of the Bagiya Barbeque. The documents revealed that the ITDC, which ran the Ashok Yatri Niwas, had given the restaurant premises, located on the western lawns of the hotel grounds, on lease to a private consortium – M/s Excel Hotels Inc. Sushil Sharma, the former DPYC president, was one of five proprietors of the consortium, which ostensibly operated from a corporate office at 159 Kamla Market. A three-year license agreement had been entered into with Excel Hotels on 10 November 1994, which was due to expire in 1997.

Sushil Sharma's partners in M/s Excel Hotels Inc. were Vinod Kumar Nagpal – otherwise a general manager of Hotel Oriental Delux on Padam Singh Road – Ram Prasad Sachdeva, Lalit Sachdeva and R.P. Malik, a former administrative officer of Delhi District Courts. Keshav Kumar, a resident of Uttam Nagar in West Delhi who claimed to have been a general secretary of the DPYC, worked for the owners of the Bagiya as its manager. He had no written employment contract, there was no formal order or documentation to validate his position – he reported directly to Sushil Sharma.

Niranjan also had his men examine the restaurant and its environs in the light of day. The lawns to the left of the main entrance to Ashok Yatri Niwas from Ashoka Road, with its landscaped terraces, decorative shrubs and arches, man-made waterways and waterfalls, were used as the entertainment and outdoor catering area for the Bagiya. Chairs and tables were laid out for customers amidst decorative wooden-plank arches erected in different styles and designs around the lawns.

The Bagiya was far from the simple garden that its name suggests. At least, it was far from the tidy, ideal garden, and more like a cluttered backyard. In the wake of the investigation, with all the burned wood and material, it was even more of a mess. Stacked haphazardly around the garden complex and against the hotel compound wall were clusters of Congress party propaganda material and equipment – used posters and pamphlets, parts of hoardings and kiosks, bundles of flags and buntings and bamboo poles and other scaffolding used to erect platforms, public address stages and overhead welcome arches. Given its location, the complex was evidently convenient as an improvised storage facility for the party.

Officers quizzed the operators of the three small shops adjacent to the hotel compound about the goings-on in the Bagiya to see if they could find any further clues. These shops were just outside the boundary wall of the Ashok Yatri Niwas on Janpath Lane, beside a Mother Dairy milk booth. Anaro Devi, the lady who had raised the alarm the night before, managed one of them, dispensing fresh vegetables to the households in the neighbourhood. Anaro, it seems, was a regular supplier of vegetables to the Bagiya Barbeque.

At around 9.30 a.m., Commissioner Nikhil Kumar visited the Bagiya as he had promised. I made sure I was there before he arrived. A commissioner's visit to a scene of occurrence is rare. But Nikhil was a hands-on field man, and he never baulked at a spot visit, despite an extremely busy schedule. He was one of those rare, energetic individuals who seems to be in ten different places at once.

The visit was a low-key affair: no members of the press were present, as news of the crime had not yet swept the city, as it would in just a few hours. A thoughtful man who listened more than he spoke and whose words therefore always carried weight, Nikhil was mostly quiet, apart from a few brief questions. As I guided him through the Bagiya and made mention of the details of the crime, I wondered whether there was going to be a repeat order to place Constable Kunju under suspension for inadequate action. But he didn't say a word about it.

THE TANDOOR MURDER   27

Perhaps the enormity of the crime and the magnitude of the contribution of a mere constable had sunk in – even before the details were digested. Nikhil reiterated his earlier direction to bring Sushil into custody without delay and left in his Ambassador for his inspection at Paharganj. While on his way, he asked me over the wireless to quickly send him a note on Constable Kunju's actions, which is the standard procedure when a superior officer wishes to issue a citation.

My tension eased. I had deeply appreciated Kunju's extraordinary initiative and doggedness in bringing the gruesome murder to light and wanted his role in uncovering the crime to be duly acknowledged. Back in my office on the third floor of Delhi Police Headquarters, I drafted a report on the sequence of events post haste and despatched it to the commissioner's office, with the hope that only good would come of it.

And it did. In just a few hours, the administrative wing had completed the formalities of paper work and procedures for a citation. Late in the afternoon, Constable Abdul Nazeer Kunju of Connaught Place police station was summoned to the commissioner's salubrious office at Delhi Police Headquarters at Indraprastha Estate.

I was there before him and occupied one of the comfortable chairs opposite Commissioner Nikhil Kumar. He always seemed quite some distance away over the veritable plateau of his expansive desk, which dwarfed the usual paraphernalia found on any office table: a desk calendar, a cylindrical pen-holder with more than a dozen pens, notepads and all manner of trinkets – not to forget the stack of files and documents on one side.

On an extension table to Nikhil's left sat an array of telephones and wireless equipment. A framed portrait of Mahatma Gandhi looked benignly down from the wall behind his chair and against the wall to his right, mounted on a shining brass base, were two crossed flags: the Indian tricolour and an Ashoka lion crest with laurels set against a red and indigo field – the Delhi Police flag. In an alcove immediately to the left of the main room, two large television screens were installed in the commissioner's direct line of vision. One streamed visual media from news channels and the other displayed the Press Trust of India (PTI) ticker that presented quick grabs of the latest news from the wires.

Constable Kunju was ushered into the office by Nikhil's staff officer. The pageantry of the occasion and the sheer opulence of the room were clearly overwhelming for him. Though he was quiet, his eyes shone as he approached the commissioner's desk and saluted. Just hours earlier, he had been an unheralded beat constable. Now, a rare honour, an out-of-turn promotion, was to be bestowed on him.

After a few warm words with Kunju, Nikhil looked towards his aide, who produced the award for him. He rose from his chair, and handed me one of the insignia. We approached Kunju from opposite sides and at once pinned the three downward-pointing, black-striped red chevrons on each shirt sleeve, just below the shoulder. 'Congratulations on a fine job. Your initiative is commendable,' Nikhil said, and beamed a warm smile. 'I'm proud of you. You've done a fabulous job, preventing a murder from being covered up,' I added. Kunju's countenance was radiant with his well-deserved recognition. He was now Head Constable Abdul Nazeer Kunju.

That same afternoon, the commissioner of police announced to the media that a reward of one lakh rupees would be given to anyone providing information that could lead to Sushil's arrest.

⚖️

Meanwhile, and indeed throughout the day, the police were making concerted efforts to locate Sushil. A systematic search was organised at all guesthouses and hotels in Delhi, with the help of the local police and other agencies. Following unsuccessful searches in and around Delhi, raiding parties were despatched to other cities, and they swooped on Sushil's contacts – his relatives, friends and sympathisers – as information came to light. No lead was ignored;

any address Sushil could take refuge at was investigated – especially in Karol Bagh, South Extension, Jama Masjid and the surrounding areas.

Unlikely though it seemed, the possibility that he had gone to Chandigarh, as his parents had suggested, was not ignored either. Yudhvir Dadwal, the then Chandigarh police chief, was requested to mount a search for him, and a Delhi Police team was sent to assist the local police.

As the day progressed and there was still no information about his whereabouts, a nationwide 'wanted' alert was sounded for Sushil's arrest. As is routine, his descriptive roll (height, build, weight, complexion, distinguishing features, etc.) was flashed on wireless to all police stations in the country and his photograph sent to the print media and the television channels to be disseminated – especially on Doordarshan, the national television channel.

Information on Sushil's associates was collected and they were subjected to questioning by different investigation teams. Police surveillance was mounted at the addresses of Sushil's business partners, associates, family members and friends. Known telephone numbers were all put under observation to intercept any calls from Sushil.

Keshav Kumar was produced before Dharam Raj Singh, the area metropolitan magistrate at Patiala House, a little after 2 p.m. – well before the deadline; a suspect is supposed to be produced in court within twenty-four hours of being taken into custody. In a serious case such as this, the police usually ask for ten to fifteen days of police remand, expecting only five, which is exactly what the magistrate ordered. If Keshav did not cooperate within these five days, an extension would have to be sought. Five days are, at any rate, a long time for an accused to be subjected to skilled interrogation. And, by now, the police had formed a special team of crack investigators and interrogators to work on the case.

Aditya Arya, supported by Additional DCP Dinesh Bhat at the proximate supervisory level, led the special team. The core group comprised five assistant commissioners of police, nine inspectors and other ancillary staff. All of them were considered particularly adept at their respective jobs, and were now deputed to take up full-time investigation and monitoring of this major case.

V.K. Nagpal, Ram Prakash Sachdeva, Lalit Sachdeva and R.P. Malik – Sushil's partners in M/s Excel Hotels, the Bagiya enterprise – were called in for questioning. Nagpal, who was away in Dehra Dun, was summoned to Delhi.

During his initial interrogation, Keshav had tried to sell a story implicating Nagpal as the one who had brought the bundled-up corpse to the hotel. But this possibility was quickly ruled out by the quantum of evidence already pointing to Sushil having done so. With Keshav's hedging and a dearth of leads in the case, we became increasingly aware of the dead ends we were encountering in our quest to find the fugitive.

One by one the partners were questioned, with no measure of success. No one could provide any clue to Sushil's possible whereabouts. His associates and friends were questioned, but they all expressed complete ignorance – feigned or otherwise – about his movements. No one came forward to help the police or provide any pertinent clues.

Aditya's team anticipated that Sushil would tap his close associates in the political arena. Many of them were from the youth wing of the party, of which he had been a high-profile office-bearer, and others were mentors, senior party figures he was known to or was rumoured to be close to, who were credited with nurturing his political ascendency.

Indeed, the team considered every contingency and took action accordingly, as the police does in such cases. To thwart any attempt Sushil might make to escape the country via its porous eastern border with neighbouring Nepal – a traditional escape route for criminals on the run, as it is less than six hours' drive east from Delhi – a police team with Sushil's photograph was rushed to the Nepal border. The Ministry of Home and the Ministry of External Affairs were asked to approach the Nepal government with requests for cooperation. They promptly requested their Nepali counterparts to arrest and hand over Sushil to Delhi Police in the event of his arriving in Nepal or attempting to use Kathmandu as a route for fleeing to another destination.

Photographs were sent to all the other border check posts too, to international airports, sea ports and other land ports of exit, with requests to locate and intercept Sushil Sharma should he be sighted. His passport number and descriptive roll were also provided to the Foreigner Regional Registration Offices (FRROs), with a request to prevent him from boarding any international flight. Even the Interpol division of the Central Bureau of Investigation (CBI) was alerted and briefed.

All this while, the artful questioning and tactful handling of Keshav continued. In the years since, the general public has become privy to all manner of harsh interrogation techniques, thanks mainly to the US and the scandals of 'rendition' in the wake of the 11 September 2001 terrorist attacks on the World Trade Center. After shocking reports of 'water boarding' – not to forget the publication of barbarous shots of soldiers grinning beside hooded captives with electrical wires connected to their limbs and appendages – many have perhaps reached the conclusion that torture is routine. Worse, some may assume it is necessary in the process of interrogation.

My experience of decades in law enforcement tells me that the third degree is not part of proper policing. A skilled interrogator can elicit information from a suspect without resorting to violence. Keshav's interrogation illustrates this point perfectly.

Keshav was taken to the Tilak Marg station for questioning, as the Connaught Place police station was then operating in temporary buildings and had no suitable rooms. Keshav, although confined in a room, was not subjected to harsh interrogation. He was, however, relentlessly questioned by one or two officers, whose clear objective was to convince him to become a police witness. This was, without doubt, the most commonsensical course of action under the circumstances. Logic and common sense, however, would prove to be elusive throughout this case.

When Keshav was initially taken into custody, his first reaction was, '*Hum kuchh nahin bol sake. Hum bhi khareede huey ghulam hain* (I can't say anything. I am obliged not to.)' He feigned ignorance of the murder and even tried to lead investigators astray with false stories. He seemed to be protecting Sushil Sharma, but whether this was born of misplaced loyalty or fear, they could not tell – at least not at this stage of the case. When they kept at him relentlessly, though, telling him that his part in the crime could finish him and his whole family – including the future of his children – he changed tack.

He began divulging information, bit by bit, which ironed out many contradictions. Most significantly, he disclosed the identity of the victim. The human remains amidst the ashes on the tandoor were, he assured them, those of Ravi Naina Sahni.

He told the interrogators that he had not looked at the face in the bundle before placing the body on the tandoor. 'I was so busy with the work that I simply failed to see her face. But the structure and the body was without doubt hers.' It was incomprehensible to the investigators that Keshav, along with Sushil, could place the human bundle on the black plastic sheet, build a pyre atop the tandoor and hoist the body onto it – and in the process have its blood smear his clothes – without noticing the face. He seemed to be imparting the bare minimum of information that would keep investigators from implicating him in the murder.

Nevertheless, Keshav's account gave a chilling insight into the prime murder suspect's character. He told police interrogators that after he had bought packets of butter at Sushil's behest so the body would burn quickly, and as Naina's body burned, Sushil had paused and reflected on his appalling crime. He had placed his pistol on a table, poured several glasses of water over his head and lamented, '*Yeh maine kya kar diya? Yeh mujhse kya ho gaya?* (What have I done? How could I have done this?)'. He poured several more litres of water over himself, as if to cleanse the stain of guilt from his mind.

From Keshav's description, it was clear that Sushil's remorse had not caused him to lose his composure. He had been directing operations at the restaurant with startling efficiency before he left Keshav to fend for himself. That he had told Keshav to get some butter so the corpse could burn faster evinced a peculiar clarity of thought and astonishing cunning. Without any shadow of doubt, it demonstrated a clear criminal intent to destroy all evidence of the murder.

Sushil's actions had been as bold as they were tenacious. Even after Kunju doused the fire and uncovered his sickening crime, he had made a last-ditch effort to burn the corpse. Then he had vanished, as the police discovered the burning corpse and arrested Keshav.

A profile emerged of a Jekyll and Hyde character – an assessment later confirmed by those who knew Sharma. Shades of fearsome black were interspersed with greys and whites in this complex man's psyche.

Keshav revealed to the police that the victim, Ravi Naina Sahni, was living with Sushil Sharma as his wife, in a flat whose existence was barely even known to his friends. Sushil, Keshav told interrogators, kept his affair with Naina quiet, not wanting even his close associates to know about his clandestine marital life. For some reason, Sushil had convinced himself that public knowledge of his relationship would be detrimental to his political ambitions.

The first-floor flat where the couple lived was in the DIZ (Delhi Imperial Zone) area of Mandir Marg. Keshav claimed not to know the address, but he said it had an air conditioner. Investigators could not tell at the time whether this was a major breakthrough or yet another attempt by their wily captive to frustrate, or at least delay them.

4

The Crime Scene

As the crucial first twenty-four hours of the investigation were drawing to a close, the investigating team may have been sobered by its lack of progress in tracking the prime suspect, but it was buoyed by a clear indication of the victim's identity. Following Keshav's disclosure about Sushil's secret pad, the police combed the entire DIZ colony around Mandir Marg. They looked for the one clue to the premises Keshav had provided: that the first-floor flat Sushil and Naina shared was the only one in its immediate neighbourhood with an air conditioner installed in one of its windows.

As its name indicates, Mandir Marg is dotted with temples, including one of Delhi's famous landmarks – the colourful Birla Mandir or Laxminarayan Temple. The Kali Bari of the Bengalis is also prominent. The street boasts some of the oldest and most famous schools of Delhi, like Harcourt Butler and St. Thomas Girls. The circular bustling shopping centres of Gole Market and Bhagat Singh Market service the residents of this neighbourhood.

The DIZ area is generally known as the 'babus' colony', as many employees of the Central government reside there. It was originally the residential centre for Indian staff of the Imperial Secretariat, in the last decades of British rule. The DIZ area adjoins the LBZ or the Lutyens Bungalow Zone in the heart of the city and is surrounded by Connaught Place, Paharganj and the Institutional Area.

A sprawling colony conveniently located near major hospitals, educational institutions and temples, the DIZ consisted mainly of old squares, such as Havelock Square and Dalhousie Square. These had mostly been rebuilt with nondescript four-storeyed concrete apartment buildings which, although sturdily built and functional, were not equipped with such luxuries as lifts. The colony was peaceful, neat and clean.

In those years, an air conditioner was a rare luxury for apartment dwellers; most government workers, on comparatively meagre salaries, cooled themselves in Delhi's heat with ceiling fans and water-fed air coolers. An apartment with an air conditioner would surely stand out from the others in the colony. By late evening of 3 July, team members had spotted a first-floor flat with an air conditioner in its window. It was flat 8/2A in Sector II of the DIZ area, off Mandir Marg, located some two kilometres from the Bagiya Barbeque restaurant.

The premises were found locked, the day's newspapers still on the floor in front of the main entrance. There was no activity outside, nor any indication of movement inside. Neighbours were not particularly forthcoming and seemed to have scant knowledge of the flat's occupants beyond superficial descriptions. 'The occupants of apartment 2A are not sociable,' one of the neighbours said. 'The couple keep to themselves. They give the impression that they belong to a higher class by their lifestyle,' said another. 'The lady never mixes with anyone.' No one knew where either of the two had gone.

Police noted a Maruti car with the registration plate DAC-3283, parked below in the apartment compound. Enquiries among the neighbours revealed that this was the car usually driven by the lady of the house. It was locked.

The police mounted a watch, hoping to surprise the prime suspect or anyone else who turned up. While investigators thought it unlikely that Sushil would show up, the police can never rely on assumptions. Nothing is taken for granted in an investigation.

There was no indication of Sushil Sharma's movements after he fled the crime scene late on 2 July, that is, until the morning of 4 July. While patrolling in the Malcha Marg Market of Delhi's Diplomatic Enclave, beat Constable Mukesh Kumar of Chanakyapuri police station spotted a white Maruti car parked on the roadside. The car appeared to have been locked and abandoned in front of ANZ Grindlays Bank, next to Fujia restaurant on Malcha Marg. He recalled a lookout for a similar car that was posted on the police station bulletin board, on the basis of a message flashed earlier to all police stations by the PCR. Mukesh Kumar lost no time in informing his superiors about the car and kept watch over it.

A number of police personnel from the local station rushed to the spot and gave the vehicle a cursory examination. They quickly established that the car with the number plate DL-2CA-1872 was registered in the name of Inder Mani Sharma, already identified as Sushil Sharma's father. It was the car that Sushil had driven to the Bagiya late in the evening, on 2 July.

Inspector Niranjan reached Malcha Marg in minutes with SI V.K. Rastogi and ASI Dayanand and immediately summoned a team of experts from CFSL. Officers opened the car in the presence of witnesses and forensic experts went over it with a fine-tooth comb.

They quickly saw indications that this was the very car that had transported the body to the Bagiya. There were some pale red spots in the dickey that resembled dried blood. Swabs were taken of these. A few strands of hair were detected around the left front side and also in the rear of the car. More were found in the dickey. An 'ABBA' wristwatch was in the dashboard. All these pieces of evidence were sealed as exhibits in the presence of the police officers and sent for examination.

That same morning, the gory case of the 'tandoor murder' hit the headlines. Given the sensational nature of the case, all the newspapers carried it on their front pages. News had reached the print media community only on 3 July, to fill the columns of newspapers the following day. Delhi's evening tabloids had been the first to break the story, with predictably salacious titles. The most egregious of these was 'Gang raped and killed – Chopped and burnt for good measure' – a truly disgraceful piece of journalism that only served to mislead and alarm the public.

It was not as if people weren't alarmed already. The burning of human flesh on a tandoor, an oven ubiquitous in restaurants and caterers' kitchens, suggested a repugnant crime. The very thought of eating anything from a tandoor evoked revulsion. Visions of roasted human flesh adorning a tandoori platter would haunt people throughout the country, particularly in Delhi.

For reporters though, it was cause for great excitement. While all of the media – print, radio and television – covered the case widely, the newspapers went berserk with their hysterical reportage. The involvement of a powerful politician only fuelled their natural inclination for hyperbole.

The morning papers of 4 July vied with each other in their lurid coverage of this 'macabre incident' and 'gruesome murder cover-up'. Reporters gave vent to their imagination, and speculation ran rife. Indian journalism has its own inimitable style, which may best be described as 'sensationalising', and 'colourful'. The Delhi contingent of journalists, who are quite capable of peddling conjecture as news, are masters of this style. Some of their articles on the tandoor murder verged on fantasy.

The outcome of all this was a distorted public perception of the crime and misinformation that would linger for years. One column reported the police 'not ruling out' the victim's gang rape 'before she was hacked to death'. Another went so far as to report that foreign missions had been approached to ascertain if any European women had gone missing. This, merely on the basis of the fair skin of the corpse found on the tandoor.

Screaming banner headlines immediately under the masthead grabbed the public's attention, and journalists could not pass up this opportunity to pontificate. They waxed lyrical on the sad state of society, holding forth in florid language on the depths to which morality had plummeted. The utter shock and horror of a terrorised community was expressed at great length. The incident had shattered the very sense of security in the nation's capital, the media declared. Never mind that the crime, which was far from a random killing of a member of the public, had been quickly and efficiently detected by the police, and the perpetrator was being vigorously pursued.

The news was especially shocking for a group of guests in the Ashok Yatri Niwas. Watching television in the lobby of the hotel, they were horrified when the screen flashed a news ticker of the day's headlines: 'Woman's body burnt in hotel's tandoor.' Seeing the focus settle on an event in their own proximity, they picked up the day's newspaper and were aghast to discover that the tandoor in question was on the other side of the hotel lobby. While they had been sleeping the previous night in the hotel's safe, luxurious rooms, criminals had been incinerating a murdered woman's body just metres away; and worse, they had done so on a tandoor that may well have cooked food for some of them. 'To be told an incident like this took place next door is kind of scary,' said one of the patrons.

Some newspapers carried related stories; even the ITDC was not spared attention: 'ITDC hotels have surprisingly provided sites for curious deaths. The post-mortem episode on Sunday lends the chain greater dubiousness. Sex, sleaze, politics, rivalry, jealousy, revenge or mere aberration are quoted as instigating forces, mostly to divert attention from the gruesome fact of the murder most foul.'[15] Much to the dismay of the ITDC management, one paper researched and published a list of murders that had taken place in ITDC hotels.

Of all the dramatis personae in the case, Head Constable Kunju fared the best in the media – and deservedly so. *The Tribune* perhaps best encapsulated his contribution:

> Constable Abdul Nazeer, who was put on an extended patrol duty, has emerged as a symbol of man's uncompromising conscience in this sordid drama of intrigue, gore and grime. Had he allowed

his intrepidity, enterprise and sense of duty to be clouded by the tricks of the criminal's henchmen, the real story would have been reduced to ashes with the body in the tandoor.[16]

Later in the year, on 14 December, Kunju would be honoured in an article in the 'Metropolitan' section of the *Hindustan Times*, being lauded among six 'who have not only excelled in their respective fields but set new social norms'. Featuring a friendly looking caricature, the article described him as a 'conscientious and dutiful person' whose actions had changed the image of Delhi Police.

Most policemen try to avoid media attention for fear of being trapped by wily journalists into saying something unintended or detrimental to an investigation. There is, it must be said, a dearth of training for officers in handling the media. Besides, if a police officer on a high-profile case such as the tandoor murder were to be at the beck and call of every reporter, he would be too busy talking to attend to his work.

Even so, I made myself available to the media as much as I could. Additionally, the Press Relations Officer (PRO) and two sub-inspector press officers liaised with the media from Delhi Police Headquarters. The PRO's room was regularly packed for briefings, and so it remained for the tandoor murder.

The media barrage in some ways aided the investigation. Sharma's photograph was regularly broadcast. With his likeness in almost every newspaper of the land, it would be difficult for him to travel incognito or stay anywhere for long without being recognised.

It also gave the police an opportunity to be forthright with the public in a manner that would best serve justice. I was convinced that any hesitation in identifying the accused positively and publicly would only work to his advantage. Sharma had already shown himself to be a master strategist, and the following months and years would prove him to be a formidable adversary. Procrastinating would provide him with a tactical advantage; he would attempt to use his influence and political clout to circumvent the due process of law.

Thus, along with providing the particulars of the crime to reporters in my very first interactions with them on 3 July, I unambiguously named Sushil Sharma as the suspected perpetrator.

This, and the deft handling of the police media briefings, ensured that Sushil Sharma became a social and political pariah. At the risk of being accused of conducting a trial by media (which did happen at a later stage in the case), the message was loud and clear: There was little doubt of Sushil Sharma's involvement in the reprehensible crime and anyone supporting or harbouring him would be dealt with accordingly by the police.

Just as the morning newspapers of 4 July were being read over morning tea, and Delhi homes and workplaces were abuzz with talk of the tandoor murder, the police took Keshav to apartment 8/2A – the flat with the air conditioner in the window. Keshav promptly identified it as the place where Sushil had been living with his wife Naina Sahni.

The police watch posted at the site the previous night had nothing to report; all had been quiet, and no one had as much as approached the flat. A special team led by Chief Investigating Officer Inspector Niranjan Singh, the SHO of Mandir Marg police station, Inspector Suraj Prakash and SI Jagat Singh of Connaught Place police station, arrived at the apartment. Niranjan now decided to inspect the flat in the presence of an independent witness. Dhir Singh Chauhan, an upstanding member of the public, was asked to attend for this purpose. Officers broke open the lock on the front door and we entered the home of the chief suspect – and the victim.

The front door opened into a compact, sparsely furnished living room. The immediate impression was of modest amenities; it had been designed to meet the needs, if not the wants, of a lower-level government functionary. Niranjan walked gingerly to the left corner of the living room and lifted the telephone receiver from its cradle. A dial tone buzzed – the line was connected.

Abutting the living room was the dining area, which housed a round dining table; to the right was a small kitchen. A door from the dining room led into the bedroom, which was crowded with furniture. A double bed sat adjacent to the wall beside the door, with a cupboard and a chest of drawers positioned along the opposite wall. An air conditioner filled a window on the left outer wall and to its right was an ensuite bathroom.

We were cautious in our preliminary survey, careful not to disturb evidence. The survey revealed many telltale signs of violence and disturbance, as well as indications of a hasty departure. Hurried, largely futile attempts had evidently been made to clean the floor and furniture. Investigators found dried blood in places throughout the apartment, proof of the grisly acts that had been committed within its walls.

The walls themselves had a tale to tell. There was a bullet mark on one wall, and a bullet hole in the plywood cover in the window above the air conditioner. Lead from a discharged bullet was found on the bedroom carpet, just under the bed. Four spent handgun cartridges lay in two bowls on a dressing table, with another on the floor, near a stool on which a telephone sat.

A dried pool of blood with splatters around it sullied the bedroom carpet. There were tufts of long, broken hair stuck in it. The cotton mattress of the double bed was bare and heavily bloodstained in one corner. Electrical wires leading to the air conditioner near the wall were spattered with blood. Blood was also found on the cupboard, the wooden rack, and on the chatai[17] lying between the double bed and the cupboard. A bloodied cloth had been left in the bathroom.

Someone had placed a near-empty glass tumbler of tomato soup on the cupboard, and beside it stood an empty bottle of vodka. An air-pistol was found under the cupboard. Bundles of documents, some of which were sale records of the Bagiya Barbeque restaurant, were stacked atop the cupboard. Torn pieces of a letter written in Hindi and English lay scattered in the wastepaper basket.

The police crime team and other experts from CFSL lifted samples of blood and inspected the scene further. Considering the high-profile nature of the case, the most senior government forensic functionary in the country, Dr V.N. Sehgal, the director of CFSL, visited the apartment at Mandir Marg with his colleague Dr S.K. Singh.

Photographers took innumerable shots of the scene. A ballistic expert from CFSL, Senior Scientific Officer (SSO) Roop Singh, visited the following day. He collected the cartridges and the discharged bullet from the scene for forensic analysis. He noted that they were of a .32 calibre weapon and had been recently fired.

The physical evidence spoke of an appalling crime in the apartment, but the home and its contents told other stories. Poignant indications of a full, if troubled, marital life remained throughout – the proof of love, hope and dreams before murder ended it all. Personal correspondence and papers described achievements and affections, some frankly recording the logic and sorrow of complicated lives. A cherry-coloured diary declared boldly in red: 'Sushil Sharma loves Naina – Naina loves Sushil'.

For the first time, we glimpsed likenesses of the living Naina, a vivacious-looking young woman in her late twenties, looking back at us from photographs in the apartment. In some of the photographs, she gazed into the camera coyly, lovingly, doubtless at the man who would later take her life. A small album held photographs of the couple's families, and group photographs showed Naina and Sushil together. There were photographs, too, of Naina with her family, some taken with a woman later identified as Sushil Sharma's mother.

There were bills such as one would expect to find: from the Bagiya, for the telephone and other miscellaneous services. Papers relating to Naina's car, registration number DAC 3283, were also in the apartment, along with letters and assorted documents. A cheque made out to the Prime Minister's Relief Fund was also found during the thorough search that the forensic team conducted.

The usual police formalities were ensured, and the police seized many of these items as exhibits, which would later serve to support an account of events that was just beginning to take shape.

Among the items seized and sealed were two video cassettes of the Hindi films *Bombay* and *Policewala Gunda*. The local video movie supplier Pradeep Sharma, of 10 Jain Mandir Marg, later confirmed he had supplied them to the lady of the house, Naina Sahni, on 2 July. Jagdish Taneja of Music Mahal at Udhyan Marg confirmed that these cassettes had gone to Naina Sahni from his shop via Pradeep Sharma of Aditi Cables.

Perhaps galvanised by the shocking news of the murder, some of the neighbours became more forthcoming. But no one knew where the occupants of the apartment had gone. The Gujrals and the Chaudharys, next-door neighbours, told the police they had witnessed frequent fights between the couple, and on one occasion they had seen the man dragging the lady from the ground floor up to the flat on the first floor.

In all, there was a plethora of evidence at the Mandir Marg apartment to link the murder that had obviously been committed there to the chief suspect – and the chief suspect to the garden restaurant where he had sought to destroy the evidence of his crime.

After inspecting the apartment and the car found abandoned on Malcha Marg that morning, the investigating team could now safely conclude that the murder had been committed in the bedroom of the apartment. The corpse was then removed and transported in the car to the Bagiya Barbeque restaurant.

Police later made inquires about the leasehold on the flat. How Sushil and Naina came to live in the government flat was revealing of Sushil's ways. 8/2A off Mandir Marg was allotted to J.P. Sharma, a government employee. Enquiries revealed that J.P. Sharma was Sushil's distant relative, and he had rented the flat to Sushil against the rules and regulations of government housing.

Unconfirmed reports indicated that Sushil had used his political clout to have the flat allotted to his relative, for the sole purpose of using it himself.

5
Family Trouble

Among the papers seized from the Mandir Marg house was a summons from the court of Metropolitan Magistrate H.S. Sharma, addressed to Ravi Naina, daughter of Harbhajan Singh, resident of 24/3 West Patel Nagar. The police promptly tracked down Naina's parents at that address.

In the meantime, officers had contacted Naina's colleagues at the DPYC, where she had been the general secretary. They, too, had pointed the investigating team to her family. By all accounts, Naina's parents were ordinary, hard-working, middle-class people. Her father Harbhajan Singh was a retired senior store-keeper at the Army Ordinance Depot and her mother Jaswant Kaur was a physical trainer in a west Delhi school. Her brothers ran a sanitary fittings business in Kashmere Gate.

There was every indication now that the body would be positively identified by Naina's parents as that of their missing daughter. We thus sought their cooperation, as is usual practice, to identify her burnt remains.

Naina's family were unequivocal in acknowledging that Sushil and Naina were married, and that they were staying together in the DIZ area. But they immediately rebuffed any suggestion that their daughter could have met with foul play. The body, they said, could not possibly be Naina's: she was away in the Himalayas, somewhere between Kullu and Manali in Himachal Pradesh. They based their claim, they told the police, on Naina telling them that she had planned to take a trip there, when she last met them on Friday, 30 June. This was corroborated by Naina's aunt in New Friends Colony, who said she had received a call from Naina on that same day and Naina had informed her of her plans to go to Kullu.

After the forensic examination of the apartment on 4 July, the police took Naina's parents, brothers Ranjit Singh and Manmeet Singh and bhabhi (sister-in-law) Gurbachan Kaur, to the Mandir Marg flat. On seeing the condition of the flat and reaching the inescapable conclusions to which the evidence pointed, they broke down and wept.

Though reluctant, Naina's parents, brothers and bhabhi were then prevailed upon to accompany the police to the mortuary, which was situated within a kilometre of the Mandir Marg apartment, to view the remains there.

After recording a medico-legal autopsy in respect of the charred body they had received in the early hours of 3 July, the Ram Manohar Lohia Hospital authorities had sent the body to the mortuary at the Lady Hardinge Medical College. The college hospital was responsible for conducting autopsies in the New Delhi area. In the absence of immediate identification, the corpse was stored in the mortuary's cold chamber, where it would remain for up to seventy-two hours, awaiting identification by kith and kin or a known acquaintance. This is routine procedure for police in India when dealing with an unclaimed or unidentified body.

Naina's family were tactfully ushered into the Lady Hardinge Medical College mortuary to view the charred remains. Officers are carefully briefed for such delicate events, these being among the more difficult in a police officer's line of duty and, indubitably, the most painful of any parent's or relative's life.

The family's mood was sombre, and as the body was uncovered in their presence, they quietly shed tears. Her mother seemed most affected. Although they showed signs of recognising the remains, they declined to identify them. The expression in their clouded eyes upon seeing the silver anklets recovered from the ashes indicated that these too were Naina's, but they remained steadfast in their refusal to provide positive identification. Gurbachan Kaur, Naina's bhabhi, merely conceded that Naina had 'similar' anklets.[18]

Much to our disappointment and frustration, Naina's family's hesitant and somewhat reluctant cooperation with the police investigation ended at this juncture. There was no anger or outrage over the horrific acts that took their daughter's life and sought to obliterate evidence of the crime – only tears, then denial.

It is true that the charred cadaver was a gruesome sight to behold for anyone, let alone a relative. But the outline of Naina's features was still discernible, at least to someone who knew her. Surely, too, they had recognised her anklets even if they had been truly unable to see beyond the ruination of her body by the fire. In any event, the dire state of the apartment – and that no one had heard from Naina in several days – should have been enough to convince her family that she had come to harm.

Our immediate, and most charitable, thought was that Naina's parents, brothers and bhabhi were reluctant to accept that she was no more; they were clutching at straws – and the hope that Naina would still return from a trip to Kullu. The family's confoundingly non-committal approach to their daughter's murder as events unfolded would leave us nonplussed, however, as would their steadfast refusal to believe anything adverse about Sushil.

Astoundingly, Naina's parents even suggested that Sushil be brought to the mortuary. Only if he identified the charred body as Naina's in their presence, they declared, would they accept that these were her remains.

Their peculiar behaviour left much to conjecture but ultimately, unlike the physical details of the crime, an understanding of these emotional aspects remained elusive. I had seen countless families of murder victims over the years: some shell-shocked, some vengeful, and almost all expressing grief for their loss. But I had never encountered a family so ambivalent, so detached from the murder of their loved one, as Ravi Naina Sahni's.

Later, Naina's close relations would have no qualms about telling the police it would not be possible for them to stand witness against Sushil Sharma: the family was greatly indebted to him.

Perhaps Naina's parents were too beholden to Sushil to confront the truth of his crime – or they were simply afraid of him.[19] I have also often wondered whether they had, in some senses, abandoned their daughter long before her murder.[20] Naina's lifestyle, as we would discover, was a cause of concern for her parents and siblings. Her habits, which were decidedly 'modern', probably horrified the somewhat conservative family. Harbhajan Singh and his wife may have viewed Sushil Sharma's arrival on the scene as the best chance of making an honest woman of her. Sadly, they may even have apportioned some blame to Naina herself for her terrible fate.

Their reasons for failing to identify her body, at any rate, were neither of consequence nor of any consolation insofar as the progress of the investigation was concerned. But it could prove detrimental to the investigation's credibility. Also, if the body was not formally identified, it would certainly impede our work. The team needed to find someone, preferably a close associate of the deceased, who could positively identify the remains.

Investigators turned to the DPYC, where Naina had been the general secretary alongside Sushil as the president. They learned that Naina had had a long-term romantic relationship with Matloob Karim of Turkman Gate, who had previously served on the committee with Naina and Sushil as one of the organisation's general secretaries. The pair had reportedly lived together, and though they had parted, they had done so amicably and kept in touch.[21]

Matloob, it seemed, had remained Naina's confidant until her death. Indeed, investigators would later discover that her speaking with him had precipitated her murder. At this stage of the case, however, Matloob was only seen as the best hope for a positive identification of the corpse, and on 5 July, he was taken to the mortuary.

Matloob recognised his friend and former lover's remains at the morgue and sobbed. Without any hesitation, he formally identified the remains as Naina's on the basis of his personal knowledge of the victim, from the structure of her nose, forehead and hair, a clump of which had survived the flames. Matloob was likewise positive about the anklets, which he identified as Naina's.

He later said, 'I could immediately recognise the body as that of Naina … Her face and hair were not burnt. Naina always used to make a bun above her shoulders. That typical bun was still there when I saw the body.'[22]

Matloob further revealed to the police that Sushil and Naina's relationship had recently deteriorated, and they often clashed. Sushil, he said, would at times beat Naina. Matloob's description of marital discord erupting into violence – with Naina inevitably bearing the brunt of it – matched what their neighbours at the apartment complex had said.

Unsurprisingly, the print media was quick to seize on Matloob's involvement with the murder victim. Sniffing a prime opportunity for salacious copy, crime reporters began digging into Naina's and Sushil's pasts, and in no time prurient stories of their exploits and conquests at university were public fare. Matloob himself was not spared the depredations of this 'proactive investigative journalism'; his alleged love life with Naina before Sushil came onto the scene was unearthed and laid painfully bare in the capital's dailies in the coming days.[23]

Nevertheless, Matloob had done his duty to the deceased, something her own family had resiled from; his grief at her death was evidently sincere. And crucially, Matloob's willing assistance allowed the police to move the investigation forward. Having secured his formal identification, the police could press for an autopsy to be conducted on the corpse – now identified as the mortal remains of Ravi Naina Sharma, de facto wife of Sushil Sharma.

6

Murder Most Foul

The monsoon's advance signals a primal battle between the forces of nature – fire and water. The moist winds bring promise of comfort and blunt the heat, but summer will not release its grip on the land so easily.

Delhi is steaming. Those who can afford to, take shelter behind desert air coolers which, while a boon in the scorching dry heat of April and May, offer less relief in the sultry months of July and August.

Still, the whirring of cooler fans in apartment windows – complimented by the distant rumbling of traffic and punctuated by the odd raucous dialogue from behind closed doors – is the soundtrack of this Sunday evening in Mandir Marg. The streets are all but deserted; everyone is going about their lives, finishing the day's chores, making dinner or simply relaxing with the only affordable pastime in those days – television.

At apartment 8/2A, DIZ Sector-II, Mandir Marg, Ravi Naina has retreated to her bedroom and the comfort of her air conditioner. She is perhaps the only one in the apartment block enjoying such a luxury. Naina pours herself a drink – her favourite, a Bloody Mary made with the usual vodka, but with tomato soup in place of tomato juice – and settles down for the evening.

She is contemplating a future far away, and there is no place for her husband in her plans. Intelligent, ambitious and strikingly attractive, Naina has managed to graduate from university, obtain a pilot's licence, hold a position in the Congress party and run a successful boutique – all before reaching thirty. Her relationships with men, however, are a different story and have been less than fulfilling: two attempts to find lasting love have left her disillusioned. At least one man, her first serious love, still supports her dreams. Now, she hopes to make a life for herself alone in Australia and she has enlisted his help to achieve this. It is a brave step, emigrating to a land far removed from Delhi but one where her talents and charm might serve her well.

At about seven in the evening, Naina dials Jagdish Taneja at the video library in the neighbourhood and asks him to deliver two cassettes. She then rings up her confidant and former lover, Matloob Karim, at his residence. She asks him whether he has visited Ram Swaroop, the travel consultant in Jor Bagh, to collect her visa for Australia. Matloob tells her he will in a day or two, and with that they end the conversation.

Naina's live-in partner, paramour, lover and unofficial husband Sushil Sharma drives into the apartment complex at around 8.15 p.m., parks his car and lets himself into the apartment. There is no loving welcome from Naina, but she quietly offers him a drink. The simmering tension between the two is palpable, even as Sushil pours the drink and both partake in their favourite tipple. There isn't much exchange of conversation – not for the moment, anyway.

Sushil is tense. For some time now he has doubted Naina's fidelity, and he may have reason for doing so. The consummate politician that he is, he senses keenly the changed tenor of their relationship, and he can feel her drawing away from him. That his political fortunes have recently ebbed is also gnawing at him. While the fact that he has forsaken her by refusing to acknowledge their relationship publicly eludes him, Sushil is roiling inside that his Naina is forsaking him just when he needs her support the most.

He is stung, too, by her displays of arrogance and rebelliousness, which have become all too frequent of late. A couple of months ago, she had raised her hand at him, and he still dwells grimly on it, his mind dark and clouded with jealousy. As their relationship has deteriorated, he has maintained a surveillance on her. Whether real or imagined, Sushil sees signs of Naina's betrayal everywhere.

At 8.30 p.m., Pradeep Sharma, the video shop attendant, arrives and delivers the two cassettes. Pradeep sees Naina and Sushil together in the house, but notices nothing untoward. As the videowala departs, Sushil goes to the telephone in the outer room of their small flat. Bringing the receiver to his ear, he presses the redial button and listens silently. A man answers with a 'hello' at the other end. Sushil immediately recognises Matloob Karim's voice. His heart chills and then hardens as he replaces the receiver.

Seething, he strides into the bedroom and confronts Naina. Why, he asks, is she still carrying on with Matloob? Why has she not shunned him and put an end to their relationship? Naina replies curtly that it is none of his business. He has absolutely no right to interfere in her private life, she says acidly.

Naina's retort adds fuel to Sushil's burning anger, which is fast growing to levels beyond his control. He feels anguished, his thoughts are straying towards the irrational – as they have so many times in the past, when he has entertained a desire to be rid of her. His mind has time and again toyed with various scenarios, juggling and weighing the different possibilities, the avenues and means by which he can eliminate her.

He observes Naina and finds her in a suitably inebriated state. The liquor that has emboldened his agitated mind has merely stupefied hers. A dark inner voice, the kind that a man in his senses recoils from, goads him to act: Now is the time to do it.

Quietly he goes to the chest of drawers, opens one, takes out his revolver and inspects it, then loads it with four cartridges. In cold blood, without a second thought, he turns around and aims at Naina's head, firing three times at point-blank range. Two of the bullets find their mark in Naina's head and neck. The third bullet misses and hits the plywood by the air conditioner.

Naina falls, bleeding profusely. She writhes in pain on the bed for a moment, and is still. She dies almost instantaneously.

The drone and rattle of desert coolers and the assortment of sounds within the flats – of ordinary family life and favourite Sunday television soap operas – continue unabated even after Naina's killing. The noise of the discharging pistol and the bullet ricocheting against the bedroom wall is lost in the din of colony life; not one neighbour hears the fatal shots. Though the inhabitants of the four-storeyed tenements live cheek by jowl, everyone remains oblivious to the end of a promising young life in their midst – at least until the police descend on the apartment block in force and newspapers break the story a day later.

Sushil gathers his wits about him. He calms his nerves by drinking cold water from the fridge. His mind is racing, contemplating the next move: how to dispose of Naina's body.

The first thought that comes to his mind is to dump the body into the river Yamuna. That, he feels, should be easy. And then he can make good his escape. Escape? Where to? Well, that's secondary – first things first!

He looks around him and acts hurriedly, making a desperate attempt to remove all signs of the killing. He bundles up the body in the same bed sheet on which Naina had fallen and then wraps it in the plastic sheet that covers the dining table. He washes the room to clean it of the splattered blood, and changes his own bloodstained clothes. Peering outside, he satisfies himself that there is no one around and that nobody has been alarmed by the sound of gunfire.

He scurries downstairs and backs his Maruti close to the staircase, then runs back to the apartment. He drags the bundle with the dead body through the flat to the main door, the connecting first-floor corridor, and then down the stairs to the ground floor. Folding down the rear seat of his 800cc white Maruti car, he hoists the bundle into the dickey.

Sushil's silken white kurta pyjama is badly stained. Blood had spattered on it the moment he shot Naina. He has smeared it further while hauling her corpse through the apartment, down the stairs and into the car. He hurries upstairs to the apartment and changes into another white kurta pyjama. Back in the car in no time, he drives away. It is now past 9.30 p.m. on Sunday, 2 July 1995.

Whether by divine dispensation or coincidence, Jagdev Singh, a neighbour from the next block, witnesses Sushil loading the bundle into the dickey. Amba Dass, a head constable patrolling in the area, sees Sushil driving away in his car. Neither man thinks much of it until later.

Sushil drives from Mandir Marg to Kali Bari and Gole Dak Khana, down Ashoka Road to Firoz Shah Road and onwards. Turning right past the Railway Tilak Bridge, he drives along Indraprastha Marg, past the front of Delhi Police Headquarters plaza and reaches the ITO bridge, which stretches across the broad, polluted expanse of the Yamuna river and its floodplains to Vikas Marg.

But his hopes of ridding himself of the body in the Yamuna are now dashed. The bridge is full of traffic and heavily congested, with vehicles moving bumper to bumper, even at this late hour. He realises that he will almost certainly be exposed and apprehended should he attempt to dump the body into the river.

Sushil's mind is working overtime for a solution. In a sudden brainwave, he thinks of the tandoor at the Bagiya restaurant. Yes, he tells himself, he can dispose of the body by burning it on the tandoor. At the end of the bridge over the Yamuna, he performs a U-turn and drives back to Ashoka Road.

Sushil reaches the Bagiya at 10.15 p.m. and parks his car in the parking space just inside the main gate. Mahesh Prasad, a security guard, sees the car enter and makes the relevant entry of the car number along with the time of arrival in the register. Philip Paul, who performs at the Bagiya in the evenings with his wife Nisha, is entering the restaurant and notices Sushil in the car.

Sushil beckons Keshav Kumar, the manager of the Bagiya Barbeque, and tells him that there has been a major mishap – that he has committed a massive blunder. He wants the restaurant to be closed quickly and the staff sent off, so he can dispose of the incriminating bundle by burning it on the tandoor.

Keshav understands. He is horrified, disgusted even, but his loyalty to Sushil compels him to go inside the restaurant and act on his boss's command. This man has seen him through some of the most difficult times of his life, and he will not desert him now.

Karan Singh, Sushil's former employee, sees Sushil speaking to Keshav in the car. He comes to the car to greet him, broaching the subject of some outstanding wages. Sushil fobs him off by asking him to come another day and take the payment. Karan leaves.

Sushil continues to remain seated in the car, watched by Sultan Singh, one of the security guards, who is standing near the hotel gate. In the meantime, Keshav asks the customers present in the restaurant to finish their dinner quickly. He extinguishes the restaurant lights, even as they gulp down the remainder of their food. A customer, Narendra Nath Gupta, is astonished to find himself suddenly sitting in a darkened restaurant. The patrons are effectively forced to leave.

Keshav asks all the staff and workers too, to leave for the day. Philip and Nisha, the husband-wife duo, are surprised. They see Sushil sitting in the car as they leave. The staff members are given ₹25 each by Keshav in lieu of the dinner normally provided to them at the restaurant.

Once the customers and the staff have left, Keshav approaches Sushil, who reverses the car to the steps of the restaurant. Keshav brings a large black polythene tarpaulin and together they unload the bundle from the dickey onto the tarpaulin. They carry it straight to the kitchen area and place it next to the tandoor. In the process, Keshav's clothes are stained here and there with blood. It is now around 10.50 p.m.

Sushil asks Keshav to draw the kanaat and fixes it to block the entry to the restaurant. They then pick up a few wooden planks that are piled on the grass around the chairs in front of the restaurant, and break them into smaller pieces. They pick up other items of wood and party propaganda material and arrange these like a pyre around the body, still bundled in the bed sheet. They place it atop the tandoor. They pile more wood around and above the bundle. Keshav then leaves at Sushil's behest and returns with four large packs of Amul butter. He places them on the bundle with the body. It is now a little past 11 p.m. Sushil sets the pyre alight, consigning Naina's body to the flames.

As Naina's body burns, Sushil pauses, the first time he has done so in the preceding two hours. He places his pistol on a table and pours several glasses of cold water over his head, to cool himself and wash away the mortal sin he has just committed. '*Yeh maine kya kar diya? Yeh mujhse kya ho gaya?* (What have I done? How could I have done this?)' The expression of regret, if it is regret, comes far too late. He pours more cold water over himself.

Keshav stokes the blazing fire, while Sushil positions himself near the entrance at the kanaat. The revolver is still in his pocket; if need be, he will use it again. The rising flames from the makeshift pyre leap high and the billowing smoke is visible in the night sky over the Bagiya – high and far enough to catch the attention of those in the vicinity. The vegetable vendor across the lane, the elderly Anaro Devi, is alarmed by the leaping flames. As is Constable Kunju, who is on patrol and catches sight of them from a distance.

7

The Earth Shakes

While Sushil appeared to have been slippery in many of his dealings before the crime and afterwards proved most elusive, the fracas in the wake of the tandoor murder was immense and unavoidable – no less for his political colleagues and mentors. With the main accused in the tandoor murder being a prominent political figure, extravagant political reactions and a massive fallout were inevitable.

The Opposition party, not to pass up an opportunity to smear the Congress, made much of Sushil Sharma's former position in the youth wing of the party. Many in the Congress, especially those Sushil was said to be close to, ducked for cover. The Congress leadership put up a brave front while the party's damage control machinery swung into action.

Madan Lal Khurana, Delhi's Bharatiya Janata Party (BJP) chief minister, fired off a letter to the official in charge of law and order in the capital: P.K. Dave, the lieutenant governor of Delhi. The letter said that the news regarding a young lady being cut to pieces and burnt in a tandoor – that, too, in a semi-government-run establishment, an ITDC hotel – was not only sensational, it had also instilled fear in the hearts of Delhi's citizens, especially its female population, leading to a climate of terror.

Quoting from the newspapers, the chief minister pointed out that the name of a youth leader of a political party had been prominently mentioned in connection with the murder. It was, he wrote, such people who were exercising power in the ruling government at the Centre. He added that it was necessary to make an example of such anti-social elements by taking exemplary action against them.

Khurana cautioned that because of the political clout enjoyed by this former youth leader, attempts may be made to draw a pardah over the crime. He further questioned the legality of using the vacant front lawns of a government hotel to run a garden restaurant for profit. After expressing his outrage at the offences at the Bagiya Barbeque restaurant, he asked that the city police chief be told to ensure an 'impartial and fearless' investigation.

Others in the BJP also tried to gain mileage from the murder. Demanding a CBI enquiry, Delhi BJP MP Professor Vijay Kumar Malhotra declared it was a matter of shame for the Congress to have their state unit's past office-bearers allegedly involved in such heinous crimes. The deputy leader of the BJP in the Lok Sabha, Jaswant Singh, took a broader view, arguing that this murder was

> ... symptomatic of much that is buried under it. We were getting used to the criminalisation of politics, but suddenly this murder has made us acutely aware of the politicisation of crime ... What should make every thinking person sit up is the fact that the whole atmosphere is being vitiated in state after state due to the malaise which has taken Naina's life. This will have profound political implications.

Members of the smaller parties also made observations similar to those of the BJP leaders. Janata Dal National General Secretary Ramvir Singh Bidhuri stated that the alleged involvement of a Congress politician in the gruesome murder only showed what kind of people were part of the organisation. Sharad Yadav, also of the Janata Dal, observed that 'There has been degeneration in the political life of the country. There are offenders in all political parties. What is worrisome is that this number is multiplying faster than the capacity of the social system to absorb such aberrations.'

Communist Party of India General Secretary Inderjit Gupta was just as candid in his assessment of the nexus between crime and politics. Like Jaswant Singh and Sharad Yadav, he was less inclined to score political points than make a general observation about the state of politics in India. He bluntly stated that 'criminals are there in all political parties. So why be surprised if they are in the Youth Congress too! After all, it is common knowledge that there are dozens of criminals in the Congress party too.'

The talk in the capital at the time was telling. That the conscience of many among the political elite had been awakened was duly noted. Most leaders appeared to attribute the ghastly excesses of the tandoor murder less to the bestiality of the murderer than to the criminalisation of politics. The crime was now described explicitly by all classes of people as a disease, spreading not only in the Congress, but also among other parties at the centre of India's national politics.

Media scrutiny, nonetheless, fell squarely on Sharma and his role in the ruling party. *The Pioneer*, reporting on 'The suspects, the victim and their contacts', quoted Congress sources in revealing that Sushil, said to be a loyalist of R.K. Dhawan, had used his 'good offices' to help Deep Chand Bandhu become president of the Delhi Pradesh Congress Committee (DPCC). A photograph prominently displayed alongside the article showed Sushil and Keshav with the erstwhile cinema idol Rajesh Khanna at the latter's Congress victory procession after winning the by-election for the Lok Sabha seat of New Delhi in 1992.

Keshav, being almost insignificant in the political firmament, attracted much less attention in the media. It did emerge, however, that he was sometimes referred to in Congress circles as 'mini Tytler',[24] for his resemblance to Jagdish Tytler, the controversial Central minister. This was, it must be said, a dubious compliment, and an eerie coincidence considering the allegations they faced.[25]

Senior party figures were soon to regret Keshav's likeness and his new-found prominence. A photograph in *The Pioneer* depicted Keshav and Sushil with Congress luminaries Priyanka Gandhi,

Ramesh Chennitala and R.K. Dhawan. It would be hard to quantify the effect these images had on the public. Suffice it to say the photographs of the men who had only a few days ago burned the body of a slain woman on a tandoor, standing close and in good cheer to senior Congress leaders, was devastating for the party.

Perhaps unsurprisingly, the tandoor murder elicited a strong response from several Congress leaders too. Congress spokesman V.N. Gadgil declared, 'We condemn all such acts'. Reacting to reports about Sharma's involvement, he said, 'Let the investigation be complete, we will not hesitate to take action.'

Maninderjeet Singh (M.S.) Bitta, the incumbent Indian Youth Congress president and Sushil's implacable foe, saw no reason to wait for the investigation. He lost no time in announcing to the media that Sushil Sharma had been expelled from the Youth Congress for misconduct and undesirable activities. He went on to call Sushil a disgrace to the organization: he had indulged in immoral activities and was responsible for fostering indiscipline. M.S. Bitta also made a veiled but unmistakeable reference to Sushil's alleged womanising within the Youth Congress.[26]

Some of Sushil's former colleagues were more circumspect, and everyone in the Congress sought to depoliticise the murder. While expressing shock at the appalling crime, All India Mahila Congress President Girija Vyas demanded punishment for the culprits 'regardless of the political party they belong to'. DPYC President Jagdish Yadav, Sharma's successor and staunch opponent, who had taken the post of president in January of that year, was far less reserved. Indeed, Yadav was among the most vehement of all political figures in his condemnation of Sharma and Keshav. 'All those involved in the act,' he declared, 'should be hanged to death. Nothing less ... can deter people from committing such ghastly acts.'

But perhaps the most emotive of all political statements, which also made a concerted effort to link the outrage of the tandoor murder to the Congress party in general, was the action by the Mahila Morcha (the women's wing of the BJP) on Wednesday,

5 July. Shouting slogans and waving placards emblazoned with slogans like 'Hang the Congress murderers' and 'Women are not things to be burned alive', members of the Delhi Mahila Morcha, led by its president Prem Gupta, marched from the party's national headquarters towards Home Minister S.B. Chauhan's office. Ms Gupta grandly declared that no woman was safe from the goonda elements in the Congress, who were protected by the powerful in the party. The demonstration was stopped by the police at Windsor Place, though a delegation later delivered a memorandum to the minister's office, demanding firm action against the perpetrators of the tandoor murder.

Not to be outdone, the DPYC held its own, more sizeable, demonstration a day later. The assembly was surely called with the intention of deflecting the political aspect of the issue, and to emphasise the disgust within the Congress over the murder. Led by Jagdish Yadav, the procession marched to the front of Delhi Police Headquarters at Indraprastha Estate. With placards hoisted aloft over the crowd reading 'Punish the Murderers', fists raised in the air and chanting in a manner similar to their BJP counterparts, the Youth Congress protesters demanded that Sushil Sharma be brought to justice.

The ITDC, in the meantime, announced that the licence granted to the owners of the Bagiya would be terminated. ITDC Managing Director Anil Bhandari also promised that an enquiry would be held to contemplate preventive measures against such 'gruesome and unthinkable' incidents. The security arrangements at ITDC hotels would be tightened, he declared, adding that 'legal experts would be consulted on filing a suit for damages against the owners of Bagiya.'

Beyond the obvious, it seemed the ITDC had good reason for terminating its contract with Excel Hotels. *The Pioneer* reported that a Delhi businessman had disclosed to the paper that despite his company being the lowest bidder for the contract to run the Bagiya Barbeque restaurant, Excel Hotels – which was not even in the original list of bidders – was given the contract at the last moment.

Predictably, the vice-president of the hotels division of ITDC, M.D. Kapoor, denied that the restaurant contract had been awarded due to the political connections of the partners: 'We floated an open tender ... all bidders had equal opportunity ... One of the partners has a long experience in the business,' he said.

Few were convinced by ITDC's desperate attempts to rally under media fire. For the press, and for much of the public, the circumstances surrounding the murder were almost as sinister as the crime itself. An *Indian Express* editorial was particularly scathing about the blatant political manipulation that had led to Excel Hotels receiving the ITDC contract. It pointed to the 'obnoxious political culture' of the Youth Congress that both this incident and the tandoor murder evinced. The article also suggested that the brazenness of the murder cover-up showed that the offenders were accustomed to getting away with serious criminal acts.

Finally, the editorial argued that the circumstances surrounding the tandoor murder were symptomatic of a historical malaise within the Congress. The crime, it argued, was redolent of the 'lumpen behaviour associated with Sanjay Gandhi' during the Emergency.[27]

An editorial in the *Tribune* on the same day – with laudable foresight, as it turned out – underlined the importance of speedy, unhindered justice; not just for the victim, but for the city and society at large:

> ... And here begins the inescapable duty of the Delhi Government and the citizens who know something about the crime. The facts must be brought out into the open and the killer must be punished without legal or other procedural delays. Delhi is becoming the crime capital of India. Such a murder does not kill one Naina Sahni. It kills a vital part of our social organism.[28]

The reference to the 'lumpen behaviour associated with Sanjay Gandhi' did not need to be any more explicit for Delhi's residents to know what the writer intended. While the Emergency[29] had occurred nearly two decades earlier, and Sanjay Gandhi had died fifteen years before the tandoor murder, on 23 June 1980, the excesses of Indira Gandhi's younger son and his henchmen were etched deeply in the collective memory of the nation's capital.

A capricious, vindictive man, Sanjay Gandhi never held high office, yet ran a parallel government by virtue of his hold over the Congress party machinery. He presided over a de facto police state during the twenty-one months of the Emergency in 1975–77. Delhiites still shudder at the mere mention of his brutal slum demolitions and forced sterilisation programme.

Like the memory, the man's influence lingered with those he had fostered in the party organisation. It was these same 'party brokers' who would mentor a new generation of Congress politicians. Indeed, R.K. Dhawan, who was a close associate of Sanjay Gandhi and a key figure in the Emergency, was said to be one of Sushil Sharma's mentors in the Congress.[30] Sushil's activities and notoriety had probably caught the attention of party recruiters while he was still a student of Delhi University.

Student power in India is hardly a recent phenomenon. Inder Sharma, the doyen of the travel industry in India, was the first to bring to my attention the heady mix of student and mainstream politics in the country. It was, as Inder told me, first effectively harnessed by the Father of the Nation, Mahatma Gandhi, during the Quit India Movement of 1942. Post Independence, however, Pandit Jawaharlal Nehru, the first prime minister of India, was wary about the then National Students Congress becoming involved, or even taking too much interest, in politics. He was very particular that student unions should concentrate only on academic matters. Under Nehru, the National Students' Congress was renamed and reconstituted as the National Students' Union of India (NSUI).

Nevertheless, students continued to take an active interest in politics. The nation witnessed their might in 1977, when, led by Jayaprakash Narayan, they were instrumental in ousting Indira

Gandhi during the Janata wave. In many Indian states, student power has asserted itself strongly, even playing a key role in toppling governments.

In the state of Assam, student agitators went so far as to take the reins of power themselves, governing from 1985 to 1989 and later, from 1996 to 2001, with the Asom Gana Parishad (Assam People's Association or AGP), being formed from the Assam Students' Union (AASU). That the 'secret killings' – state-sponsored murder – took place in Assam under the AGP amply exemplifies the criminality of some who have risen to power via student politics.

The political power of students has, in any event, only increased with time, after legislative changes and with an increasingly demographically young nation. Prime Minister Rajiv Gandhi championed the Sixty-first Amendment of the Constitution of India, which was passed by the Lok Sabha in December 1988, lowering the voting age from twenty-one years to eighteen. This brought a veritable sea of youngsters, many of them students, into the electorate.

A youthful population – around 41 per cent of India is below the age of twenty years[31] – has spurred major political parties to form 'youth cells' to harness youth power and mobilise youngsters for party interests. The aim of student bodies is ostensibly to project and protect students' interests – to pursue objectives which genuinely affect students' lives, such as better transportation, improved facilities on campus or reforms in the education system. Such matters have tended to become secondary, however, for young student representatives busy proving themselves to their seniors in the party proper. Many student representatives are, it would appear, involved in student politics just so they can fulfil their future political aspirations.

Youthful energy and attractiveness are a powerful combination, sure to lure potential supporters. And so, more and more parties actively and openly give support, both financial and otherwise, to student candidates contesting university elections. The bosses of major political parties make no bones about predicating their fate in any upcoming elections on the performance of their student wings.

Strangely, the winner and the loser sing totally different tunes before and after each election: the loser without fail decries the tendency of political parties to involve students for political gain, to the detriment of their academic pursuits.

⚖

Sushil Sharma, Matloob Karim and Naina Sahni started their careers at Delhi University. They began as members of NSUI, the youth wing of the Delhi Pradesh Congress, in a time of political instability and turmoil.

An aggressive separatist movement had engulfed Punjab in the initial years of the 1980s and been brutally suppressed. Operation Blue Star, the army attack on militants at Amritsar's sacred shrine, the Golden Temple, in early June 1984, broke the back of the insurrection, but it was to have grave repercussions for the nation. Prime Minister Indira Gandhi was assassinated by her two Sikh bodyguards on 31 October 1984, and terrible anti-Sikh riots followed. The upheaval of those times only served to vitiate youth politics, which most law enforcers thought of as a bastion for rogues and opportunists.

In 1984, Matloob Karim was nominated general secretary of NSUI and Naina Sahni was made the convener of its women's wing. They first met during a meeting of the office bearers of NSUI in Delhi University, and before long a romantic relationship blossomed. Around the same time, Naina met Sushil Sharma. In 1986, when Sharma became the president of NSUI, he nominated Naina as the DPYC general secretary, and they held their respective offices until 16 January 1995.

Youth politics was particularly beset with questionable and criminal behaviour during the years in which Sushil Sharma was DPYC president, and he was in the thick of it. Perhaps the most alarming event for the Youth Congress before the tandoor murder was the deadly car bomb attack on 11 September 1993 at the Indian Youth Congress premises on Raisina Road by Sikh Khalistan

Liberation Force militants. The attack was aimed squarely at Maninderjeet Singh Bitta, the president of the Youth Congress, who had been severely injured in another bombing in Amritsar, Punjab, the previous year. Though Bitta escaped with relatively minor injuries, nine people perished in the Delhi attack, including his two bodyguards, and thirty-six others were wounded.

While this incident did not involve Sushil Sharma, it evinces the prevalent state of affairs and the involvement of youthful leaders in decidedly sinister activities. Youth, it must be said, was – and still is – a misnomer; Sushil Sharma, for one, was a hardened political campaigner entering his fourth decade when he was replaced as president of the DPYC by Jagdish Yadav.

'Junior' would be a more apt description. Junior members of the party, such as Sharma, wielded the whip and did all manner of legwork for their seniors and mentors – hence the political paraphernalia stored at the Bagiya Barbeque restaurant. Perhaps the obvious use of influence in awarding the restaurant contract to Excel Hotels was among the lesser of Sushil Sharma's sins before 2 July 1995.

8

Getaway

The last half hour of 2 July 1995 marked the end of Sushil Sharma's life as a young, up-and-coming politician and businessman. He would start the new day, almost exactly at the hour of midnight, as a fugitive from the law, a man reviled and pursued for his odious crime. He would now be the focus of public attention for the very worst reasons.

He had little time to consider the enormity of the sudden change in his circumstances and, if he had, it would not have been in his nature to dwell long on it without plotting and manoeuvring. A man of strategy and action whose skills had made many beholden to him, Sushil would now rely on those very skills to evade justice and thwart every attempt to hold him accountable for his actions.

On the night in question, Sushil senses imminent trouble the moment he sees Constable Kunju at the kanaat in front of the Bagiya. Like any predator, Sushil can sum up a man in seconds and Kunju, he sees, is not your ordinary beat cop. With Kunju's few words, Sushil can discern the constable's quiet implacability: he will not be fobbed off or cowed by the mere mention of political contacts – and he will not entertain a bribe. As Kunju leaves with his companion, Sushil directs Keshav to stoke the fire; to burn the corpse as quickly as possible. He will try to hold off anyone who comes to the front of the Bagiya as best he can. His .32 calibre pistol, the murder weapon, is still in his possession, concealed beneath his kurta. But he knows that it would be utter madness to use it again this night.

When Sushil sees Kunju and Chander Pal leap from the wall at the back of the restaurant kitchen and confront Keshav, he curses under his breath, knowing it will be only minutes before they discover his terrible secret amidst the charred logs and party banners on the tandoor. Never one to capitulate or submit to an inevitable fate, he holds back, waiting to see how the situation plays out. There is still some slight chance that they will not notice that the old party hoardings, pamphlets and logs are actually a makeshift pyre for a murdered woman.

He watches from behind the canvas screen as Kunju and Chander Pal douse the fire. He takes pains to appear inconspicuous or, at least, a dispassionate observer. Like most political types, he is nothing if not a shrewd actor. He thinks better of trying to block Sub-inspector (SI) Rajesh Kumar, PCR Head Constable Majid Khan and Constable Rajbir Singh, who join Kunju and Chander Pal in quelling the blaze with buckets of water.

He weighs the situation. The body has been burning now for something like forty minutes – hardly enough time, he reckons, to have reduced Naina's remains to bare, blackened bones, which was the purpose of the fire in the first instance. The best he can hope for now is that the corpse has burned beyond recognition, for the police are very likely to at least prod the fire to take a look at what Keshav has been burning.

The police, he sees, are for now more concerned that the fire has spread, and they take Keshav outside, so that they can access the hotel's second storey. An impassive Keshav doesn't acknowledge Sushil as they pass him.

Sushil seizes his last opportunity to remove traces of his crime. Once they are out of sight, he rushes to the kitchen. After stuffing some more party pamphlets that were lying around into the steaming mess atop the tandoor, he pours some used cooking oil over the ignominious pyre for his murdered wife. Just as the flames rise again in the kitchen, he hears alarmed voices above him. Glancing upwards, he sees the constable who had leapt over the back wall peering down at him from the adjacent first-floor terrace of the hotel. Even at this distance, he can read the alarm, the anger in his face. Sushil moves quickly, not running, but quickly enough, and is out of the Bagiya in seconds. He strides to his car near the entry gate, unlocks and opens the door, and sits in the driver's seat in one smooth movement. He revs up the engine and drives away, straight to his erstwhile marital home on Mandir Marg.

Back in the apartment, he takes stock of his situation and acts with urgency. Keshav will not squeal on him – he is sure of this – but he cannot linger.

Feverishly, he tries to locate and remove any visible bloodstains, and other telltale signs of the crime. He wants no evidence left behind, but time is against him. He quickly sets to washing the bloodstained clothes he was wearing when he shot Naina. He has singed his second kurta in places, while setting the pyre alight and stoking it. But there is no time for him to change his clothes again.

Sushil knows he must get far away. His mind is racing, wracked with imaginings of his capture. Delhi, the city where he had found his place and promise of great success, is no longer safe. He has to make good his escape, but where can he go?

He opens a black briefcase on the bed where, only hours ago, Naina had breathed her last. He packs some clothes in the briefcase, then adds the kurta pyjama he had been wearing earlier, when he shot Naina, into a small black polythene bag. He stuffs the bag into the briefcase on top of his fresh clothes.

Next, he plucks out wads of cash – something he is never short of – from the cupboard. He puts the notes, amounting to around 2.25 lakh, in a compartment in the briefcase. Opening the cylinder of his revolver, he picks the three spent cartridges from it, reloads the chambers and shuts the cylinder. He places the revolver amongst the clothes, takes some extra cartridges and his arms license, too. He then fills a blue shoulder bag with more clothes.

He surveys the flat one final time. Having satisfied himself that he has done whatever he can to remove evidence of the murder, he quietly eases himself out of the flat, locks the front door and leaves. An escape plan has begun to take shape in his mind, and for that he needs help. He drives straight to Gujarat Bhavan, a well-kept complex surrounded by elegant gardens on Kautilya Marg in Chanakyapuri. It is now after two in the morning.

Sushil parks his Maruti in the parking lot at the Bhavan and walks towards the guest quarters overlooking a manicured lawn, taking pains to appear inconspicuous. The security personnel and the reception staff at the Bhavan see him entering the building. He hurries up the stairs, two at a time, to the first floor, to room number 20 where his friend, D. Kishore Rao, an IAS officer of the Gujarat cadre, is staying.

Rao, a jovial, engaging man, has been in touch with Sushil ever since he met him through Ashok Gandhi, a businessman in Bombay with interests in Vadodara (Baroda) in Gujarat. Theirs is not an especially close relationship, but there is mutual respect.

A deputy secretary holding charge of the post of Director, Sports, Youth and Cultural Activities in Gujarat, Rao has just been to the Lal Bahadur Shastri National Academy of Administration in Mussoorie for a three-week short-duration refresher course. He is staying for a day in Delhi on his way back to Ahmedabad. Rao had spent time with Sushil some hours earlier on Sunday, asking his advice and seeking his help in connection with a personal service problem and transfer issues.

Sushil knocks on the door and is greeted by Rao, who is barely awake. Despite his drowsy state, Rao immediately senses that Sushil is abnormally tense, even disturbed. Sushil then tells him, '*Kuch gadbad hai* (Something has gone wrong). I am tired, I want to rest.' He walks straight to the cot and lies down, covering his face with the blanket. But try as he might, he cannot sleep. He proceeds to give Rao an explanation for his visit at this odd hour. He tells him that he had a quarrel with his wife, in the course of which she sustained an injury.

Rao tries to get some sleep as he has to catch an early morning flight to Ahmedabad. But Sushil cannot sleep. The tension within him is acute. Last evening's sequence of events plays its reel of horror: of him shooting his love dead and hauling the body away to the restaurant, her dishonourable cremation – and the twist of fate leading to Keshav's arrest. The fear of apprehension torments him.

D.K. Rao wakes up early for his flight. Bahadur, the room attendant, brings him tea at half-past four. Rao offers tea to Sushil, but he declines, saying he will call for it later when he wants it. The tension within him does not abate as the hours pass, and he has no appetite.

Before Rao leaves, Sushil requests him to book the room for two more days in the name of his friend Jai Prakash. Rao is familiar with Jai Prakash, a tall, powerfully built man who is a former Hind Kesari wrestling champion, former Olympic wrestler and erstwhile DPCC sports cell chief. In good faith, Rao obliges and makes an advance payment of ₹400 to the receptionist.

Rao leaves for the airport at five in the morning. Now alone in the room at the Bhavan, Sushil feels isolated, plagued by fear.

Past daybreak, around 6 a.m., Sushil calls up Jai Prakash Pehlwan and asks him to come immediately to Gujarat Bhavan. He confesses to Jai Prakash that he has committed a serious mistake. After he has rung off, he dials the number of Ram Prakash Sachdeva, his business partner, and confides his predicament to him.

When Jai Prakash reaches Gujarat Bhavan at around 7.15 a.m., Sushil narrates to him the previous night's episode – as much, at least, as he deems necessary. He presents a sorry picture of himself, looking profoundly depressed, and expresses a desire to commit suicide. At the same time, he seeks Jai Prakash's help in this, his hour of grave adversity.

Jai Prakash is Sushil's de facto bodyguard and a fearsome character: Sheer physical presence and the still, assured gaze of a fighter have their uses in politics. He has been involved in some murky business in his time, and sees the underbelly of the capital at close quarters.[32] But even he is mortified at this turn of events. He is shocked, too, at the sight of his friend – who is usually the one extending support to others – reduced to this pitiful state.

Jai Prakash is more troubled still when he learns that the room at the Bhavan has been booked in his name and protests bitterly to Sushil. To mollify him, Sushil has the reservation changed so that it is in the name of Ram Prakash instead of Jai Prakash.

Jai Prakash advises Sushil to remove his car immediately from the premises. By now it is 8 a.m. The two men venture out of the room. On the way down to the car park, Sushil asks the Bhavan staff to buy him toiletries and washing powder. Sushil shows Jai Prakash his car in the Bhavan compound. With Jai Prakash following in his own vehicle, Sushil drives his car to the nearby Malcha Marg Market beyond Carmel Convent in Chanakyapuri's commercial complex. The fashionable market is all but deserted; shutters are down on the shops, and the couple of shopkeepers readying themselves for the day's trading pay him no attention. He parks the car, locks it, crosses the road and gets into Jai Prakash's car.

They confer for a while, Jai Prakash trying to calm his friend and offer comfort – without becoming too deeply involved in the horrendous situation that Sushil has created. Jai Prakash then drops Sushil at the taxi stand outside Uttar Pradesh Niwas. Sushil takes a taxi and heads for Geeta Colony, a well-heeled residential area, across the Yamuna in East Delhi. As the taxi crosses the ITO bridge, he reflects on how events might have transpired had he waited and dumped Naina's body there in the early hours, when no one was around to see him.

He reaches the Geeta Colony residence of his friend and business partner, Ram Prakash Sachdeva, at around 8.45 a.m. Sachdeva is an avuncular character; far more considered in his approach than Sushil and his hotheaded younger friends. Sushil recounts an expurgated version of the previous night's events to Ram Prakash, and seeks his advice and help.

Sachdeva, in the meantime, has received telephone calls from

R.P. Malik and Lalit Sachdeva, the other partners of Excel Hotels, telling him that something is seriously amiss at the Bagiya. He has already learnt from them that the police have called them and Kavita Arora to the station – and that they are likely to call him too, any moment.

Even as Sushil is discussing his dilemma with him, Sachdeva receives a telephone call from ACP Alok Kumar. It is now 9.45 a.m. Alok Kumar apprises him of the discovery of the burnt corpse at the Bagiya and asks Sachdeva to report to Connaught Place police station for questioning and clarification. Sachdeva agrees to report at the station – but he does not reveal to ACP Alok Kumar that Sushil is in his house.[33]

Sushil is now seized with terror, knowing that the police are in hot pursuit. Ram Prakash advises Sushil to leave Delhi immediately and arrange a credible alibi for himself. Sushil asks Sachdeva to keep the cash he is carrying, but Sachdeva declines and tells him to hold onto the money: It will come in handy, he says.

Sushil has no clear plan, but he knows that he must go far, and for this he needs cash. He departs from Sachdeva's house without delay. Neighbours who know Sushil see him emerge from Sachdeva's home and enter the taxi, which has been waiting for him. Sushil returns to Gujarat Bhavan and the room attendant brings him the washing powder, soap, toothpaste and shampoo he had ordered earlier. As he hands them to Sushil, Bahadur notices Sushil's white kurta has burn marks on the sleeves. This naturally strikes him as odd, but it slips his mind after he leaves the room. He will realise the significance of the marks later.

Sushil now takes his first shower since the murder. He scrubs himself squeaky clean, as if somehow this will cleanse him of his foul crime. As he dries himself, he takes from the plastic bag the clothes he had worn at the time of the murder. The thought that Naina's blood remains on them still nags at his mind. Once again, he goes through the ritual of washing the clothes, scrubbing them, trying to remove any traces of blood that may still stain them.

Sushil puts the wet kurta pyjama back in the black plastic bag.

Then he heads downstairs with the bag and steps out. He surveys the peaceful grounds of the Bhavan. After satisfying himself that nobody is observing him, Sushil shoves the plastic bag under a rock in a garden bed and walks back into the building.

He asks the reception staff to arrange a taxi for 2.30 p.m. and waits in his room. He packs the second, singed white kurta pyjama in his bag. Upon the taxi's arrival, he instructs the driver to take him to Vasant Kunj. The staff at the Bhavan witness his movements. Although the room is still reserved for his use, he will not return there.

The taxi passes through the vast government residential complexes, their monotonous yellow houses covering the suburban expanse between Delhi and the airport. It reaches Munirka village, short of Vasant Kunj, around 3 p.m., and with the intention of concealing his destination from the driver, Sushil asks him to park some distance away. He walks the few steps to his friend Rishi Raj Rathi's office, where Rathi greets him warmly though he, like D.K. Rao, immediately knows something has gone awry.

Along with Jai Prakash, Rathi has been close to Sushil for some time, and he has never seen his friend in such a state. Rishi Raj, like Jai Prakash, has a reputation for toughness in his haunts of Munirka and Okhla – and a penchant, some would later claim, for extortion and land grabbing.[34] He is Sushil's friend of last resort; his last hope.

Tea is brought in. Sushil cannot take more than a few sips. Once again, he relates some version of the dreadful happenings at Mandir Marg and the Bagiya, confiding in part to Rathi. He implores his friend to take him to Jaipur, Rajasthan, in his car; he cannot let a taxi driver know his movements and whereabouts, he says. Rishi Raj demurs: Jaipur is a good many hours away, some 300 kilometres' drive, and his absence would be noted, but he assures Sushil he will help him flee Delhi. They hatch a plan together to get Sushil far from the capital; away from the net that the police, by now, must surely have cast for him.

Sushil returns to the waiting taxi and travels in it to the nearby

C-II flats of Vasant Kunj, where he alights and dismisses the taxi after paying the driver ₹200. Rishi Raj, who has followed him in his red Maruti car, now pulls up beside him, and Sushil gets into the passenger seat, by his side. They proceed towards Gurgaon via Mahipalpur, where the outer reaches of Delhi's urban sprawl are teeming with new developments. Driving along the National Highway, they traverse the wasteland beyond the suburbs, and reach Rangpuri on Delhi's outskirts at around 5 p.m.

Sushil's mind is still in turmoil. The thought of the wet clothes in his bag gnaws at him. It is as if the two kurta pyjamas he had worn the previous night represent the moral burden of his crimes, which is haunting him now, as it surely will for the rest of his days. Just past Rangpuri Chowk, Sushil asks Rishi Raj to take the car into a kachcha side road, with the excuse of answering nature's call. He walks into the thick scrub that has grown over the dug-up and abandoned brick-kiln fields. He discards the incriminating kurta pyjama here, throwing the garments out into the pitted jungle.

He returns to the car and they continue on their way, reaching the Gurgaon roundabout at around 6 p.m. At the cab stand in the vicinity, Rishi Raj negotiates for a taxi to go to Jaipur. Sushil is not happy with the exorbitant fares the taxi drivers are demanding and finally settles for a private car, registration number DAV-296, which is being run unlawfully as a commercial taxi. It will, he surmises, attract less attention than a taxi.

Rishi Raj offers some comforting words and a farewell as Sushil sits in the car. He sees his friend slump in the back seat and watches for some moments as the car heads south-west towards Jaipur, into the bleak lands on the edge of the Thar desert. Worry lingers, as much for himself as for his friend, even when Sushil is long gone. In a sombre mood, he returns to his house in Munirka. It is as if Sushil has somehow left some of his troubles behind with him.

The driver, of course, is happily unaware of the drama of the preceding hours. Jagdish Prasad, known to his family and friends as Billu, is happy to have such a long trip for the evening. The twenty-one-year-old lad is enjoying his first job away from his village, driving his uncle's personal car as a taxi. The only drawback is that he must be constantly on the lookout for local transport department officers and the police. Any encounter with these, he knows, will mean parting with some of the trip's earnings as a fine or a bribe – even with his uncle's impressive contacts. He tries to blend in with the traffic, hoping and praying that he will not be stopped at a police checkpost.

The first indication Billu has that this is no ordinary passenger is the prolonged, unnatural silence in the car. Almost everyone strikes up a conversation at some stage of such a long journey, even if to enquire about the distance remaining and the time. Not this man. The lack of words, the darkness and the droning of tyres on the tarmac lend an eeriness to their enforced intimacy. Billu is unnerved, but also intrigued.

In the rear-view mirror, he steals an occasional glance. But for his profile in the half darkness, the man seems barely present. It is only when some wayside lights illuminate the inside of the car that Billu can discern his tension, his preoccupied expression. More than once, he catches a glimpse of the man's dark, hollow eyes staring back at him. He thinks better of trying to engage his passenger in any chit-chat, and maintains a respectful silence.

Sushil notices the driver observing him, peering at him from time to time in the rear-view mirror. Normally, he would have snapped at the driver to keep his eyes on the road, or even ticked him off for such insolence. But he has no wish to draw attention to himself, and says nothing. The driver is the least of his worries. While the murder continues to haunt him, his mind is shuffling through various scenarios. He knows he has to make his next move boldly. For though he has evaded the manhunt which has now begun in earnest in Delhi, he is far from safe.

The manhunt for Sushil Sharma had not abated since the early hours of 3 July, but officers had little to show for their efforts. In all, more than 300 people had been picked up for questioning in as many as fifty raids in the days following Sushil's hasty departure from the crime scene. This was backed up by a systematic checking of public places: hotels, guest houses and even state Bhavans. Homes, businesses and workplaces of relatives, friends, partners and sympathisers were not spared either.

Although the investigation of the tandoor murder and the hunt for the prime murder suspect was largely routine police work, the scale of it took its toll. The investigating officers found responding to the innumerable tip-offs from the public – telephonic or otherwise – a burdensome task in itself.

Some provided what they called clues to Sushil's whereabouts; others seemed to have their own axe to grind, or just wanted to be part of the drama. And yet nothing, not even the most insignificant titbit of information could be ignored, however unlikely the prospect of it being material to the case. Preserving the evidence and systematically recording the interrogations for verification and cross verification that would help build a water-tight case was also a colossal undertaking. I admired Aditya Arya's patience and diligence, his meticulousness in ensuring this was done.

While investigations were progressing on many fronts, the need to keep the hungry public informed with appropriate details was not forgotten, lest disinformation or misinformation hamper the process. Conversely, officers took pains not to part with too much information, which could be detrimental to the interests of further investigation.

There was unprecedented interest in the tandoor murder. Telegrams, letters, telephone calls and even personal representations from members of the public urged the police to act bravely, without fear or favour. There were fervent pleas for justice and fair play. Most people were apprehensive that the police might try to cover up the beastly crime under political or government pressure, especially in view of Sushil's powerful contacts.

We gave assurances to the public, to the political leaders and the media, of the police being unbiased and non-partisan in their handling of the case, and made it abundantly clear that there would be no succumbing to any kind of pressure, however high-placed the source of it may be. All and sundry were made aware that the police would ensure fair and impartial investigations and arrest the accused at the earliest.

As the police followed leads from the public and handled the media, the team continued to investigate all known contacts of the fugitive. Extensive enquiries were made about Sushil and Naina's friends and relatives, but to little avail.

The team again grilled Sushil's parents and members of his family at Maurya Enclave in Pitampura. They maintained their earlier claim that Sushil had gone out of Delhi, and they seemed genuinely unaware of his movements beyond this fact.

They were decidedly cagey about one thing, though. Although Sushil's parents initially denied he was married, photographs that the police had seized during a search of their Pitampura house showed Sushil and Naina celebrating the karva chauth festival with them. Confronted with this evidence, they recanted, offering the officers a vague explanation that the couple had got married secretly in a simple ceremony at a temple three years earlier. No tangible proof of the marriage seemed to exist.

9

Medical Complications

Controversy in the media and in the political arena in the wake of the tandoor murder was only to be expected: News of a high-profile figure in the ruling party burning his wife's body on a restaurant tandoor was sure to create a furore. That the controversy – along with other, unseen factors – could unduly influence the investigation was fast becoming apparent in the days after Sushil Sharma absconded. Particularly troubling was the way in which seasoned professionals involved in the case seemed to abandon good sense and sound judgement – even professional ethics. The first to be dazzled by the media glare surrounding the case, or perhaps other factors beyond our knowledge, was a doctor.

Inspector Niranjan Singh, the investigating officer, had made out an application for an autopsy on the body of an unknown deceased woman in the early hours of 3 July. As soon as Matloob Karim formally identified the body as that of Ravi Naina Sahni on 5 July, the autopsy could proceed, and Constables Jai Chand and Karan Singh produced the body before the examining forensic pathologist at the Lady Hardinge Medical College, on the very same day.

The inquest papers and a report of investigations already conducted under provisions of Section 174 of the Criminal Procedure Code, detailing the history of the case, were also provided to the doctor. Along with these was the detailed submission of Sub-inspector Jawahar Singh, which had been compiled by Inspector Niranjan Singh.

The application enumerated numerous clear directions for the forensic pathologist, including the following:

1. To preserve the blood, viscera, hair, skull, teeth and pieces of burnt clothes that were stuck to the body.
2. To ascertain the cause and time of death, whether the deceased was burnt ante or post-mortem, whether she was pregnant, and whether she had ever given birth to a child.
3. To take a vaginal swab and samples for DNA and blood plasma identification.

Also included in the application was a specific request that the body be X-rayed before the post-mortem. This would determine if the deceased had sustained any injury from a firearm or a sharp instrument that had left bullets or blade tips in the body. The examining doctor's opinion was sought, too, on whether the limbs of the corpse had been amputated. SI Jawahar Singh specially detailed for the examining doctor all routine procedures required by the police and assured him that any assistance he required would be immediately provided.

The post-mortem examination of the mortal remains of Ravi Naina Sahni was recorded as no. 230 of 1995. Dr Murari Prasad Sarangi, associate professor in the Department of Forensic Medicine and Toxicology at the Lady Hardinge Medical College, conducted the examination between 2.30 p.m. and 3.30 p.m. on 5 July, after studying the papers provided. Crucially, he failed to X-ray the charred remains of the body, despite the explicit request for this in the application.

Worse was in store for us. Even though the autopsy was conducted on 5 July, the doctor's report was not given promptly, and the investigating team awaited its submission with bated breath. This was, after all, the most prominent murder investigation in the country. On 7 July, instead of the report we so keenly awaited, we were given a rude shock. Dr Sarangi gave an interview to *Newstrack,* the video news magazine – even before formally submitting the post-mortem report to the investigating team. As if this was not bad enough, he played to the gallery, giving a vivid description of how Naina's legs had been cut below the knees and her hands chopped off at the shoulders.[35]

In speaking out of turn to the media, Dr Sarangi had breached all established norms of ethics and procedure. Naturally, the media was all agog at Dr Sarangi's revelations and he was quoted liberally. Many of his so-called findings were, however, quite contrary to the evidence at the crime scenes and what we had already conveyed in our media briefings. The doctor was publicly negating our well-considered reconstruction of the crime and sequence of events – and we had no report at hand by which we could counter or even evaluate his claims.

The investigating team was obviously most unimpressed with Dr Sarangi and, through gritted teeth, prevailed upon him to furnish his report without delay. We finally obtained the report on 8 July.

In the post-mortem report, Dr Sarangi had written his findings in the routine fashion, on the prescribed post-mortem form. He had described the human remains and recorded his observations in minute detail. But despite his attention to anatomical minutiae, he seemed to have neglected the imperatives of a post-mortem.

Dr Sarangi noted that twenty-nine teeth were present in the remains (a normal adult mouth has thirty-two teeth). Both incisors were missing in the upper jaw, and the lateral incisors were, he stated, also missing in the lower jaw. The eyelids and the face were charred and the eyeballs destroyed. The ears, nose and lips were likewise charred, and the teeth exposed and studded with soot. Other natural orifices were also studded with soot particles. The usual post-mortem changes were noted as not being elicitable given the extensive charring of the body.

The report noted that the corpse was charred beyond identification and had attained a pugilistic attitude (with the limbs in front of the body as if in a defensive pose) owing to coagulation of muscle proteins. The skull bone was exposed, partly burnt and blackened. It showed multiple post-mortem cracks, with a few strands of partially burnt hair and a metal hair clip attached to the hair.

Dr Sarangi's report also described the external injuries. He found that the right leg had been amputated 23 cm below the knee; the bones of both legs were exposed, being cut from the front and showing bevelling below and inwards. The patella (knee cap) bone was missing on the right limb. The distal phalanges of the right hand had been chopped off and were missing. The left upper limb, too, was amputated just below the elbow. The left thigh was chopped off 28 cm below the left interior and superior iliac spine, the underlying thigh bone having been cut from the back, showing bevelling upwards.

The examination revealed that the scalp tissue was mostly burnt, except over a small area in the occipital region, where a few strands of burnt hair were still attached. The underlying skull bone showed multiple post-mortem heat cracks; it was partly charred and blackened. A reddish-white heat haematoma was present in the brain matter, more on the left cerebral hemisphere above the dura. The haematoma had adhered to the endocranium on this side. The brain meninges were intact and pale in appearance. The brain was shrunken and its substance looked pale but there was, he stated, no brain injury or haemorrhage.

The crown rump length of the body was 83 cm, weighing 28 kg in all. In the neck, the trachea, bronchi and oesophagus along with the pharynx, larynx and tracheal rings were intact, but the mucosa of the tracheal rings was pale and smeared with black soot particles. The thyroid bone was intact, but the blood vessels in the neck had collapsed due to extensive burns.

Extensive burns were also noted in the report on the thoracic cage; the intercostal muscles and diaphragm were burnt, more on the left side than the right. The plural cavities and lungs showed the pleurae studded with carbon particles. To the naked eye, there was no sign of inflammation; both lungs were shrunken, desiccated and pale. The heart showed patent coronary blood vessels. Its chambers were empty, but the heart musculature was intact, looking pale.

In the lower thoracic region, the abdominal and pelvic walls were burnt; the peritoneum partly so. The stomach contained about 500 millilitres of a brownish semi-liquid substance which smelt alcoholic, the doctor noted. The bowels looked pale. The pancreas, and the small and large intestines were shrunken, desiccated and protruding outside the abdominal cavity. No injury or abnormality in the abdominal organs was noticed – the liver, spleen and kidneys were intact but shrunken. The external genitals were burnt and destroyed. The uterus was intact and non gravid (the deceased was not pregnant), and showed no injury.

From his examination, which was done merely with the naked eye, Dr Sarangi found no evidence of firearm injuries, and stated so categorically in the report.

Dr Sarangi preserved vaginal swabs to exclude recent sexual activity. He took other required samples for routine chemical, biological and serological examination, including of the stomach contents and hair. Some sample tissues of the lungs, liver and kidneys were also kept for histopathological examination in the laboratory.

In accordance with the request of the investigating officer in the application, the skull was separated for the purpose of conducting a skull superimposition test. This would be required, along with a DNA test, to confirm the identity of the deceased as Ravi Naina Sahni.

Pending receipt of the chemical analyses and the histopathological reports, Dr Sarangi provisionally concluded that the death, to the best of his knowledge, was instantaneous and due to haemorrhagic shock (essentially, lack of blood flow, thus oxygen, to the tissues), consequent to ante-mortem injuries. Burns present on the dead body appeared most probably to have been inflicted post-mortem, his report stated. His final opinion as to the cause of death, at any rate, would be given after histopathological examination of the tissues from the lungs, liver and kidneys, and examination of the viscera and blood samples.

The investigating team examined the post-mortem report critically, and noted that it was confoundingly vague as to the cause of death. 'Haemorrhagic shock' can occur as the result of a vast multitude of medical conditions and events, and Dr Sarangi had not specified the ante-mortem injuries which might have caused it. Finding the injuries that caused death is surely essential for a post-mortem; far more important, one would think, than mere anatomical observations.

From a prosecution viewpoint, the report was a disaster. It was cursory, ambiguous, riven with contradictions, and at odds with the crime scene evidence and the established facts of the case. Dr Sarangi himself could not explain these contradictions or clarify the ambiguities, even after the investigating officers had spoken with him at length.

The police listed some of the ambiguities and contradictions in the report. First, the burn injuries present appeared to have been inflicted post-mortem. Dr Sarangi had, however, found soot particles in the trachea, which indicated that the victim may still have been breathing while suffering the burns. There seemed no other explanation for the presence of soot particles in the trachea. This cast some doubt on whether the burn injuries were ante-mortem or post-mortem. Other injuries on the body were also not classified clearly as ante-mortem or post-mortem.

Second, the autopsy report indicated the cause of death to be 'apparently instantaneous and due to haemorrhagic [shock] consequent to ante-mortem injuries'. But Dr Sarangi had failed to mention which of the ante-mortem injuries were sufficient to cause death.

Third, police investigators were aghast that Dr Sarangi appeared to exclude the possibility of firearm injuries to the deceased. This was quite incongruous with the evidence in the bedroom of the

Mandir Marg apartment, which was surely the scene of Ravi Naina Sahni's murder. The recovery of a bullet and spent cartridges of a matching calibre – and the telltale spatters of blood in the bedroom of the apartment – clearly indicated a homicide with a firearm. In the absence of an X-ray examination, the investigating team could not fathom Dr Sarangi's finding.

We were mystified as to why the doctor had failed to X-ray the body – and indignant that he had failed to do so, despite Inspector Niranjan Singh's repeated requests and even DCP Aditya Arya's intervention. It scarce needs explaining to a lay person, let alone a forensic expert, that an X-ray is capable of revealing bullet fragments within the cadaver that may not be discernible to the naked eye. It was later learned that Dr Sarangi had not complied with the request to X-ray the remains simply because the X-ray machine at the Lady Hardinge Medical College was not functioning.

Fourth, the post-mortem report asserted that the upper and lower limbs of the body had been chopped off, without providing the evidence upon which this conclusion was based. Further, Dr Sarangi did not detail any relevant injuries on the cadaver to justify his opinion that the limbs were amputated ante-mortem. And he did not mention the nature of the instrument used for the purported amputation of the limbs. We could only surmise that the good doctor's imagination had got away with him after the fanciful and gory speculations about the crime in the media.

There were further discrepancies in Dr Sarangi's report. It noted that the stomach contents smelt of alcohol, an observation which CFSL negated in their examination of the viscera. Furthermore, and most disturbingly, CFSL analysis of the specimens revealed that Dr Sarangi had preserved common saline solution in place of sample blood – surely a callous and unprofessional act.[36]

In view of the shortcomings in Dr Sarangi's conduct of the autopsy and the contradictions and ambiguities in his report, we immediately moved the Delhi Government to constitute a board of medico-legal experts to examine the matter and conduct a second autopsy on the cadaver. The cadaver was preserved in the cold chamber of the mortuary at Lady Hardinge Medical College, pending an official decision on our request.

Thankfully, the government lost no time in constituting a high-profile board[37] for the purpose of conducting a second, more thorough and conclusive, autopsy. The board comprised the most eminent forensic doctors and senior medico-legal experts in Delhi: Dr Bharat Singh,[38] the medical superintendent of Delhi's Deen Dayal Upadhyay Hospital, Dr T.D. Dogra, professor and head of forensic medicine at AIIMS and Dr S.K. Khanna, professor of forensic medicine at the Maulana Azad Medical College, Delhi.

This panel of expert forensic pathologists met on 12 July and conducted a second autopsy at Police Hospital, otherwise referred to as Civil Hospital. Naturally, there was some intrigue in the media at this turn of events. Countering the media onslaught, Commissioner Nikhil Kumar declared that Delhi Police would request 'not only a second autopsy; we will go in for a third post-mortem too, if necessary!'

In their findings after the second autopsy, the board clearly opined the cause of death to be due to a firearm injury to the head, which was sufficient to cause death under normal circumstances. They based their findings substantially on the X-ray examination the charred remains were subjected to at Civil Hospital.

The second autopsy found a large gap in the left side of the skull, extending from the frontal to the occipital region, with the outer table in this region burnt and charred. In the X-ray plates, the board observed the presence of two metal pieces: one in the back of the right ear (mastoid region), and the other on the left side of the neck near the spine, in the soft tissues of the cervical stump.

During the dissection that followed the X-ray, a deformed bullet was found in the soft tissues adjacent to the lower cervical vertebrae of the cervical stump on the left side. The report noted extravasation of blood in the surrounding area (the flow of blood into tissue surrounding blood vessels, i.e., internal bleeding), with the nose portion of the bullet pointing towards the left outer surface of the neck. A bullet track with infiltration of blood was found, running obliquely in the spinal column adjacent to the site where the bullet was lodged. The direction of the track was from above and from the right to the left side.

The doctors on the panel also dissected the right mastoid area of the skull to locate the other bullet. The X-ray image indicated that the outer table of the skull above the mastoid process was bulging outwards with the metal piece within, and as they dissected this, they could see the outer tip of the metal piece protruding from the bulge. On further dissection, they saw it was a deformed bullet, and it was found embedded in the bone, with its nose portion pointing outwards and its base towards the medial side. There was extravasation in the surrounding area.

The second post-mortem report further clarified that 'no soot particles were found on the mucosal surface [of the upper respiratory tract], which was showing bluish-black discoloration, due to decomposition.' This, too, was clearly contrary to Dr Sarangi's findings.

The board categorically opined that the death was due to coma, consequent upon the firearm injury to the head.

Regarding the burns, the board found that they were post-mortem in nature. It further determined that the firearm injuries were caused by a handgun and were ante-mortem in nature. In view of the extensive burns sustained by the cadaver post-mortem, the board's report stated it was not possible to give the exact location of the entry wounds of the bullets. On the basis of the track and location of the bullet metal, however, the entry wound in the head could have been in the left temple region, and the entry wound of the bullet in the neck could have been in the right upper part of the neck. The report stated it was not possible to comment on the range of fire because of the extensive burns the body had sustained post-mortem.

The board members found that there were deep burns extending to muscles in all the limbs: the bones were exposed and burnt in places, and distal parts of the limbs were missing. They were categorical in stating that there was no evidence of any cuts around the distal burnt ends of the bones. They declared that it was not possible to comment on whether the distal portions of the limbs had been chopped off or separated due to burns. The doctors also opined that the soot detected in the trachea during the first autopsy could very well be artefactual; that is, deposited there during the burning, rather than inhaled.

To our great relief, the second autopsy report made complete sense: it was congruous with the crime scene evidence and our painstaking reconstruction of the crime. The entire exercise of requesting and undertaking a second autopsy, though, entailed bracing ourselves against media attacks, likely alleging inefficiency, incompetence and collusion.

We had little choice but to give at least a partial explanation to the press for this unusual turn of events – without revealing information that would jeopardise the case. Aditya Arya explained in a media briefing that anomalies in the first autopsy had led us to sanction a second autopsy, and I mentioned that in the first, no X-ray had been performed on the corpse to detect bullets. Never one to mince his words, Aditya said, 'We were not satisfied at all … If [Dr Sarangi's] report could not satisfy me, how can we satisfy our defence counsel?'[39]

The second post-mortem itself admonished Dr Sarangi, albeit gently, by stating the obvious: 'Dr Sarangi had given his report without conducting the X-ray, which seems to be the main reason behind his failure to see the bullet marks.' It offered no explanation, however, for how Dr Sarangi had concluded that the body's limbs had been severed.[40]

Stung by the public criticism of his autopsy, Dr Sarangi took perhaps the least prudent course available to him – which was to go on the offensive, in print. He airily suggested in an interview with *The Statesman* that 'authenticity cannot be attached to the second post-mortem report' because, he declared, he 'had already conducted a thorough forensic examination'.[41] He stuck doggedly to his statement that injuries were inflicted on the deceased while she was still alive, and she had died from loss of blood.

Unsurprisingly, he avoided any discussion of the three bullets he would have been able to detect with a simple X-ray. The likely effect of these, shot into the deceased's head at point blank range, seemed to have eluded the learned gentleman entirely.

The investigating team was up in arms, annoyed at having to justify the two, contradictory autopsies before even preparing the charge sheet against Sharma and Keshav. The press was already mercilessly speculating on the reasons for the second post-mortem, the accuracy and authenticity of both autopsies and the reasons for Dr Sarangi's conclusions in the first post-mortem report. Reporters were even questioning the motives of the establishment for sanctioning the second autopsy. Now we had little choice but to silence this loose cannon before it sank our otherwise watertight forensic case.

It was a job best left to the experts. The doctors on the board, who had been mild in their criticism in the report, were far less reserved in their interviews. The day after Dr Sarangi's ill-considered interview with *The Statesman* was published, *The Patriot* gave column space to their response. One of the doctors who conducted the second autopsy bluntly stated to the paper that 'either the doctors who performed the first autopsy were not experienced or they have deliberately tried to hide the facts'.[42]

It didn't take a skilled professional to conclude that Dr Sarangi had seriously botched up the autopsy, and the media turned on him. Reporters hinted that rather than a mere matter of negligence, 'pressure' had been exerted on Dr Sarangi, which suggested a 'wider conspiracy to throw investigations off track'. For this, it was suggested, Dr Sarangi faced the prospect of grave charges under the Evidence Act.[43]

Folly and hubris seemed the most likely explanation for Dr Sarangi's behaviour. At the very least, he appeared more concerned with savouring his fifteen minutes of fame than performing his duty with due skill, care and diligence. At this stage of the investigation, the reasons for Dr Sarangi conducting such a patently incompetent post-mortem were not important. Even so, I forwarded a detailed report to the medical department enumerating the irregularities and ineptitudes of the autopsy.

The serious breach in ethics and protocol of Dr Sarangi's interviews with *Newstrack* and the print media, even before he had furnished the post-mortem report to the investigating officer, was stressed in my report. Had we not taken prompt and decisive action, his baffling conduct could well have scuppered our case. My report concluded with a request that the competent authority take proper legal and departmental action against Dr Sarangi, as it deemed fit.[44]

We had weathered the brief media blitz over the two autopsies with some aplomb, but the lasting damage to our case against Sushil Sharma was another matter. We knew that however watertight our case may be, clever defence counsel would concentrate its attack on the perceived uncertainty posed by two vastly different autopsy reports, in their inevitable quest to sink it. But that would be later.

The autopsy imbroglio gave us cause to reflect on a broader issue. Had the investigating team not assiduously inspected the crime scene and found the bullet lead, the spent cartridges and the bullet holes in the apartment before the first post-mortem, it would not have been possible to make out a convincing case for a second examination. We noted with no small regret that there was no system to check any mistakes, connivance or arbitrariness in post-mortems.

It is interesting to note that like the tandoor murder itself, many plots and sub-plots surrounding the case were still playing out years, even decades later. As late as October 2012, Dr Murari Prasad Sarangi was involved in a case against the Ministry of Health and Family Welfare, questioning his dismissal from the position of professor of forensic medicine at Lady Hardinge Medical College.[45]

It is not clear whether the fiasco of his post-mortem of Naina Sahni's remains contributed to his dismissal. But it certainly could not have helped his cause.

10

Opening Gambit

Sometimes a law enforcement officer has to be patient. Despite an unusually large manhunt and exhaustive inquiries, the investigating team had no actionable intelligence as to Sushil's whereabouts in the first few days after Kunju's discovery. With every raid coming up short in Delhi, the likelihood that he had evaded the police dragnet and fled the capital left us with little to do. All of Sushil's contacts, family members and associates were under surveillance and telephone taps were in place. The police were on the lookout for him everywhere, including the borders and at airports, and with his face in almost every newspaper in the land, some member of the public was sure to spot him.

We put ourselves in the shoes of the fugitive to anticipate the likely steps he would take to evade arrest. We were fairly sure he would apply for anticipatory bail – this is almost de rigueur for a well-heeled offender facing imminent arrest – so we moved the Delhi High Court for a caveat against the grant of such bail without first informing Delhi Police and making us a party to the proceedings. This caveat was granted by the High Court on 7 July.

Under Indian criminal law, a person who apprehends that a move is afoot to arrest him on false or trumped-up charges may apply for anticipatory bail under Section 438 of the Criminal Procedure Code. The accusations against Sushil Sharma were anything but false or trumped up. Courts, however, often give the benefit of the doubt to an alleged offender, and anticipatory bail is quite a regular feature, even a bugbear, of criminal law in India. The caveat would allow us to present salient features of the overwhelming circumstantial evidence against Sushil, so he could be denied anticipatory bail. Or so we thought.

The first news of Sushil after he fled the Bagiya late on 2 July came from Madras on 7 July, the very day the Delhi High Court granted us the caveat. On the afternoon of that day, the *Hindustan Times* tabloid supplement, 'Evening News', quoting the Press Trust of India (PTI), reported that Sushil Sharma had been granted bail by a court in Madras. When contacted by our investigating team, PTI confirmed the news immediately.

Sushil Sharma, we discovered, had been granted interim anticipatory bail by a principal district and sessions judge in Madras. Far from being immediately informed of his application and given an opportunity to respond as the caveat mandated, we had learned of this development in the case through the newspapers, like other Delhi residents. The granting of interim bail to the offender was a major blow to Delhi Police and a serious embarrassment. And the manner of us hearing of it was, needless to say, humiliating.

The caveat granted by the High Court had debarred any court anywhere from granting anticipatory bail without first informing Delhi Police. Sadly, this order had no practical effect at the time of Sushil Sharma's hearing in Madras. He had moved the court before Delhi Police could arrange for the information on the caveat to reach concerned quarters elsewhere in the country. Sushil was a step ahead of us, as he had been since the discovery of the body on the tandoor.

Apparently, the matter of granting interim anticipatory bail was all over in the court of the principal sessions judge in Madras in less than five minutes. The whole charade smacked of pre-planned mala fide collusion. The application had been lodged that same morning at 10.30 a.m. Upon Sushil's advocate presenting the bail application before the court at 3.15 p.m., City Public Prosecutor E. Raja promptly told the presiding judge that no case against the applicant had been registered in Madras City.[46] M. Gopalaswamy, the judge in question, then granted Sushil the anticipatory bail he sought.

On hearing of this troubling development, I hastened to speak to the commissioner of police, Madras, by telephone. In confirmation of our discussion, I sent him a wireless message that Sushil Sharma was wanted in case FIR no. 486/95 u/s 302/201/34 IPC of Connaught Place police station, New Delhi. He was reportedly staying at 38 Natesa Iyer Street, Thyagaraya Nagar, Madras 17 – the address provided by him in his bail application. I requested the commissioner to arrest Sushil and consult with us for further action.

In Delhi, Commissioner Nikhil Kumar convened a high-level meeting to discuss strategies to counter Sharma's latest move. The investigating team's distress at being so cunningly outmanoeuvred was palpable. We were indignant that the system had been blatantly manipulated and were resolved to undo Sushil's contrived legal protection. His actions were, we knew, simply ploys to avoid arrest and deny physical custody to Delhi Police.

The deceit inherent in his application and its submissions was nauseating, if predictable. Sushil had contended that he was a popular political figure by virtue of having been the former president of the DPYC. His rivals were jealous of him, he stated, and wished to stall his political rise. They had consequently falsely implicated him in a case in Delhi with the intention of tarnishing his image before the forthcoming elections. The case related to the suspicious death of one Naina Sahni, of which, he asserted, he had no knowledge.

He further submitted that he would need to approach the appropriate court to seek regular anticipatory bail, but in the meantime feared arrest by Delhi Police through the commissioner of police, Madras. This, he maintained in his application, would subject him to much shame and disgrace.

Sushil named the inspector in charge of Connaught Place police station in Delhi as the first respondent and the commissioner of police, Madras as the second respondent. The judge, Thiru M. Gopalaswamy, vide his order in Crl Misc. Petition no. 3906/95, recorded the presence of Messrs S. Ananthanarayanan, V. Shanmugam and P. Dharmaraj as counsels for the petitioner, and E. Raja, the city public prosecutor, as counsel for the second respondent.

Without calling for any report, the public prosecutor informed the court that there was no case pending against the accused in Madras. On this ground, the judge saw it fit to dismiss the petition insofar as it concerned the second respondent (the commissioner of police, Madras). The whole matter became murkier with the judge's next, more controversial, decision. He allowed the petition insofar as it concerned the first respondent – the inspector of New Delhi's Connaught Place police station – without the first respondent being given any opportunity to make a submission. Indeed, neither the second respondent, nor any representative thereof, was within his – or his court's – jurisdiction.

Nevertheless, Principal District and Sessions Judge Gopalaswamy granted Sushil Sharma interim anticipatory bail for two weeks with a direction that in the event of arrest, the petitioner be released on bail on his executing a bond for ₹5,000 with two sureties and a like sum to the satisfaction of the fifth metropolitan magistrate of Madras. He further directed the petitioner to get an appropriate order from the concerned court within two weeks.

Upon being served with the anticipatory bail orders of the court, the Madras police commissioner's office informed us in Delhi and faxed us a copy of the bail order. Delhi Police Commissioner Nikhil Kumar then telephoned Madras Police Commissioner Thiru. Rajasekharan Nair to advise him that a Delhi Police team, accompanied by counsel, would be despatched to Madras to challenge the anticipatory bail orders.

In the interim, I contacted the Delhi Government and liaised with the home ministry so that the Additional Solicitor General of India, Mr K.T.S. Tulsi, could assist us in countering these developments in Madras. Meanwhile, ACP V. Renganathan of the Crime Branch, a Tamilian whose mother tongue and knowledge of Madras were sure to be helpful, was briefed along with a team of officials. ACP Renganathan and the team travelled by air to Madras the very next day, on 8 July, with a brief to move the Madras High Court to cancel the interim bail granted to Sharma.

Even before the Delhi Police team could reach Madras, an unusual public outcry arose, in Delhi and throughout the country. Prominent people voiced their outrage against the hasty act of the principal sessions judge in Madras and the manner in which bail had been granted to Sharma – who was, after all, wanted in a most egregious murder case. The consensus was that in such serious cases, the courts should exercise the utmost restraint in granting anticipatory bail and that Sushil had circumvented the due processes of law – that he had secured bail through deception and cunning.

'Decision surprises legal experts,' *The Times of India* reported in a headline. In this article, the former chief justice of the Delhi High Court, Rajinder Sachar, voiced his bemusement at the grant of anticipatory bail in a case which had drawn so much publicity. Pran Nath Lekhi, the eminent lawyer and outspoken activist, quipped, 'What can be done when [the] administration and police also want to aid an accused! This tendency for obtaining bail from other states has become quite rampant.' He recalled the case of Captain Satish Sharma, who had obtained bail from the Delhi High Court to avoid an arrest warrant issued against him in Uttar Pradesh. R.D. Jolly, a senior public prosecutor, decried the obvious manipulation in Sushil Sharma being granted anticipatory bail.

The media was critical of Delhi Police for not having had any inkling of the anticipatory bail application, despite the so-called country-wide alert for Sharma. The *Express News Service* headline[47] 'Fugitive Y.C. chief stays one step ahead' was apt, uncomfortably so for the investigating team. Speculation was rife, too, that Sushil could still be holed up in Delhi, being shielded by someone prominent, even as he was manipulating matters elsewhere to keep him from the long arm of the law.

Some associations of lawyers were not content with issuing critical statements. They demanded action. A group in Delhi sent a telegram to the chief justice of Madras High Court, asking the court to treat the telegram as a PIL[48] application and cancel the anticipatory bail it had granted. The All-India Lawyers' Forum for Civil Liberties took a similar stance. In a telegraphic message to the chief justice of India, Justice A.M. Ahmadi, the forum requested that he summon the bail-granting records from Madras and cancel the anticipatory bail immediately.[49] In the message, O.P. Saxena, the president of the forum, pointed out that the granting of bail to Sushil Sharma by the Madras court was without jurisdiction and contrary to the law.

Given the commotion, it was inevitable that political parties would join the fray. A spokesman of the Delhi state committee of the CPI(M) expressed serious concern over the granting of bail on the basis of gross misrepresentation of facts, among which was a false residential address. He alleged that the bail had been moved at the behest of a politician with influence.

It later emerged that Sushil had paid his advocate Ananthanarayanan one and a half lakh rupees just to manage his anticipatory bail – an extortionate sum in 1995 for this brief procedural matter. But Sushil hadn't been able to secure the two sureties required to execute his bond immediately. The local address given in his bail application was, unsurprisingly, bogus; neighbours told journalists on the prowl that Sushil had never stayed there. The actual resident, Dr Saraswati, was a popular local astrologer who ran the Kadalangudi Astrological and Indological Research Centre, which was patronised by some political leaders.

Dr Saraswati expressed surprise at the fact that Ananthanarayanan, whose own home was a few kilometres away in Devaki Ammal Street, Shenoy Nagar, had given her address in Natesa Iyer Street as Sushil's. She declared that she had nothing to do with Sushil. Annoyed by the harassment of continual enquiries in person and over the telephone, she even took up the matter with Advocate General R. Krishnamurthy. After Krishnamurthy's intervention, the city police commissioner assured Dr Saraswati that the residents of the house would not be troubled.

It was later hinted in the press that Sushil had consulted Dr Saraswati, although she would deny this. She had apparently told Sushil that he was in a difficult phase astrologically, and this would persist for the following six months. There could not have been a greater understatement.

Ananthanarayanan, meanwhile, was being hounded by reporters. They soon dug up his Congress connections: He was the election agent of the Congress member of parliament for Central Madras, Mr Era Anbarasu, and neighbours revealed that a Congress flag had previously flown in front of his Devaki Ammal Street home. The flagpole was now conspicuously bare. Besieged by the media, Ananthanarayanan declared that he would have had Sushil execute the bail bond on the day of the hearing itself, had he known the case would attract so much attention in the media. Claiming that he enjoyed professional immunity to protect his client's interests under Section 126 of the Indian Evidence Act, he refused to disclose Sushil's whereabouts, or even whether he was in Madras.

Journalists hovered around the court and the Arumbakkam residence of Metropolitan Magistrate Vijayendra Rani, in the hope of accosting or, at the very least, catching a glimpse of Sushil when he executed the bail bond.

The surge of public reaction and adverse publicity inevitably evoked a response from Principal District and Sessions Judge Gopalaswamy. Gopalaswamy was one of the six judges whose names had been recommended to the chief justice of India for elevation to the Madras High Court and the furore surrounding his bail decision had done him no favour. He made a statement to the press to clarify his position. 'In a single day, we pass several dozen bail applications,' he told reporters, while justifying his decision on the grounds that granting Sushil bail was well within the law. Sushil's bail was, he stressed, only temporary, to enable the applicant to reach the competent court.[50]

The judge courted controversy, however, by declaring that the magnitude of the alleged offence was immaterial, as anticipatory bail did not distinguish between a greater and a lesser offence. He emphasised that granting bail 'is entirely within [the judge's] personal discretion'.

Naturally, the media would not leave it at that. Everything in this case, it seemed, was newsworthy, and the more tenacious media efforts often yielded more than the reporters had hoped for. They didn't have to look far in this instance. The judge, they quickly discovered, had a worrying penchant for granting bail all too easily. Gopalaswamy was the very same judge who had granted bail to five alleged offenders in January of the same year in another controversial case. The five had allegedly murdered Food Corporation of India (FCI) Director Neelkanta by hurling petrol bombs at him.

Justice Shivappa of the Madras High Court had felt constrained in that case to cancel the bail order, observing that 'before granting bail in non-bailable offences, [the lower court] should take into consideration the nature, seriousness and the gravity of the offence, the reasonable apprehension of witnesses being tampered with, and the larger interest of the public'.[51]

Perhaps in reaction to the media furore in the wake of Sharma's grant of anticipatory bail, the Madras High Court now became involved, ostensibly in response to a telegram addressed to its chief justice on 8 July by P.D. Joseph of Putham Madan Kunnu in Thiroor, Thrissur district, Kerala. Upon reading in the newspaper about the bail order for Sushil Sharma, Joseph had fired off a telegram which declared that the 'impugned order appeared to have been obtained by deception, thwarting the process of law'. He requested the chief justice of Madras High Court to 'intervene and cancel the bail, treating this telegram as a writ.'

On 9 July, the registry placed P.D. Joseph's telegram before the chief justice. He promptly acceded to the request, treating the telegram as an urgent PIL (Public Interest Litigation) issue, and called for the relevant records from the registrar, City Civil Court, Madras.

The day after this latest development in the drama in Madras, a hard-hitting editorial in *The Statesman* denounced the anticipatory bail fiasco, castigating the relevant judge: 'The Principal Sessions Judge in Madras, Mr. M. Gopalaswamy, broke new ground,' it declared, 'when he granted anticipatory bail for two weeks to the prime accused in the Naina Sahni murder case in the capital, to enable him to consult his lawyers.' It elaborated:

> ... The power of anticipatory bail, under Section 438(1) of the Criminal Procedure Code, has to be exercised sparingly and in exceptional cases. It was incorporated in the Code on the advice of the Law Commission which sought to prevent 'influential persons from trying to implicate their rivals in false cases ... by getting them detained in jail for some days ...'
>
> ... An essential condition [for anticipatory bail] is that the application should be made to court within whose jurisdiction the offence is committed and not before a court under whose jurisdiction the applicant resides ... Further, the general principle is that the applicant must surrender before the court ... The reason for moving a court out of jurisdiction is not difficult to understand. The public prosecutor in Madras did not oppose bail as Sharma was not wanted by the State police.

The editorial did not lose this opportunity to denounce the political clique in Delhi which had nurtured Sushil Sharma:

> ... Sharma is the archetypical member of the gang that Sanjay Gandhi had around him and several of them still hold positions of power and influence. Their distinguishing mark is arrogance ... the grant of anticipatory bail in the ... case reminds one of the words of the 1985 judgement in Yoginder Kumar's case – 'an abuse of the judicial process and would shake the confidence of the general public in the judiciary'.[52]

The wheels of justice were now turning, at any rate – and turning quickly. On Monday, 10 July, the registrar at Madras High Court collected the relevant records from the Sessions Court and placed them before the chief justice, along with clippings of relevant news items in different local newspapers. Considering the seriousness of the offence and the adverse publicity in the case, the chief justice ordered that it be placed before the double bench of Justices Arunachalam and Thangamani.

Having perused the records, Justice Arunachalam and Justice Thangamani observed that this order granting interim anticipatory bail had been passed in great haste, without any attempt to find out the nature of the allegations against the petitioner and without even ordering notice to the first respondent, the inspector of Connaught Place police station.

Justice Arunachalam and Justice Thangamani ordered that the interim bail granted by the principal sessions judge, City Civil and Sessions Court Madras in criminal Misc. Petition no. 3906 of 1995, be suspended forthwith. The matter was then listed for 12 July, after urgent notices to respondents (Delhi Police, Madras Police, as well as the petitioner and his advocate).

Curiously, just as the learned judges were contemplating this matter in the Madras High Court, another application surfaced in the court of Principal Sessions Judge Gopalaswamy. Practising advocates Professor S. Krishnaswamy and Rathi Devi moved the court to take action to cancel the anticipatory bail granted on 7 July by Judge Gopalaswamy himself. The application was ostensibly made in cognizance of the deception in Sushil Sharma's earlier application to the honourable court.

It was surely the bombardment from all sides following his grant of anticipatory bail that prompted this application. But it was unclear whether the applicants were assisting Judge Gopalaswamy to tread the right path or were simply assisting him in salvaging whatever honour he could from the debacle. Be that as it may, the judge himself lost no time in retracting his earlier order.

The city public prosecutor, at least, seemed to go along with the pretence that all was well within the Madras judiciary. He wrote to the commissioner of police, Madras, about this development, with some elaborate bureaucratic posturing that could only be construed as a face-saving exercise. In the letter, he informed the commissioner that just as Judge Gopalaswamy was in the process of dictating his decision, notice was received from the High Court that it had stayed his earlier anticipatory bail order.

ACP V. Renganathan had meanwhile reached Madras and moved a petition in the Madras High Court. Through V.J. Gopalan, the senior Central government standing counsel at Madras, he placed before the court Delhi Police's version of events.

With the required formalities attended to and clearances obtained, Additional Solicitor General Tulsi was briefed and rushed to Madras to represent Delhi Police. He appeared on the appointed date, 12 July, and argued for the cancellation of the bail, the operation of which had already been suspended by the Madras High Court on 10 July.

In its editorial 'Crime and Congress', *The Indian Express* applauded the Madras High Court's decision to rescind Sushil Sharma's extraordinary bail. It also took aim at the unsavoury culture in the Youth Congress, noting, once again, the influence of 'Sanjay Gandhi's notorious political style' in Sharma's actions.[53]

The public discourse about the tandoor murder had already veered far from the events of 2 July at Mandir Marg and the Bagiya Barbeque. Although, to the press as to the public, the case was a sensational murder that could very well have been sparked by a domestic dispute, it invoked issues well beyond crime and punishment. To the general public, Sushil Sharma seemed the very embodiment of brash, arrogant criminality that held sway in the nation's capital. For many, the murder, along with its botched, ghastly cover-up, was a symptom of moral degeneracy in the Congress and in politics at large, rather than the terrible moral failures of a desperate man.

11

The Noose Draws Tight

The contrived interim anticipatory bail, perhaps Sushil's last hope of evading arrest, stood for little more than two days before common sense prevailed in the Madras judiciary on 10 July. The outcome of the hearing two days later was, it seemed, a foregone conclusion. Indeed, Honourable Justice J. Arunachalam would describe the chicanery of 7 July in his judgement as 'an episode which shocked the judicial conscience of this court and led as well to justifiable public lamentation'.[54] Events were now turning in our favour.

Late in the evening of 10 July, we heard contradictory accounts from Karnataka police sources that agreed in one crucial respect: Sushil Sharma was in custody in Bangalore. First came Karnataka Police's claim that they had arrested Sushil; then we heard that he had surrendered in a Bangalore court. Later, we were told that he had surrendered not in a court, but to the police. Through our sources, we determined that Sushil was indeed in custody. The means by which this had happened was not as important as the end itself. Our relief was immeasurable.

Sometimes it takes a little time for the truth to emerge. It seems that Sushil had a harrowing, rather Kafkaesque day. The courts being closed for the weekend following the issuing of the interim anticipatory bail, Sushil and his advocate had reached Bangalore on 9 July and stayed the night at the Pai Vihar Hotel, a comfortable middle-class establishment on Old Taluk Cutchery (O.T.C.) Road in central Bangalore. The next morning Sushil appeared in the Principal City Civil and Sessions Court in Bangalore with his advocate, Ananthanarayanan. There, he filed a petition asking to surrender to the court.

The presiding judge, Bangalore Principal Sessions Judge Mohammad Anwar, was taken aback. Bewildered by Sushil's curious plea, and probably aware of the countrywide sensation over the tandoor murder and Sharma's notoriety, he promptly rejected the petition. Bizarrely, India's most famous absconder was then sent from the court back onto Bangalore's leafy streets, a free man. And Delhi Police was none the wiser.

The least the learned judge could have done, one would think, was to have his staff telephone the police.

Sushil's Catch-22 situation – which was, it must be said, of his own making – did not end there. After he and his advocate were allowed to walk out of the Principal City Civil and Sessions Court, they beat a path to the seniormost officers of Bangalore City Police. First, they went to the police commissioner's office on Infantry Road, where Ananthanarayanan sought a personal interview with Commissioner T. Srinivasalu. The commissioner's staff informed the advocate that he was busy in meetings. Ananthanarayanan, it seems, did not disclose the reason for his request, and the commissioner's staff apparently didn't recognise Sushil.

The pair left the commissioner's office and made their way through the complex to the office of Additional Commissioner A.R. Infant who was, it appears, indisposed. No one from the additional commissioner's office recognised Sushil either, which is perhaps not surprising, given that he had taken some pains to change his appearance after his flight from Delhi. Nonplussed by the baffling response of the judge and their inability to even speak with senior police officials, the pair gave thought to their next move as they left the commissionerate.

It was then that they got their first break of the day. An inspector of police from the Bangalore Rural District had seen Sushil and Ananthanarayanan in court and had witnessed the drama of the judge refusing to entertain Sushil's surrender petition. Sniffing an opportunity, he had telephoned his boss S.K. Venugopal, the superintendent of police of the Bangalore Rural District. After getting Venugopal's approval, the inspector eagerly set off to track down Sushil and his lawyer, and encountered them just as they stepped outside the commissionerate. After a brief discussion, he came to an agreement with them, and Ananthanarayanan and Sushil were soon on their way to Hoskote, the inspector's own beat, some 25 km north-east of central Bangalore.

Today, Hoskote is a satellite town of Bangalore, all but consumed by urban sprawl. At the time, though, it was a sleepy rural town surrounded by open fields, featuring a reservoir constructed in the fifteenth century and a number of attractive temples. As the sun set on a very strange day, Sushil and his advocate reached Hoskote. After walking in and out of court and the offices of senior police officials in Bangalore, Sushil had finally managed to find someone who would accept his surrender in Karnataka. By 6.10 p.m., he was formally in police custody. And, at least for the moment, he was far from the clutches of Delhi Police.

This was, of course, the objective of Sushil's peculiar approaches to the judiciary and Bangalore Police.

For a fugitive such as Sushil, surrendering before a court and being remanded to judicial custody is usually preferable to police custody. More often than not, wanted criminals resort to this legal manoeuvre when their intention is to avoid custody by the agency investigating their misdeeds. Sometimes they wish to save themselves from interrogation; perhaps they fear torture at the hands of the investigating police. In every case, they want to deny the investigating officers any opportunity to extract information or a confession.

By surrendering in a court of jurisdiction distant from Delhi, Sushil's lawyer could argue, with at least some hope of success, against police custody remand. He could make a plea that Sushil not be handed over to Delhi Police – not to any police for that matter – but be remanded to judicial custody. With Sushil in judicial custody in Karnataka – and Karnataka being governed by a party inimical to the ruling party at the Centre – he could try to manipulate matters. With some persuasion, Karnataka might well refuse custody transfer, or at least frustrate our attempts to bring him into the custody of Delhi Police. This, we feared, would delay the investigations and dilute the evidentiary impact enough to hamper Sharma's prosecution.

The superintendent's eagerness to accept Sushil's surrender hinted at motives that were not altogether pure either. I would later discover that after promptly recording his arrest and informing Delhi, Bangalore Rural District Police just as quickly contacted the press, and, on the following day, would luxuriate in the media spotlight. It seemed that few were immune to the lure of instant publicity that the case promised. Sushil's surrender was a fillip for the police and their town, which had perhaps not commanded such widespread attention since the Battle of Ooscota (Hoskote) on 22 August 1768, during the First Anglo-Mysore War.

Late in the evening of 10 July, a meeting of our high-level team of investigators in Delhi discussed strategy threadbare, while charting the next course of action to counter Sushil's moves. As our deliberations continued well into the night, a consensus emerged that we must immediately send a police party to Karnataka. We decided, too, that this could not be any ordinary deputation. It must comprise a select group of police officers to face the challenges that would likely meet us in Bangalore, some 1,740 km south, a world away from Delhi.

The deputation to Bangalore, the meeting decided, would include an assistant commissioner from the crime branch, Raj Mohinder Singh, along with Inspector Niranjan Singh. And I would lead the team, for two practical reasons: First, we felt that less senior officers might be bullied or overawed. Also, I hailed from Karnataka and spoke the local language, Kannada. Indeed, Bangalore was my second home: I had gone to university there (St. Joseph's College and Government Law College) and practised law at Bangalore Cantonment's Mayo Hall Courts. My local knowledge would lend me considerable advantage.

That the director general of police, Karnataka, Francis T.R. Colaso, was a close friend and like an elder brother to me would work in my favour too. Or so we thought.

Having settled this, the investigators toiled late into the evening to prepare the papers for Bangalore. Metropolitan Magistrate Dharam Raj Singh was most obliging in providing us with a production and transit warrant in the middle of the night from his residence.

At the airport security lounge the next morning, as I waited for the Bangalore flight to be announced, I bumped into Additional Solicitor General K.T.S. Tulsi. The anticipatory bail matter was coming up before the Division Bench of Madras High Court the following day, 12 July, and Tulsi was heading to Madras to represent Delhi Police at this hearing. ACP Renganathan had already made progress in Madras, having been despatched there immediately after hearing about Sushil's ploy of securing bail.

Tulsi and I sat together in the lounge over a coffee and chatted about the events which were unfolding rapidly before us. We pondered the likely implications of Sushil's surrender and our prospects for success. While Tulsi was supremely confident he would prevail in Madras, he was more than a little concerned, as was I, that political intrigues could derail us in Bangalore.

When the announcement was made for my Indian Airlines flight, I wished Tulsi all the best and boarded the plane with my team. Just as we took off for Bangalore, Tulsi was boarding his plane to Madras. It was as if we were tactically closing in on Sharma in a pincer movement: Tulsi from Madras, and my team 284 km due west, in Bangalore.

In the plane, I was in for another unexpected encounter: with Girja Shankar Kaura, the gentlemanly, bespectacled crime reporter from the *Hindustan Times*. He must have noticed my startled expression when I saw him and said with a soft smile, 'We had to work all night to see that we were on the plane with you, sir.' How he had learned of our plans, which had only been finalised hours before, I could not fathom, but then some of our journalists are actually quite smart. The *Hindustan Times* had truly exceeded themselves in pulling strings to place Girja on the flight with us. Girja's instructions, he told me, were to tail me for the duration of our time in Bangalore. The newspaper bosses knew that our trip there would be newsworthy. Just how newsworthy, even we could not imagine.

A liaison officer from Bangalore Police met us at HAL Airport, and we were provided with police vehicles: a trusty Ambassador for me, and a four-wheel-drive for my team. Francis Colaso, the director general of Karnataka Police, true to his word, had made all the necessary arrangements for us. I was somewhat disappointed to discover that Francis himself was away on an inspection tour to Coorg. I couldn't tell whether this was a tactical move, or he simply had a pressing engagement he had to fulfil. At any rate, he had left his personal regrets to me for his absence. Without losing time, we set off for Hoskote on the outskirts of Bangalore.

The drive to Hoskote had its picturesque moments, but much of the open, rugged countryside of my youth was gone. Colonies, residences and commercial establishments had mushroomed across the landscape in the years that I had been away from Bangalore. I witnessed the change regretfully. The scenic wilderness I remembered from my college days, had been desecrated. I am not one to stand in the way of progress, but its riding roughshod over the glorious Karnataka landscape was a rude shock for me.

The day was to hold other unpleasant surprises. As the Ambassador drew near the Hoskote District Court complex, the bedlam there had me quite taken aback. I had not anticipated the large congregation of reporters and journalists, television cameras and crews, nor was I prepared for the innumerable spectators thronging outside and crammed within the courtroom. It seemed strangely incongruous in sleepy, rural Karnataka; almost surreal.

One would have expected a motley assortment of local television and press personnel, but certainly not the presence of international media. We were taken aback by the unprecedented number of news crews, including those from foreign networks and news agencies, including the BBC, ABC, ANI and CNN. One of my reporter friends later told me there were no less than eighty-four correspondents covering the story. I couldn't verify this, but given the clamour of the day, it seems plausible. Obviously, the case had garnered significant worldwide attention and notoriety.

As a senior police officer, I avoided unnecessary contact with the media: it tended to cause me trouble of one kind or another. Granted, press briefings held in a controlled environment were integral to our successful pursuit of the fugitive, and we couldn't have conducted the case thus far without them. Avoiding or managing the media in Hoskote, however, was quite impossible. With Sushil in another jurisdiction, where our writ was dependent as much on goodwill as legal authority, we were quite unprepared for what was in store for us. The media clamour in Hoskote, it quickly became apparent, had actually been encouraged; engineered, even. And the drama that ensued for me afterwards would be an object lesson in exactly how much trouble the media can cause.

In any event, the outsized media presence and the public interest in the hearing generated a bizarre atmosphere at the Hoskote District Court complex. It was as if the crowd was awaiting the arrival of a cinema superstar or rock band, rather than a political-fixer-turned-murderer's appearance in court. It highlighted a particular aspect of human nature that the police officer all too often confronts: a prurient interest in the darker happenings in life, which goads normal people to gawk at traffic accidents and flock to public executions. Sushil Sharma's life had all the elements of a film script: sex, money, power, fame and violence, but little art or subtlety – and, it seemed, nothing to redeem it. The less enlightened among us were enthralled.

A certain Mr Gowda, a local resident, seemed to speak for many when he told Girja, 'We want to have a look at the man who could be so cruel as to murder the very person he loved very much once upon a time and then push her body into the tandoor.'[55] When the Bangalore Rural Police arrived at the gates to the court complex with Sushil in a Tata Sumo, they were very nearly overcome by the crowd.

Reporting on the carnivalesque scene at Hoskote, our shadow Girja Shankar Kaura wrote in his article the following day:

> The one man with the biggest smile on his face in this small town was the tea stall owner outside the District Courts. He had never seen such a crowd. There were all kinds of people: Policemen, reporters, photographers, onlookers … and everyone wanted a hot cup of tea.
>
> And everyone wanted to catch a glimpse of Sushil Sharma, who with his one deed has hogged so much publicity, something no other public figure has managed in recent times.
>
> An air of expectancy prevailed at the Hoskote District Courts where the office of the First Class Magistrate is situated. The local judge had to give a final judgement on whether to hand over the former Delhi Pradesh Youth Congress president to the Delhi Police team. Even though Sushil Sharma had not committed any crime in Bangalore or Hoskote, still the media attention which the case had received in the last nine days had generated enough interest in the public here. They thronged the small District Courts.

The drama of the event engulfed me as soon as I alighted from the police Ambassador. In the sea of jostling bodies that covered the dusty, open expanse before the court complex gates, I was mobbed. Cameras flashed and I was bombarded with questions – each journalist wanting to get his question heard as the tapes and film rolled. 'Mr Pereira, Sushil Sharma claims he has been framed, falsely accused, with not an iota of evidence against him. Tell us what evidence you have against him. Do you have any?' Without hesitation came my blunt reply: 'There is enough evidence to hang him; however, every soul is innocent unless proven guilty in a court of law.'

My sound bite was frank, if not particularly diplomatic. But few could have anticipated the fallout of this short sentence, which was correct in both the figurative and literal senses. We had a veritable mountain of evidence against Sushil Sharma – enough to hang him – and now, the press had elicited four words with which others would attempt to hang me. But more on that later.

We had been ambushed at Hoskote. It was only after the hearing that I came to know that far from keeping Sushil away from the media as we had requested, the Bangalore Police had given reporters full access to him. They had even gone so far as to let the press interview Sharma and his lawyer – no holds barred.

Never one to waste an opportunity, Sushil had waxed lyrical, telling the media how he had been framed; how the murder was a political conspiracy against him and was the brainchild of Youth Congress President Maninderjeet Singh Bitta. He asserted that '[Keshav] is also framing me. He is giving statements under pressure from Bitta.'[56] Sushil swore that on the night of the murder he was on a pilgrimage in Ajmer Sharif, and he only learned of the murder on the following Thursday evening. With a melodramatic flourish, he proclaimed to the media, 'I am innocent. I am a holy man. If I am guilty, I should be hanged.'[57]

Someone from the force had seen fit to convey to the media that Sushil had told the police that 'his life was in danger' when he surrendered. Perhaps Francis Colaso's absence from Bangalore was in anticipation of this injudiciousness – not that he had any part in it.

Even without the sideshows, the hearing was a formidable event. The courtroom itself, designed to accommodate perhaps twenty people, was crammed with twice that number. It was standing room only, for all. And the cameramen and news crews, along with a myriad spectators, were left outside. Soon the proceedings were underway. The poor magistrate, a slim man who seemed to be in his mid-thirties, was evidently more accustomed to rural quietude than international attention. He looked like an actor thrust upon a stage, in the glare of the spotlight without a script. The audience was there for a performance; he had to deliver. The gallery was shoulder to shoulder and chest to back with spectators and scribes.

He seemed to quickly gather his wits, despite the enormous pressure on him. He knew he must decide prudently in this high-profile case – and arguments were fired from each side hard and fast – or he might suffer the ignominy that Judge M. Gopalaswamy had merited just days earlier.

It was only as the action in the courtroom heated up that I realised the Bangalore Rural Police were playing a game of their own. While they were not particularly hostile and indeed gave the appearance of being helpful, they were far from supportive of our efforts. I had neither time nor inclination to ponder their motives then. Our task was simply to secure custody of Sushil Sharma for Delhi Police on the strength of the transit and production warrant issued by the Delhi magistrate. We were determined not to be distracted by the drama of the event, which aside from being an annoyance, threatened to interfere with our mission.

And there was plenty of drama to be had. This was the biggest show in town; even a bit player without any connection to the main plot could enjoy his interlude. The Bangalore Rural Police had brought Sushil to the court in handcuffs. This was promptly – and predictably – objected to by Manjunath, the secretary of the Hoskote Advocates' Association, who appeared as if on cue.

Regular handcuffing of prisoners, for reasons elucidated earlier, is all but proscribed in India. And it barely seemed warranted here anyway, given that Sharma had gone to some pains the previous day to surrender. This gaffe allowed the magistrate to take the high ground, to reprimand the police and order the removal of the handcuffs. Journalists and spectators alike enjoyed the show.

The Bangalore Rural Police's avoidable lapses didn't end there. They produced Sushil in court with his face concealed, his head covered with a beige-coloured muffler. Concealing the face of an accused is a procedure adopted in instances where showing him before the court could prejudice his identification in a Test

Identification Parade (TIP) or endanger his family. It beggared belief that anyone could deem this fitting under the circumstances. Sharma was a public figure whose face had featured on the front page of virtually every major daily newspaper of the land in the preceding days. It quickly became a point of contention, a pretext for Sushil's advocate S. Ananthanarayanan to raise objections against our warrant.

Unsurprisingly, Ananthanarayanan refuted Bangalore Police's assertion that 'Sushil [had] been produced with his face covered so that no witness has any opportunity of identifying him', an explanation that was barely credible to anyone. He cunningly went on to claim that this was itself an indication of torture; a sign of what was in store for Sushil. Ananthanarayanan then argued against Sushil being handed over to Delhi Police on grounds that his client would be subjected to the third degree.

The muffler, too, was ordered removed, and I saw Sushil Sharma for the first time. He barely resembled the well-fed and confident-looking man I had seen in photographs. His head was tonsured, his moustache was shaved off – he would claim, for his pilgrimage to Tirupati – and this itself had altered his appearance immeasurably. It accentuated the petulant, upturned curl of his upper lip, for one thing. His countenance and posture were those of a defeated, caged animal. As he stood hunched over, his large, dark eyes wide with fear, he seemed utterly overcome.

I was not entirely convinced, however. I already knew Sharma to be a master manipulator, a man who would use almost any means of turning a situation to his advantage. How much of this apparent fear was real and how much was contrived for effect before the assemblage, I could not tell.

There was no shortage of shenanigans in the courthouse that day. The Bangalore Rural Police gave Ananthanarayanan further cause to discredit them before the court and provide some light entertainment for the gallery. They claimed that Sushil had not surrendered, and that they had nabbed him as he was travelling in a Tamil Nadu bus, on its way from Tirupati to Bangalore. Ananthanarayanan took some delight in narrating to the court Sushil's travails the day before, trying to surrender before Judge Mohammad Anwar, and then before the most senior officers of Bangalore City Police.

The human propensity for manipulating and telling lies to suit one's own ends is universal. By claiming arrest, Bangalore Police would have hoped to garner some prestige and perhaps claim the reward for Sushil's apprehension. As it turned out, their contrivance neither benefitted them nor did any favours for Indian law enforcement's credibility.

For Delhi Police, how Sushil came to be in custody was largely irrelevant, anyhow. What mattered far more was that the most exhausting and exhaustive manhunt in recent Indian history was over. I was quoted in a paper the following day: 'For us it is immaterial whether he has surrendered or was arrested, as long as we have got him in our custody now!'

With the theatrics and manoeuvring over, the court got to the crux of the matter before it. The Delhi Police team had already submitted to the court the 'body warrant' for the transit remand. This was necessary for us to travel with Sushil to Delhi and produce him before the Judicial Magistrate's Court of New Delhi. We stood firm and presented our arguments on the strength of the transit warrant. It sought reasonable custody remand for the travel time involved in transporting Sushil to Delhi.

We stressed throughout that no party, other than the accused, of course, had a locus standi (standing or right before the court) to intervene or interfere in this. We countered spurious arguments that we could not execute the warrant on the mere grounds that the accused had chosen to surrender here, in another jurisdiction. We emphasised in our court submission that these arguments were a transparent attempt by the accused to subvert and delay the due process of law. While Raj Mohinder and Niranjan were doing a sterling job of presenting the case for Delhi Police, I also addressed the court to underscore a few of their points.

First Class Judicial Magistrate K.N. Laxminarayana took his time to ponder the matter before him. He was involved in what was surely one of the most prominent hearings of his magistracy. He must have been painfully aware that any misstep on his part would be detrimental to his career. As he carefully weighed the counsels' arguments, I sensed that he was quite clear that Sushil was, in spite of his advocate's well-framed arguments, simply trying to use devious means to evade the long arm of the law.

After much toing and froing, he recorded his order transferring Sushil's custody to the Delhi team with a four-day remand. This was given in cognizance of the three-day train journey to Delhi.

Curiously, all this while, the Bangalore Rural Police seemed to be sitting on the fence, doing the bare minimum to assist their Delhi colleagues. Their procrastination in actually transferring custody of Sushil to the Delhi team after the court orders were made was particularly exasperating. Even after the magistrate's order was made, stamped and issued, they took their time sending Sushil to a hospital for a medical check-up as ordered by the magistrate.

The peculiar indifference, too, of S.K. Venugopal, the superintendent of the Bangalore Rural District – despite the Delhi team being led by a senior officer, an additional commissioner – left us underwhelmed. In police circles, visiting officers of another force are usually afforded every courtesy. In Hoskote, our reception was decidedly cool.

I couldn't help but make a mental note of all this, concluding that such behaviour could only result from some hidden agendas and machinations. Perhaps Superintendent Venugopal was simply responding to whispers from the corridors of power. Karnataka Chief Minister Deve Gowda was a staunch opponent of the Congress government at the Centre. His party would not be unhappy if Sushil's case caused the Congress further embarrassment.

The next day's papers provided some insight into the Karnataka government's role in the whole murky affair. Karnataka Home Minister P.G.R. Sindhia informed the press that after Sushil Sharma surrendered before Bangalore Rural Police, he himself had convened a meeting of Home Secretary R.N.A. Muthanna and other top police officials and discussed the issue. A clipping from 'Evening News' threw light on the matter, while I was still in Bangalore:

> ... the surrender of Sharma before the superintendent of Police S.K. Venugopal of Hoskote, near Bangalore was a well planned move on his part and he must have used his alibis ... planned his move carefully and used his contacts before he surrendered to the police, after which he was formally arrested. With Sharma's arrest the biggest manhunt for a criminal in the Capital in the recent past comes to an end.[58]

Having won our battle and secured Sushil's custody, I left the nitty-gritty of paperwork and other follow-up to Raj Mohinder and Niranjan. I concentrated on some crucial matters, and a few petty personal ones that demanded my attention too. I lost no time in searching out a telephone booth in the Hoskote marketplace, adjacent to the court complex, from where I telephoned Commissioner Nikhil Kumar in Delhi. 'Good show!' he said enthusiastically when I informed him of the success of our mission. Prompted by his appreciation, I visited K.C. Das on Church Street to pick up a few boxes of his favourite sweets. There were other things I sought too: some of our Mangalorean delicacies – chaklis, murkus and other salty savouries; and also the extraordinary flavoured sausages from the Bangalore Ham Shop on South Parade, which are my own childhood favourites.

I grabbed the opportunity, too, to pop into Ligoury Court on Palmgrove Road en route to the airport and see my mother, even if briefly. My mother had been staying with me in Delhi until a few days prior to our Bangalore mission and my nephew Rohan had accompanied her on the journey back to Bangalore.

I arrived at my mother's bungalow to find Rohan holding centre stage in the lounge room. He was recounting with eloquent relish his first-hand experiences of the tandoor case before a bevy of pretty cousins and friends. While the experience of witnessing the crime scene early on 3 July was no doubt etched deep in his mind, he seemed to have quite recovered from its shock. That fate had played its hand and the case followed him to Bangalore fired his imagination – and made him the focus of eager ears and sparkling eyes.

From Ligoury Court, I headed to the police chief's house beside St. Martha's Hospital on Nripatunga Road for a brief visit. There, I asked Carmel, Francis Colaso's wife, to convey my heartfelt thanks to him for the assistance he had rendered to us from behind the scenes. I knew that had it not been for Francis's intervention, our task of securing Sushil's custody would not have been achieved. It occurred to me that the trouble we had to go to, to secure Sharma's custody, had been at least in part due to the undercurrents and machinations of the powers that be. They were, it seems, piqued that they had been unable to frustrate us.

Meanwhile, Raj Mohinder concentrated on ensuring there was no loophole left in our paperwork that might later benefit the accused. And Niranjan busied himself talking to – or should I say, coaxing and gently interrogating – Sushil in the offices of Bangalore Rural District Police. He was able to win Sushil's confidence enough for him to provide us with some important information. On the basis of Sushil's disclosures, Niranjan took the assistance of Bangalore Police to go to the Pai Vihar Hotel. There, he took Sushil's briefcase from room number 110, where Sushil had stayed along with Ananthanarayanan.

The briefcase contained a German-make Arminius .32 bore revolver, serial number 1277725, with four live cartridges; an arms licence – no. NWA-no. 10038 – in his name, issued by DCP/Licensing, Delhi, valid up to 24.1.1997 with 'All India' endorsement; his passport, no. A-3455-94, issued from Delhi; one pair of Cartier golden-finish spectacles; a letterhead of the Bagiya Barbeque; a

Canara Bank cheque book in the name of Sushil Sharma and Prem Lata Sharma; a copy of FIR no. 141/85 PS Darya Ganj against Sushil Sharma and Ramesh Handa (in which he had once been proclaimed an offender), and the keys of his Maruti car.

All these were seized, with Niranjan taking pains to ensure that Bangalore Police officers were witness to the seizure. We were quite sure the Arminius .32 bore revolver was the murder weapon, and the other items were obviously material to our case. Sushil also produced a shoulder bag containing his clothes and other personal items, which were seized in the presence of ACP Raj Mohinder Singh and Hoskote Circle Inspector K.L. Puttathimme Gowda.

Having secured Sushil's custody and recovered what was almost certainly the murder weapon, it seemed pointless to remain in Bangalore any longer. Sushil had already confirmed our crime scene reconstruction that had been postulated on the basis of circumstantial evidence, and Niranjan had elicited Sushil's admission of guilt. It was crucial for us to get back to Delhi without wasting any more of our precious remand time.

We had originally planned to take Sushil by train to Delhi so we would have ample opportunity to question him during the journey. Now that Sushil had spilled the beans on his crime, we abandoned this plan. It would, we agreed, be in our favour to take him back by the next available flight. Commissioner Nikhil Kumar concurred with us when I sought his permission for us to fly to Delhi that very evening. Bangalore Rural Police assisted us in arranging the tickets.

I joined my colleagues at HAL Airport with plenty of time for Indian Airlines flight IC 404, which was scheduled to leave at around 8 p.m. Sushil, flanked by Niranjan and Raj Mohinder, arrived in an Ambassador under heavy police escort. The local police had seen to it that we were allowed use of the VIP lounge and other private rooms, away from prying eyes. Despite all efforts to keep our journey with Sushil a low-key affair, I could see curiosity and awe in the faces of people in the airport concourse. We had garnered a good deal of attention – the kind that generates more.

It was enough to prompt Anita Pratap, then a correspondent for *Time* magazine, to accost me and quiz me for details. I had known Anita from church: she was part of our Sunday congregation at Sacred Heart Cathedral in Delhi, and we stopped to chat after mass from time to time. Anita happened to be at HAL Airport en route to Delhi from Colombo, after covering the latest on the war in Sri Lanka. She was intrigued to see that we had with us Sushil Sharma, the nation's most famous fugitive, and I gave her a rundown of the day's drama.

The HAL Airport interlude gave me the opportunity to speak to Niranjan about Sushil's questioning. This is where I would first meet and speak with Sushil, to hear for myself his version of events.

A well-built man of about 5' 9", Sushil was dressed in a pale blue shirt and light-coloured trousers, and wore a pair of Kolhapuri chappals (hand-crafted leather sandals). He was carrying a black briefcase and a travel bag with his clothes and a few personal effects. He looked every bit the prosperous, upwardly mobile, middle-class young man he once was – except for his demeanour. He was utterly cowed down, the fear of a cornered rat writ large in his eyes. Doubtless, this was the nadir of his life. He spoke freely, ostensibly regretful and repentant, grovelling for mercy and leniency.

Meanwhile, Girja Shankar was hovering quietly somewhere in the background. He seemed to have been with us all the way – even on the flight back to Delhi. He wrote of our trip:

> … Niranjan Singh sat almost poker faced. He kept nodding while scribbling furiously. Once in a while he would rest his spectacles on his forehead, listen to Sushil, then put them back on and start writing again. And at times he would glance around especially at the passengers sitting in the rows right in front and behind him to see if anyone was eavesdropping … I strained hard to listen, but failed to catch the conversation between the police official and the suspect. Sushil kept talking in a very low tone and all I could hear once in a while was Niranjan Singh telling him '*Sach sach batha* (tell me the truth)'. In the meantime … Mr Pereira took

off his long boots and sat with his feet up on the cabin wall. He was reluctant to divulge anything, but said the prime suspect was already 'singing like a canary'. Mr. Pereira said that, 'Sushil Sharma was now lamenting his fate. Earlier he was trying to sell us all kinds of stories. But once we caught him in a contradiction, he was on his way.'[59]

Though Girja Shankar was suitably unobtrusive – we barely registered his presence throughout – his piece was a fair account of our trip. After a hectic day, Raj Mohinder and I were happy to leave the interviewing of Sushil to Niranjan. We sat nine rows ahead of them, and I stretched my legs and relaxed. We would need to be ready to dodge the media onslaught in Delhi.

DCP Aditya Arya had worked with the IGI Airport DCP, Rajesh Kumar Gupta, to prevent the kind of melee we had encountered in Hoskote. When we landed at Indira Gandhi International Airport at around 11.30 p.m., we were ushered through the VIP gate, where we were promptly mobbed by the waiting media. We made a decision to allow Sushil to be photographed, which was possible at the VIP gate without disrupting routine airport operations. We also hatched a plan to ensure that the press would stay at the airport after Sushil had left, which would allow the convoy taking him to make a clean getaway.

While Sushil was the star of the show and the lensmen were flashing away to their delight, I announced that I would be remaining behind to take questions from the assembled reporters. After the photojournalists had satisfied themselves taking shots of a bemused, haunted-looking Sushil, he was bundled into a nondescript silver-coloured Maruti sedan and driven away in a well-guarded convoy. The press corps felt compelled to stay behind to question me.

The convoy took Sushil to the fairly secluded Diplomatic Security Force building in the diplomatic enclave of Chanakyapuri, where he was to be held until his remand hearing. There, he would be well away from the public gaze. The building was located across the road from Gujarat Bhavan and was a short distance from where he had abandoned his car on Malcha Marg on the morning of 3 July.

From the airport, my driver took me home in my police Ambassador. This was as much a ruse to mislead any newshounds who might have tailed me from the airport as it was an opportunity to take a break. The last thing we needed was reporters milling around the Diplomatic Security Force building, harassing our officers for a scoop on Sushil's interrogation.

I sat down with a cup of tea in my house and pondered the day's developments. The media scrum and public hysteria at Hoskote was an ominous sign. We would have to be especially vigilant when we took Sushil to his remand hearing.

After a quick freshen up, I headed out to Chanakyapuri. Minutes after I reached the building, Commissioner Nikhil Kumar arrived, dressed casually in a white kurta pyjama with a light shawl. His home on Akbar Road was close by and, even at this late hour, he was keen to see the offender whose flight had prompted what would perhaps be the most extensive manhunt of his storied career.

A room full of investigating officers witnessed the ensuing drama. Sushil, perhaps in the most pathetic and remorseful state we would see him, fell at Nikhil Kumar's feet, begging for mercy, his palms pressed together and his head almost touching the ground.

Nikhil remained clam but there was steel in his eyes as he stood above the distraught captive.

'*Yeh kya kiya tum ne?* (What have you done?)'

'*Galti ho gayee* (It was a mistake)', was Sushil's mumbled answer.

It was as if Sushil was pleading for forgiveness from a priest or a father. Sadly, his contrition would not last – whether it was real or contrived.

Addressing a press conference the next day, Commissioner Nikhil Kumar recapitulated the police efforts over the preceding ten days to nab Sushil. Answering questions, he confirmed that Sushil's statements and claims would be verified – especially his claims of going to Ajmer, Madras and Tirupati. He made a point of declaring that Sushil was forced to surrender as the Delhi Police chase had become too intense for him; he knew he would not be able to keep out of the police dragnet for long. Nikhil assured the gathering of reporters that there was no way Sushil could have escaped the country, as 'we had taken all precautions and possible steps to alert the international airports and the seaports'.

The commissioner highlighted the fact that this had been one of the biggest manhunts ever, with over twenty-five raids carried out every day, on an average, in the capital and elsewhere. 'One day the information was so strong that even I, accompanied by two additional commissioners, had to be present with a raiding party during a raid at a house in Janakpuri,' he said.

With Sushil in custody, officers of the investigating team could now catch their breath. We would discover in the coming months that our troubles over Sushil had just begun.

12

The Circus Comes to Town

It would be tempting to depict Sushil Sharma as a depraved archvillain running rampant in Congress backrooms until he overstepped the mark with Naina's killing. This was, at least, the tenor of the many sensational media reports in the weeks following the discovery of Naina Sahni's body. The truth, however, was more complicated and more disturbing – as it often is.

It appears obvious now that the man lived two parallel lives, which intersected in places but were ultimately impossible to reconcile. One was the drinking, womanising, hot-headed political manipulator, and the other a serious, pious Hindu who cared deeply about his family and inspired loyalty in his friends and associates. It need scarcely be mentioned that it was the former character who lived with Naina Sahni at the Mandir Marg apartment.

In the period preceding the tandoor murder, Sushil was purportedly living with his father Inder Mani Sharma and mother Prem Lata in Maurya Enclave of Pitampura in north-west Delhi. It was here that his other avatar was at play. How much of either was a construct – or whether both were expressions of a deeply troubled psyche – we can only guess.

Sushil Sharma was born on Saturday, 24 January 1959, in Sitaram Bazar, a historic area within the walled city of Old Delhi, all narrow lanes and markets. India's first prime minister Jawaharlal Nehru had married Kamala Kaul there in 1916. The Sharmas, an educated lower-middle-class family, lived in a small rented house on a corner of Nai Sarak. Sushil was one of four children. He had two sisters, Suman and Anju, and a brother who died in an accident some eight years before the tandoor murder.

Sushil's father Inder Mani, a bank clerk who later rose to the position of deputy manager, hailed from the small town of Aurangabad in Bulandshahr district of Uttar Pradesh, some 120 km by road from the capital. Sushil received his primary education at the Marwari Primary School and went on to finish his schooling from Ludlow Castle I in Civil Lines.

By all accounts, Sushil was a fairly quiet boy, and teachers at the school could not place him. An old-timer at the school who did remember Sushil volunteered that 'He was mild-mannered, and like most students, went unnoticed'. Reacting to the tandoor murder, this person then lamented, 'This is the first such incident in the history of the school'.

But Sushil apparently had an impetuous and ambitious streak, which would begin to manifest itself as he emerged from high school. It seems his non-academic activities kept him from excelling in school and, later, from securing admission to Delhi University's more sought-after colleges. He finally settled for Satyawati College, considered a second-tier institution in 1977. Back in the day, the college was in Timarpur on Mall Road, across from the main Delhi University campus.

A young man evidently cut out for a political career, Sushil thrived in the fertile training ground of student politics, with its agitations, elections and campus intrigues. His charisma and uncanny ability to attract support by means fair or foul did not go unnoticed; he made an indelible impression on Congress hawks scouting the campuses for fresh talent.

Sushil became president of the students' union in his second year of college. He and his gang of supporters were infamous for beating up other students. The PCR received numerous complaints against them, which warranted police visits to the college. The complaints led to no action because they were considered the result of minor skirmishes between student groups.

Sushil joined the NSUI and contested for the post of vice-president at the Delhi University Students' Union elections of 1979. He polled a mere third. It was rumoured that he threatened the winning candidate of the Students' Federation of India (SFI), Amitabh Roy, with a knife in the counting room, after the results became known.[60]

This was perhaps the first of Sushil's violent acts in public. It was likely the first, too, in which he demonstrated his unsettling affinity for weapons, which became his instrument of intimidation as much as a mode of expressing rage. He earned the epithet 'chakumaar' (slasher) in these early years, for his habit of slashing the posters of rival candidates.[61]

Far from being deterred by the loss in his first election, Sushil redoubled his efforts to hold elected office in the NSUI. Along with a loyal cadre of supporters, he set out to dominate politics on campus. His henchmen, who according to a former student, 'used to go around threatening rival candidates that they would be kidnapped if they didn't withdraw', were pivotal to his success.[62]

Student politics was, and is, an often deadly business: shootings, stabbings, abduction – some of the worse premeditated criminal acts – are not uncommon in elections and during on-campus power struggles. In 1981, some miscreants belonging to the NSUI, which at the campus level was more or less controlled by Sushil Sharma, allegedly stabbed the president of Shyam Lal College in Shahdara to death[63] in a skirmish between rival groups of students. Although Sushil and his group of supporters were linked to the murder, he managed to keep himself out of the FIR. His confederates were charge-sheeted.

In 1981 he became president of the Delhi unit of the NSUI and held that position till 1983. In 1985, a case of assault was booked against him for an incident at the Delhi Police Headquarters. Sushil, along with shop owner Ramesh Handa and fifteen-odd Youth Congress activists, had barged into DCP Traffic A.S. Khan's office, shouting anti-police slogans. There, the group allegedly broke some furniture and manhandled the DCP's orderly, Head Constable Kishore, even tearing his uniform.[64]

It was a stunt typical of youth political cadres in those years. Handa was running an auto accessory fitting shop in Connaught Place, and the traffic police regularly towed away any cars that were illegally parked in front of his shop. Sushil and Handa hoped to browbeat the traffic police into giving Handa his way – at the expense of other commuters. That the mob accompanying them got off scot free, without even being apprehended at the scene, shows the kind of impunity with which the youth cadres operated.

Throughout, Sushil and his student goons were more than ready to show their usefulness to their political masters. During the 15 March 1988 Bharat bandh, Congress party youth led by Sushil reportedly mobilised support for the ruling establishment, brandishing knives and kattas (illegal, country-made pipe-barrel pistols). Determined to thwart the bandh, they menaced the BJP workers who were coercing shop owners and market stallholders in Chandni Chowk to keep their businesses closed.

Soon afterwards, Sushil was involved in an incident at the Bangla Sweet House in Gole Market. Accounts indicate that he fired on an adversary in front of numerous witnesses. The Mandir Marg police, who reached the spot in response to the PCR call, could do little more than record the incident in the daily diary of the police station. Nobody seemed willing to speak against Sharma.

In 1989, Sushil was elevated to the position of president of the Delhi unit of the Youth Congress. As with the rest of Sushil's political career, his appointment was not without controversy. The incumbent president, Mukul Wasnik, had reportedly received a telephone call from the party high command while at a conference in Pyongyang, ordering him to appoint Sushil.[65]

It was around this time that Sushil began to associate closely with

Naina Sahni, whom he appointed the general secretary of the DPYC. Party insiders were intrigued that though there were four other women office-bearers, only Naina's residential address was omitted from the office register.

As president of the DPYC, Sushil worked hard to cultivate a favourable public image. A colleague of Sushil's, who had risen to become a sitting member of the Delhi Assembly by the time of the tandoor murder, recalled that Sushil was usually very low key: 'He never smoked or consumed liquor in public and portrayed himself [as] religious minded'. He reportedly often visited the Chhatarpur temple, too.

According to submissions Sushil made in a petition to the Supreme Court, he had worked for the community at large in projects to eradicate poverty, assisted the economic improvement of the downtrodden and contributed substantially to the Congress party.[66] He claimed it was rare for a Congress worker to rise from the ranks as he had, and this evoked jealousy among his opponents in the Akhil Bharatiya Vidyarthi Parishad (ABVP) and a faction of the Congress during his university days. He also maintained that he had incurred the wrath of several Congressmen, both opponents and contestants, when he was president of the NSUI.

Naturally, Sushil's submissions were quiet on his early sources of income, which may well have been the cause of this resentment. In a cynical money-making exercise which flouted party rules, Sushil formed and appointed his own committee in the DPYC, beyond what was provided for in the executive. Each of the 300 members of this preposterously large committee was expected to pay Sushil a sizeable fee, simply for the honour of serving on it.[67]

Sushil appeared to have no qualms about giving his darker side rein, just as he had as a student politician. Chief Minister Madan Lal Khurana claimed before the press in the days following Sushil's surrender that Prime Minister A.B. Vajpayee had told him how Sharma had stoned him as a student.[68] As DPYC President, Sushil was involved in an incident in December 1991 at the residence of

Mukul Wasnik during a party function. There, he was alleged to have pointed a revolver threateningly at Parnita Azad, one of the fourteen vice-presidents of the DPYC.[69]

This suggested an ominous aggravation of his violent nature, directed as it was, at a defenceless woman. Senior party leaders apparently took no action, even when Parnita took up the matter with them.

Sushil could inspire great loyalty and he maintained close links with the movers and shakers of the party, such as R.K. Dhawan, Jitendra Prasad, Deep Chand Bandhu and the controversial tantric Chandraswamy. His following appears to have been based on his ability to solve problems, by hook or by crook, for his friends and associates. Many were in Sushil's debt, and aside from the fear he could inspire, this goes some way towards explaining the wall of silence Delhi Police encountered in the tandoor murder case.

Sushil also had close personal relationships with some of Delhi's most feared gangsters and racketeers. A photograph from 24 January 1990 surfaced in the press on the day of Sushil's second remand hearing. It showed him posing at his thirty-first birthday party with Jameel Khan, Mahipal and Tejpal Gujjar, known land-grabbers and extortionists who used to terrorise Delhi and western Uttar Pradesh.[70] By the time of the tandoor murder, Tejpal had been shot dead in an encounter[71] with Uttar Pradesh Police after murdering a head constable, and Jameel and Mahipal were in Tihar Jail.

In any event, Sushil was himself quite capable of intimidating people. Ram Niwas Dubey, Sushil's peon and cook from 1989 till April 1995, later told the police that Sushil carried his pistol with him everywhere.[72] He even celebrated New Year and Diwali by firing a few rounds from it into the air. His temper, too, was fearsome, and it got him into more and more trouble as time passed.

In 1992, Sushil was embroiled in another case, when he led a demonstration outside the Sahitya Akademi building, protesting against an award for Harinder Singh Mehboob's poetry collection *Jhanan Di Raat*. The demonstrators charged that it contained statements against Indira Gandhi and Sushil was booked for allegedly blackening the face of a public servant.[73] He was later declared a proclaimed offender[74] in 1994, after he failed to appear in court in the 1985 assault case on the DCP Traffic's orderly.

Sushil's impetuousness had seen him very nearly expelled from the Congress party, long before the tandoor murder. He had sought the party's endorsement for a Lok Sabha seat – the prestigious seat of New Delhi, no less – early in 1991, while the Congress was out of power. According to party sources, he went so far as to threaten former prime minister Rajiv Gandhi, telling him he would sabotage the elections if he was not given a party ticket.

Maninderjeet Singh Bitta, the then Indian Youth Congress president and Sushil's staunch adversary, recounted that 'an infuriated Rajiv threw him out of the office and ordered that he be immediately expelled'.[75] Gandhi's order was to be overtaken by events, however. He was assassinated just weeks later, on 21 May 1991, at Sriperumbudur, near Chennai, and Sushil continued to thrive in the party. He earned the moniker 'Mr Quick Fix' for his ability to smooth out bureaucratic and political tangles for minor industrialists and civil servants.[76] This was a sideline which earned him lucrative under-the-table payments.[77]

While Sushil's abilities brought him success, his belligerence made him bitter enemies. Around the time that he was replaced as the DPYC president by Jagdish Yadav, months before the tandoor murder, Sushil gained notoriety as a tanki-chor (water-tank thief) in Delhi Congress circles. In an astonishing display of petulance, he had ordered the removal of the water tank, wash basin, tube lights and mirrors from the Youth Congress premises on Talkatora Road, leaving the headquarters all but gutted. Yadav claimed that his predecessor had not even handed over charge, but whisked away all office records and sanitary fittings the night before he took over as DPYC chief.

Notwithstanding his obvious penchant for lawless behaviour, Sushil's criminality seemed to defy the usual convenient explanations that abound in the wake of every high-profile case. The Sharma family in Pitampura was not spared the media hounding that everyone remotely involved in the case suffered, and nothing in the family's background gave any clue to Sushil's thuggery. Everything seemed so normal, so confoundingly bland.

Even the family home was boringly middle class. Theirs was a mundane house in a nondescript Delhi Development Authority (DDA) colony. Indeed, the family was well-known in the neighbourhood for their piety. Hearing Sushil's father reciting the Ramayan Paath, a passer-by might well mistake the home for a temple.[78]

Inder Mani and Prem Lata Sharma were grief-stricken by the murder, shocked by the allegations against Sushil, and they avoided public attention as much as they could. The family was devastated that their only remaining son could have been involved in such a grisly crime. 'We are Brahmins; how could our son have done something as gory as this?' was their refrain, the neighbours said.

Friends of Sushil said his parents were decent, god-fearing people who were shattered by the murder. According to neighbours, 'They were so distraught over the news that they could not think straight. After the death of Sushil's younger brother a few years ago, this is the second tragedy to strike the family.'

For many in the colony, Sushil was a religious man, noted for his presence during navaratri. 'He came around giving us prasad,' one Pitampura resident told reporters. Before the murder, Sushil gave every appearance of being a pious, devoted son. A neighbour recalled that he used to join his parents regularly for their morning puja. 'So deep was he in his religious ceremonies,' she said, 'that during navaratras he would wash the dishes, plates and bowls after the puja.'[79]

Another neighbour declared that he was 'willing to undergo an ordeal by fire, only to swear to the respectability of this family.'[80] Most did not know Sushil well, though, and denied any knowledge of his marital status. While most neighbours could not recall seeing Naina at the house, some spoke in hushed whispers about 'another woman' frequenting with a ten- or eleven-year-old boy who address Sushil's parents as his grandparents. This woman would usually arrive at the Sharma family's home on a Friday evening and leave the following night.[81]

A senior journalist in the area said he believed that one day Sushil would represent the area in Parliament, since he was viewed by many as a successful Congressman. Shiv Mrut Singh, a tea vendor nearby, who claimed to have observed Sushil for over a decade, thought otherwise. 'He did not seem normal,' he said. 'Something in his face and demeanour gave away his real self, which everyone now knows about.'

Sushil's two married sisters, Suman and Anju, returned home to stand by their parents. The neighbours told visiting reporters that his mother Prem Lata was in a state of shock, and broke down each time anyone spoke to her. Sushil's father, they said, felt harassed by the police interrogations he was subjected to: 'One day the police had to bring him home in an ambulance, since he suffers from high blood pressure.'

As the controversies raged in the media and courtroom in the wake of the murder, the Sharma family home seemed tranquil – at least from the street. Apart from the chant of the Ramayan Paath, the only indication of activity was the chortling of children playing hide-and-seek on the balcony of the first floor of the building.

⚖

Although there were still three days of interim custody remaining, we thought it prudent to produce Sushil in court the day after our return to Delhi to seek a fresh mandate for police custody remand. If, for some reason, our bid for remand failed, we still had time to lodge an appeal while Sushil was in our custody. If a lengthier remand was granted by the Delhi magistrate, we could question Sushil without interruption.

After the tumult at Hoskote, we anticipated a maelstrom at the Delhi hearing. An elaborate bandobast was arranged to ensure that the proceedings at the court did not descend into chaos. There are ten armed battalions of police in Delhi, whose duties include securing vital installations and guarding VIP residences, among others. In addition to the local police of New Delhi district, hundreds more from the ranks of the Delhi Armed Police were deployed around the Patiala House courts complex at India Gate before the hearing. We would need each one of them.

Patiala House was the erstwhile residence of the Maharaja of Patiala, designed by Sir Edward Lutyens. It was sold by the royal family to the government in the 1970s, after privy purses were abolished under Prime Minister Indira Gandhi in 1971. Since the late 1970s, Patiala House has functioned as court buildings, and been witness to every manner of controversy. Sushil's appearance would count as among the more memorable happenings there.

Thousands of curious spectators, journalists, Youth Congress activists, demonstrators, and a battery of lawyers thronged the complex, waiting for Sushil's appearance, which was scheduled for the afternoon of 12 July. A bleary-eyed Sushil, wearing the same pale-blue shirt he had worn the day before, arrived in a police Maruti Gypsy at 3.10 p.m. He was flanked by a formidable escort, which included Additional DCP (New Delhi) D.K. Bhatt and ACP Alok Kumar. He was tethered to Niranjan with a piece of cloth so he would not be dragged away in the confusion.

All hell broke loose as the officers took Sushil towards the court building. Scores of reporters, lensmen and onlookers jostled with each other, setting off a virtual stampede which had to be controlled by the police.

A group of spectators strategically perched on the roof of the portico overlooking the court complex began to shout slogans and the air was thick with anger outside the courtroom: 'Sushil Sharma murdabad! (Down with Sushil Sharma!)' 'Yehi hai, yehi hai (It's him, it's him)'. It was a group of women activists from a voluntary organisation, voicing their disgust at the horrific crime against Naina Sahni.

Niranjan and a large detail of officers formed a phalanx around Sushil to lead him to the court complex. They were to appear at courtroom 32 of Metropolitan Magistrate Dharam Raj Singh, around which 'a massive security umbrella was thrown', as the media later reported. The preparations had been made well before Sharma's hearing, but the officers still had to elbow their way through the crowd while holding on to Sushil. It seemed that pandemonium could erupt any moment. Many people had made their way far ahead of the appointed time to the court premises, even into the gallery, determined to catch a glimpse of this fallen leader.

A photograph of Sushil arriving at the court appeared in *The Indian Express* the following day. Under the banner 'Many throng court to see Sharma', was a close-up of Sushil, sporting almost as much stubble on his face as on his tonsured head, officers pressed to him by the surrounding mob. He wore a somewhat detached expression. With the natural upward curl of his upper lip, he looked almost contemptuous. He may have been numbed by the enormity of the event – or petrified.

A huge melee was the hallmark of each of Sushil's first few court appearances. A photograph in the *Hindustan Times*, taken ten days later, at his next hearing at Patiala House, showed quite a different man. Grimacing in the crush around him, he looked more like a condemned man on the way to a public execution than an infamous offender attending court for a remand hearing. Those at the centre, including Sushil, bore the brunt of the horde as it descended on him. Only careful planning and commendable effort on the part of the police managed to keep him from harm.

That first hearing on 12 July was probably the most chaotic. The jostling among photographers, public and police personnel was no less inside the small packed courtroom – in fact, it was only exacerbated by the four walls of the courtroom. Advocates stood on benches and reporters squeezed themselves in wherever they could, in shocking violation of courtroom decorum.

Sushil was brought into court handcuffed and greeted the magistrate with his palms pressed together. Perhaps this was as much a ploy to show the handcuffs to the court as it was a sign of respect. The police escort had taken the precaution of recording in advance the reasons for the handcuffing – it was needed in view of security concerns. This did not, however, forestall the ensuing drama. Lawyer Rohit Minocha leapt into the fray, protesting loudly and demanding the removal of the handcuffs. This was done at the magistrate's bidding; the police in any case remove the handcuffs once an offender has entered the courtroom.

Even so, the magistrate declared that the use of handcuffs in the prevailing chaos was purely a matter of law and order, and quite within the discretion of the police. Thus, he stated, he would not issue any direction against their use. He further told the police that the cuffs could be applied again while taking Sushil from the court.

Minocha's tactical intervention and exhibitionism seemed to have earned him the temporary brief to represent the high-profile offender. Sushil promptly engaged him as his counsel by signing a vakalatnama,[82] which was immediately handed over to the magistrate. Responding to media queries on how he came to represent Sushil, Minocha reportedly claimed:

> I was dealing with an earlier case where Sushil was accused ... of blackening the face of a public servant while leading a demonstration in front of [the] Sahitya [Kala] Akademi in 1992. When I heard he was being produced before the court on July 12, I rushed there and Sushil agreed to sign the vakalatnama inside the court ... I felt it was my responsibility to represent my client ... and let the truth prevail.[83]

Earlier, the court complex had been alive with rumours that a senior advocate from the High Court who was considered to be close to a minister in the Central government would represent Sushil, or one of Delhi's leading criminal lawyers would take his case. This did not come to pass, at least, not at this juncture. Senior Public Prosecutor K.D. Bharadwaj and Assistant Public Prosecutor Raman Kumar represented the State.

K.D. Bharadwaj stressed our need for time to establish the sequence of events, to arrest any co-conspirators and collect other crucial evidence. We need at least ten days, he said, for further questioning and to corroborate the facts and evidence so far adduced.

While the prosecution's plea for ten days' police custody remand was not opposed by Sharma's counsel Rohit Minocha, he did make several contentious submissions to the magistrate. First, he stated that his client was a heart patient and had suffered chest pain the previous night. He argued that Sharma should therefore be given a medical examination every forty-eight hours by a private medical practitioner. Further, he expressed grave concern for his client's safety. The print media itself had made claims that suggested that he would be better off dead, just the day before. Sushil, he boldly declared, harboured a very real fear that he would be murdered while in custody, and he especially feared he would be poisoned. He therefore requested the court to order that Sushil's food be tested. He also made a plea that Sushil be questioned only in his presence.

Until this point in the proceedings, Sushil had been peering into the crowd, as if looking for a familiar face, occasionally smiling. Perhaps he was looking for family members or supporters, but there was no one. He now seemed buoyed by Minocha's advocacy, and flashing a smug grin, he eyed the battery of lawyers in the gallery and gestured, urging them to come forward to support him. This was Sushil in his element – the master of ceremonies who might well be in the dock but, in some sense at least, was still running the show.

Minocha's extraordinary pleas to the magistrate were offensive. It seemed that Sushil fancied himself a regal personage rather than a proclaimed offender accused of murder. Senior Public Prosecutor K.D. Bharadwaj vehemently opposed Minocha's pleas, especially his request to be present throughout Sushil's interrogation.

At the end of the deliberations, which lasted forty-five minutes, the magistrate acceded to the prosecution's request, and remanded Sushil to police custody for ten days, till 22 July. While granting the remand, the magistrate unhesitatingly noted that 'the complicity of [the] accused Sushil Sharma at the time of Naina Sahni's murder has been revealed by the co-accused Keshav Kumar'.

As the police surrounded Sushil to lead him from the court, he made a point of loudly proclaiming what he had told the media in Bangalore: He was innocent – the victim of a political conspiracy of M.S. Bitta's making. Labouring the point, he then shouted Bitta's name several times before he was bundled out of the room and down a staircase normally used only by court staff. Waiting below was a police Gypsy, which sped away with Sushil and the small detail of officers guarding him.

The magistrate's grant of ten days' police remand was expected in view of the seriousness of the accusations and preponderance of evidence against Sushil. But the investigating team was quite taken aback by the extraordinary provisions the magistrate included in the remand order.

The magistrate stipulated that Sushil be immediately provided medical aid at Ram Manohar Lohia Hospital, if required. He further ordered that food intended for Sharma's consumption be tested, and his advocate be present during his interrogation.

The latter condition was especially disturbing, as we feared that Sushil's advocate could mislead him or get into arguments with the police – either of which would waste our time. Though testing Sushil's food would not pose any difficulty, it niggled. The investigating team had every desire to keep Sushil alive and well so that he could be successfully prosecuted. To suggest that Delhi Police, or someone under their watch, might poison him was an insult.

We honoured the order nonetheless, complied with it in letter and spirit, despite our misgivings. If such strictures were necessary for Sushil Sharma's remand, surely they would become necessary for every other offender too.

We could not know then that this was to be the first of many requests for extraordinary 'VIP' treatment that Sushil made, all of which were readily acceded to. It was hard not to conclude that the judiciary took quite a different approach to a powerful criminal than to one from the less affluent classes – regardless of the crime.

13

Contrition and Recriminations

With Sharma in custody, we could concentrate on our investigation. We were also relieved to obtain another day's police custody remand order for Keshav Kumar – without any VIP provisions attached. This was necessary to facilitate the corroboration and confrontation of material during Sushil's questioning.

Sushil's interrogation would take place in Tilak Marg police station, which is just a few hundred metres from the courtroom in Patiala House. A special team comprising ACP Raj Mohinder Singh, Inspector Niranjan Singh (SHO, Connaught Place) and Inspector J.K. Sharma (Additional SHO, Connaught Place) interrogated Sushil.

Most of the questioning was to be done in an upstairs room at the Tilak Marg police station, which had been specially prepared for the purpose. We took great pains to ensure a conducive, even comfortable environment for the interrogation, bearing in mind the conditions imposed by the court. The room was equipped with soundproofing and air conditioning. Sushil and his interrogators would encounter no external disturbances and would escape the enervating, humid weather of the month.

We also took care to circumvent any suggestion of third degree by members of the interrogating team, by arranging video and audio recordings of the interrogation. With all our efforts, we were opening ourselves to the criticism of pampering Sharma – which is exactly what the VIP remand order entailed anyway. But we preferred to risk accusations of treating Sharma with kid gloves than be charged with brutality.

Police custody remand for Sushil was therefore not as intimidating as he may have envisaged. He seemed fresh on the morning of 13 July, after a sound sleep the previous night, followed by a bath and breakfast.

Initially, Sharma refused to cooperate. He then feigned illness or fatigue to avoid responding to questions. We would have to regularly consult doctors on his alleged conditions – ranging from stomach and chest pain to headaches – over the coming days. When the interrogators dealt with Sharma sternly, asking him to give straight answers, he would act up and make veiled threats about committing suicide. This naturally alarmed the interrogating team. We went to great lengths to ensure that he did not have any means of harming himself.

The interrogation room was padded, and we checked that his clothing, mostly a plain shirt hanging outside his trousers without a belt, did not have any components that could be used for self-harm. Abundant precautions were also taken in terms of what he ate and what he did, and a watch was maintained even while he used the toilet. His body and his clothes, too, were subjected to regular searches for fear that he may manage to procure some substance that could endanger his safety. Sushil's custodians remained vigilant throughout his police remand. Indeed, concern about possible suicidal tendencies had been one of the reasons for bringing Sushil back to Delhi by flight.

Sushil was somewhat pacified with tact, humane treatment and clever psychology. The interrogators set aside the formal questioning for a while. They began discussing his personal life and political career; they cajoled him to speak about his phenomenal rise in the political arena and other matters not relevant to the investigation. Sushil then began to settle down and talk.

We soon heard of his pride in his ascent in political circles at a young age, his ability to access power, money and status in society, at a time when most of his contemporaries were struggling in the lower echelons of their chosen fields of work. He expressed satisfaction that he had become a powerful, well-known figure in Delhi circles.

It was no surprise, then, that he was devastated by his fall from grace. He slowly revealed how his arrest and remand in police custody were a major blow to his image and status. It wounded his pride, and his anguish over his plight dominated his conversation with the interrogators for quite some time. He lamented the loss of his political career, and seemed bereft at his ruined reputation and bleak prospects.

Still, Sushil seemed to take satisfaction in making the task of the interrogators as difficult and uncomfortable as he could. At times he exuded unshakeable confidence that he would overcome his present crisis, gloating over how he had manipulated the system to get anticipatory bail in Madras. With a flourish, he declared he would go to Tihar Jail and be released on bail within two months. He would taunt the officers, telling them, 'Despite what you think, this incident has not affected my personal relations with some of the senior leaders. In their long political careers, these leaders have helped many of the present-day judges ... Do you think these judges will refuse to help me?'[84]

Sometimes he would refuse all solid food on the pretext of fasting, consuming only soup and juices. His interrogators viewed this as a calculated attempt to weaken himself, so that he could demand hospitalisation and forgo questioning.

Nonetheless, Sushil reiterated what he had earlier admitted to me and Niranjan during our questioning of him in Bangalore and on the flight back to Delhi. Not that he was consistent, or truthful. A man of extraordinary cunning, Sushil took a cue from Dr Sarangi's bungled autopsy, at one point telling investigators he had not shot Naina. He claimed instead, that in the course of a heated argument, he had hit Naina on the head, accidentally causing her death. Of course, the investigating team would have none of it. They knew that nothing Sushil said or did could be taken at face value.[85]

⚖

Even as the questioning continued within the secluded, carefully controlled environment of the interrogation room, the intrigues outside – unbridled speculation in the media and political manoeuvring – were gathering momentum.

The 'Evening News' captured the mood in the ruling Congress party in its front page column, 'Will Sushil take names?' on 11 July, the day of the Hoskote hearing. The article referred to a purported crisis meeting between the prime minister and Minister of State for Welfare K.V. Thangkabalu, who faced allegations in the press of sheltering Sushil.[86] The writer declared that 'for many in the Congress party, [Sharma] would be better off dead than alive and singing before the investigators.' Not to be outdone, the Delhi *Mid-Day's* column on the same day, 'VVIPs fear Sushil may squirt dirt on many', spoke of the 'nervous faces' in the Congress after his arrest.

The first to suffer was Sushil's sworn enemy, Youth Congress President M.S. Bitta. In Bangalore Sushil had alleged before the press that Bitta had been threatening him, and that his 'life was in danger', as Bitta had created a gang of sixty criminals 'to finish me.'[87] This was to be his refrain during many of his interactions with the press. Sushil was as intent on settling old scores as on clearing his name.

Evidently he had some success, at least in damaging Bitta's reputation and perhaps halting his rise in national politics. While there was no suggestion whatsoever of Bitta's involvement in the murder, another of Bitta's foes, Punjab Chief Minister Beant Singh, sought to capitalise on the furore. He impressed on the party high command that Bitta was not above suspicion in the matter and should therefore be removed from his post.

No measure of politicking could save Beant Singh himself, though. His fate had already been sealed months earlier, in a secret meeting of exiled Sikh militants in Lahore. A few weeks after the tandoor murder, on 31 August 1995, at 5.12 p.m., Dilawar Singh, a Sikh separatist disguised as a policeman, detonated a suicide vest beside Beant Singh's armoured Ambassador near the Punjab Government Secretariat in Chandigarh.[88] The roof of the car was blown away by the force of the explosion, and the carnage spread some 100 metres.

Beant perished along with fifteen others, including members of his security detail – and the assassin. It was the most brutal political killing since the LTTE's assassination of Rajiv Gandhi in 1991. Some of the forensic experts in this case would be sought out for their opinion on Naina Sahni's case too, but more on that later.

In the meantime, the tandoor murder and its repercussions virtually monopolised the headlines, and politicians scurried for cover. Bitta was the first to be affected but other, more powerful Congress figures would soon be in the line of fire. A report in *The Pioneer* claimed that on the night of the murder, Sushil had met former minister Madhav Singh Solanki and apprised him of Bitta's activities.[89] Although Bitta denied Sushil's allegations against him, saying 'they are an act of mockery with mala fide intention', the mere association of his name with the murder must have taken its toll.

Opposition figures rejoiced at the Congress's discomfiture in the aftermath of the murder, and some sought to actively exploit it. Delhi Chief Minister Madan Lal Khurana of the BJP, never one to pass up an opportunity for Congress-bashing, gave fulsome speeches which were lapped up eagerly by the press. His open letters to Home Minister S.B. Chavan and the police commissioner also made for riveting copy. Khurana demanded that Sushil's safety be ensured in view of apprehensions voiced in the media that he might be 'liquidated', as his presence posed 'much embarrassment to many VIPs'. Given the gravity of the situation, he demanded that the intelligence report submitted to the prime minister regarding the matter be made public.[90]

That an 'intelligence' report had been prepared for the prime minister regarding what was essentially a crime of passion gives an indication of the nail biting in the corridors of power as the case progressed.

A few days earlier, when Prime Minister Narasimha Rao was touring his native state of Andhra Pradesh, newspapers had reported his concern over rumours of 'liaisons' between Naina Sahni and 'some Central ministers'. Quoting 'reliable sources' in the Prime Minister's Office, the papers reported that Rao had ordered a 'secret' probe into Sushil and Naina's proximity to ministers.[91] This gave rise to the intelligence report that Delhi Chief Minister Madan Lal Khurana referred to in his letter to Home Minister S.B. Chavan.

It seems the 'intelligence report' was a complete dossier on Sushil Sharma's links within the party, being compiled by a top official in the Prime Minister's Office in coordination with intelligence agencies. An official was quoted as saying, 'The report is not meant as a cleansing agent for the party, but as a detailed account of who all Sushil knew and operated with. Especially since the case offered immense possibilities for political blackmail, the report is only to guard against such a possibility.'

Prime Minister Narasimha Rao himself was evidently so worried about the fallout that he asked Home Minister S.B. Chavan to personally supervise the case. Naturally, Home Secretary K. Padmanabhaiah was brought into the fray. At the best of times, the Home Ministry and Delhi Police, which functions under the ministry, share an uneasy relationship. This now came to the fore with some unseemly public posturing.

Home Secretary K. Padmanabhaiah, who was apt to chastise Delhi Police at the least opportunity, began to make ever more controversial statements. After the charge sheet was filed, he wrote a letter to Lieutenant Governor P.K. Dave, criticising Nikhil Kumar and me for 'unnecessarily shooting [our] mouth[s] off'. This, he maintained, was 'affecting the progress of the case'. He went on to ask the lieutenant governor to 'ensure that such things are not repeated' and 'police officials do not speak out of turn'.[92] In other words, he was attempting to silence the police.

He must have been under considerable pressure from his political bosses – especially considering Parliament was scheduled to debate the criminal–politician nexus the same week.

The Tribune reported that Minister of State for Home Affairs Rajesh Pilot had been restrained from supervising the tandoor murder investigation by his superior S.B. Chavan. Pilot continued to hover over the case, however, and kept the heat on Commissioner Nikhil Kumar. Pilot was, it seems, incensed at the publication of a photograph of Jai Prakash Pehlwan with two Central government ministers. He took particular exception to the photograph's purported 'selective leak' by the police.[93]

Pilot reviewed the investigation and reportedly expressed his unhappiness to Home Secretary Padmanabhaiah over Delhi Police's handling of the case. This was apparently what spurred Padmanabhaiah to shoot off his missive to Lieutenant Governor Dave, criticising Commissioner Nikhil Kumar and me. Pilot urged the police to file the charge sheet before the monsoon session of Parliament. He demanded, too, that exemplary punishment be meted out to anyone whose involvement in the macabre incident was established, 'however high and influential he may be'.[94]

Such pressure from one's superiors can give rise to lapses in one's judgement. So it was with Home Secretary Padmanabhaiah. His engagement with the issue descended into farce when he visited Sushil and Naina's Mandir Marg apartment, on Monday, 17 July. Padmanabhaiah and a host of other officials descended on the Gole Market residential complex in the afternoon, in a motorcade of government Ambassadors. They took a guided tour of the apartment with Commissioner Nikhil Kumar, and stayed there for more than an hour, chatting with Sushil and Naina's neighbours.

How his inspection of the apartment could have benefitted Padmanabhaiah, his political masters or the case is beyond my comprehension. Delhi Police Commissioner Nikhil Kumar, a hands-on manager, had felt no such need to inspect the apartment before this farce. He must have been there with Home Secretary Padmanabhaiah to maintain protocol. Surely, inspecting the apartment was a duty best left to the investigating team. If the home secretary himself was compelled to visit Sushil and Naina's 'love nest', the press and the public could only surmise that the Congress heavyweights had much to conceal. Padmanabhaiah's ill-conceived attempt at public relations backfired, giving rise to further lurid speculation in the newspapers.[95]

There was little anyone could do, in any event, to limit the damage to the Congress. While Sharma himself appeared less intent on harming the party than the press had anticipated, his arrest unleashed a wave of recriminations within the party.

'Evening News' reported on the infighting and unrest among Congress leaders in Delhi. Union Minister Jagdish Tytler, it revealed, was baying for former DPCC President H.K.L. Bhagat's blood, accusing him of bad-mouthing other Congress leaders in the wake of the murder.[96] H.K.L. Bhagat tried to turn the tables on Tytler, saying, 'I did not make him [Sushil Sharma] president – my opponents in the All-India Congress Committee [presumably Mr Jagdish Tytler and Mr R.K. Dhawan] had pushed for his candidature'.[97]

Tytler had himself experienced some of the recent public opprobrium towards the Congress. A former Sanjay Gandhi acolyte who was repeatedly accused of involvement in the anti-Sikh pogroms in 1984, Tytler now found himself being rather improbably linked to the tandoor murder. He reportedly lamented at a meeting chaired by DPCC President Deep Chand Bandhu that he had been jeered and heckled as 'Tandoorwala Tytler' while on a recent pilgrimage to Shirdi, and approached by the press in Mumbai 'as if I was the criminal'.

Perhaps the alliteration was simply too tempting for his detractors: 'Tandoorwala Tytler' had quite a ring to it. Or it may be that the tandoor murderer epitomised the thuggish Delhi politician, despised by India's increasingly educated population. At any rate,

Tytler's unsavoury dealings with Sushil, of the very sort that had the press up in arms, were just coming to light.

Tytler also resented the loose talk floating around about his association with three senior lady party members.[98] The media spotlight was now trained on the personal lives of various Congress power brokers, and he was one of many who were uncomfortable with such scrutiny. His increasingly self-conscious and awkward public attempts to justify these associations were mercifully curtailed by party members Tajdar Babar and Krishna Tirath. These wise ladies silenced him tactfully, to save him from embarrassing himself further.[99]

Sushil did make some sensational revelations, and these sparked the kind of media speculation that had Congress figures such as Tytler scurrying for cover. News reports claimed that Sushil Sharma had revealed that he had killed his wife because of her relationship with two VIPs: one of them a Central minister and the other a former minister who had been dumped from the Cabinet some time earlier. Sharma had purportedly caught Naina in a 'compromising position' with one of them, noted as a 'youthful minister', and he could not control his rage. To teach her a lesson, he kept her confined in their flat for forty days, but she refused to mend her behaviour. The press suggested he was driven to kill his wife due to her insistence on maintaining relations with the two prominent politicians.[100]

Upon seeing these oblique references to a 'youthful minister', the forty-five-year-old Minister of State for Welfare K.V. Thangkabalu felt moved to issue a public statement, denying any link with Sushil.

On the heels of this, a *Times of India* headline announced that 'Mukul Wasnik, Kalpnath deny liaison with Naina' – putting names to the earlier veiled hints of alleged romantic involvement of ministerial bigwigs with Naina.[101] Both VIPs, one the youth and welfare minister, and the other the former food minister, said they were puzzled why Sharma had named them. 'Perhaps the game is to divert attention from the real culprits,' said Wasnik. Kalpnath Rai swore in the name of God that after his first wife died, he had been living happily with his second wife. He had never, he declared, even had a nodding acquaintance with Naina, let alone taken her with him on his tours.

Other media outlets levelled equally salacious allegations, but with a different slant. They speculated that bed hopping and sharing partners to suit one's political agendas was rampant in the party, and this was very much the case with Sushil and Naina.[102] Some journalists also claimed that Sushil had revealed Naina's sexual escapades were actually of little concern to him. She had, in any case, come to him after a prolonged live-in relationship with DPYC leader Matloob Karim. Sushil was more stung, it was reported, by her seeking to desert him when his political fortunes were at an ebb, after his battles with Youth Congress chief M.S. Bitta.

Throughout, the Opposition continued to fan the flames, keeping up the heat on their Congress adversaries. BJP spokesperson K.L. Sharma demanded a thorough probe to bring out the truth about the gory incident. He expressed shock and dismay over the absolute silence maintained by Prime Minister and Congress President P.V. Narasimha Rao in connection with the murder. After all, this was, he said, the killing of one former DPYC leader by another.

The prime minister's internal intervention, nevertheless, had sent shockwaves throughout the party. All the heavyweights mentioned as Sushil's supporters were now distancing themselves from him, at least as much as they were able to. Some were simply too closely linked with him to effectively disavow him. The media speculated that DPCC President Deep Chand Bandhu was already politically isolated in view of his close political alliance with Sushil.[103]

Bandhu took every opportunity to distance himself from the case. It seems he had, despite his vehement denials, created the position of chairman of the sports cell of the DPCC for Jai Prakash Pehlwan and appointed him, at Sushil's behest.[104] His earlier claims that he had only visited the Bagiya 'two or three times' were even less convincing.[105]

For some in the party, it was largely a case of guilt by association.

The fallout from the tandoor murder did not spare the Mahila Congress and its then chief Girija Vyas, who had been a minister of state in the Rajasthan government, and at the time of the tandoor murder was a minister at the Centre in Delhi. Vyas's proximity to the then heavyweight Union Agriculture Minister Balram Jakhar also drew flak, ostensibly because he had been one of Sushil's mentors.

It seemed every Delhi politician whose name was connected with Sushil in any way would be hounded; the media was as much on the hunt for political scandal as it was for titillating revelations. Columnists wondered why the police had not questioned Youth Affairs Minister Mukul Wasnik about how and why he had appointed Sushil Sharma president of the Delhi Youth Congress in 1989 and Naina its general secretary.[106] Were the appointments made, journalists asked, on anyone's recommendation?

Congress leaders outside Delhi could not escape scrutiny, either. 'Karunakaran supports bright young boys and girls, but he cannot side with ruffians and murderers; all this about him being sympathetic to Sushil is a pack of lies,' declared a close aide of this Kerala leader, when his name was bandied about in the media.

The media was just as alert to any suggestion of political interference in the investigation of the murder, as were the BJP leaders. Responding to innumerable media queries on this score, I assured all and sundry that we were conducting a fair and impartial prosecution, and I was correctly quoted in this case: 'Mr. Pereira added that so far he had not faced any political pressure in the investigation of the case and he expected there will be none in the future. [He said,] "It is a case where everyone is interested in seeing that justice is done. On our part there will be no loophole in the investigation of the case."'

All this while, the questioning continued, and the background to the horrific murder began to take shape. Sushil told the interrogators about his marriage to Ravi Naina Sahni some three years earlier, when he was the president of the DPYC and she its general secretary. The marriage, he said, was solemnised in a temple, and both sets of parents were aware of the alliance. It was kept a secret from others, he explained, so he could make it public at a time suitable to advancing his political ambitions.

Sushil spoke of how his relationship with Naina had soured when he began to suspect her of infidelity. This, he claimed, was largely due to her refusal to sever her former romantic ties. He had married her because he had convinced himself that she would soon forget Matloob Karim. That she continued to be in touch with Matloob, despite his remonstrations, was a constant source of angst for Sushil. He was used to having his way, and Naina was openly defying him in his own home.

He said he doubted her further when he discovered she was giving his money to someone. Naina's stonewalling of his attempts to discover the person's identity only exacerbated the rage he felt towards her. Sushil nurtured his anger within till it festered. Eventually, he decided to rid himself of her.

Call it female intuition, but Naina apparently sensed his intentions.[107] Some two months earlier, when he was pondering ways to finish her off and asked her to accompany him on a holiday to Kulu and Manali, she flatly refused, he told his interrogators. His plan to hurl her to her death from one of the scenic lookouts there was thus thwarted. Later, he asked her to accompany him to Jaipur, but again, she refused.

With time, as his suspicions darkened and his heart hardened towards Naina, Sushil sensed she was planning her escape. He would check the telephone each time he returned home, he said, pressing the redial button and listening silently at the end of the line. That way, he would get to know the identity of at least one person whom she had contacted after he had left the apartment. On hearing the voice of Matloob Karim at the other end of the phone on that fateful night, he was overwhelmed with a murderous rage.

Sushil was equally unreserved in giving Niranjan and the interrogating team an account of his movements after fleeing the Bagiya late on 2 July. He mentioned contacting and staying with

D. Kishore Rao at Gujarat Bhavan, as well as seeking help from Jai Prakash Pehlwan, Ram Prakash Sachdeva and Rishi Raj Rathi to escape the police's clutches in Delhi.

Arriving in Jaipur and finding the airport closed, he had stayed at the Vatika Resort, he said, which was owned by a party contact. He then took the 7.20 a.m. ModiLuft flight to Bombay on Tuesday, 4 July. In Bombay, he stayed at the National Sports Club of India (NSCI), from where he phoned D.K. Rao, giving further details of his peculiar predicament. He wanted to ask Rao's friend Ashok Gandhi for assistance in Bombay, but despite requesting Rao to tell Gandhi to contact him at the club, he said Gandhi did not telephone him. When he rang Rao again, Rao brusquely told him to surrender to the police, and not to call him again.

Sushil then took an evening Jet Airways flight from Bombay to Madras. With the help of a party contact in Madras, he managed to get in touch with advocate Ananthanarayanan, whom he met at his home that evening. After briefing Ananthanarayanan, he took a taxi and headed to the Tirupati temple, reaching there the following morning around 10.30 a.m. At the temple, he said, he recited some prayers and tonsured his head, offering his hair to the deity.

Sushil spoke with some relish of his success in obtaining bail. He returned to Madras on 6 July and stayed with Ananthnarayanan that night. In the interim, he said, Ananthanarayanan had done some spade work, contacted the right people, and on Friday, 7 July, had managed to get him the anticipatory bail order.

It hadn't gone according to plan, of course. Ananthanarayanan had found him a hotel in Egmore, an inner-city neighbourhood of Madras, from where he could reach the court quickly to execute the bail bond. But by the time the bail order was received by Ananthanarayanan, it was 5.30 p.m. and too late to execute the bond and produce the two sureties ordered. The courts being closed on Saturday, 8 July and Sunday, 9 July, there was little he could do to make the bail order effective.

Sushil stayed holed up in Puruswalkam, another inner-city area in Madras, over the next couple of days.[108] Ananthanarayanan and Sushil then decided to travel to Bangalore, which they judged to be a relatively sympathetic jurisdiction, to surrender. Sushil had suggested they fly there, but was advised against air travel – it was far too risky for him under the circumstances – and they travelled there by road on Sunday evening.

Sushil made other, more important revelations. On 15 July, he told his custodians where he had discarded his bloodstained clothes the day after the murder, and led the police to recover them from the compound of Gujarat Bhavan. Amidst large stones under some bushes, police found his washed kurta and pyjama in a black polythene bag. In the pant pocket was his visiting card and some papers, including an Ashok Hotel health club card. He then led the police off the Jaipur National Highway towards Rangpuri, where he had dumped the other kurta pyjama. This was recovered from amongst the bushes, near the dug-up quarries in the vicinity of Ahuja Crushers. Bloodstains were still visible on the garments and there were some burnt patches around the right sleeve of the kurta.

On the same day, investigating officers took Sharma to the Bagiya and his apartment. Taking an offender to the scene of his crime is as routine a police procedure as confronting him with the physical evidence of the crime. It can help with questioning, often by shocking the offender into honesty, and it may prompt the offender's memory and help elicit a confession. Though Sushil had already confessed to committing the crime, any evidence we collected from the scene could be used in court under Section 27 of the Indian Evidence Act 1872. But more later, on the conundrum we faced here.

The day would prove to be more harrowing for Sushil than his remand hearing two days earlier. At the Bagiya, a large crowd, including overseas guests from the Ashok Yatri Niwas, gathered as the news spread that he was there. But it was at Gole Market, near the Mandir Marg apartment, that Sushil was to confront the naked hostility that many in the city felt towards him.

As officers escorted him to the apartment, an angry crowd began to gather – ordinary men and women from the neighbourhood, distracted from their everyday activities – and its ranks swelled by the minute as news spread of Sushil's arrival. To the residents of the Gole Market area, Sushil was a vile reprobate who had cruelly murdered an innocent woman. The crime scene was not an address given in a newspaper or an image on the television screen: it was their home.

Sushil now faced one of the more terrifying sights anywhere, and especially on the subcontinent: a horde of people, enraged and railing against an injustice. The crowd of hundreds began to chant 'murdabad' – and they really meant it – along with calls of 'hang him now!' The women were especially vehement in their calls for summary justice.[109] Only swift action by the police in surrounding Sushil and whisking him away saved him from the crowd.

Later in the day, officers took Sushil to the Lady Hardinge Medical College mortuary, where he was shown Naina's remains. He stayed in the mortuary for about fifteen minutes. Quoting hospital sources, *The Times of India* reported in its 16 July edition that upon seeing his wife's charred corpse, Sushil wept and cried out, 'What have I done?' He shed tears profusely throughout, repeating, 'Naina, Naina, *bahut badi galti ho gayi* (I have committed a big mistake).'[110] He seemed utterly overcome with remorse.

There was method in our taking Sushil to view the body, beyond seeking his formal identification of it. We sought to awake his conscience. And we had some hope, however faint, that he might feel moved by the sight of his wife's body to take responsibility for his crime. Given the outrageous antics of Sushil's various counsel and the behind-the-scenes skulduggery of his associates, we should have known better. All we achieved was a momentary show of repentance and an informal acknowledgement from Sushil that the cadaver was that of his murdered wife.

He quickly did a volte face on that, too. A few days later, outside the Metropolitan Magistrates' court, he told reporters that the corpse was so badly charred 'there was nothing left to identify', then added, 'it was not Naina's'. He said this in the midst of one of his usual grand performances, where he accused his nemesis Bitta of the murder and claimed he was being threatened and tortured.[111]

We were to become accustomed to such shenanigans. Sushil alternately played the wronged victim and a cool, tough political operator, depending on his mood or what best suited his interests at the time. In one of his appearances before scribes outside the court, he reportedly contended, 'I have done nothing to repent', then, turning his attention to the senior police officers present there, he said, 'I might have made a mistake, but you must help me out of this jam.'[112] The man's cockiness, his sheer gall, was almost as astonishing as his erratic behaviour.

Still, Sharma's interrogation back at the Tilak Marg police station continued to yield more details of his crime and his activities after the discovery of the corpse at the Bagiya. He also finally put to rest a crucial matter: the much publicised 'chopping' of Naina Sahni's limbs.

The presence of bones inside the tandoor at the time of the initial inspection of the restaurant had led to speculation in the media that the corpse's limbs had been amputated. It made excellent copy and reporters had liberally quoted Dr Sarangi's controversial finding in the first post-mortem, that the body had been partially dismembered. Sushil revealed that there was no such chopping of the body or the limbs.

At this stage, Sushil seemed to be telling the truth, and we had no reason to disbelieve him. It appeared likely, too, as we had learned from the second forensic examination, that the intense heat of the pyre above the tandoor – along with the stoking of the fire with poles – had caused the burnt limbs to break and distal phalanges to come off and fall inside it.

Sadly, the media's sensational 'revelations' in the wake of the murder – that the corpse had been dismembered and cast into the tandoor at the Bagiya – have proved more enduring than other, more important aspects of the case.

14

Corpus of Evidence

To almost any observer outside India, it might appear that the investigating team had all but completed its work at this point. We had the perpetrator in custody, we had a plethora of circumstantial evidence connecting him to the crime – and he had confessed to a number of senior police officers, even begging our forgiveness. To anyone not from the subcontinent, the successful prosecution of Sushil Sharma would have seemed a foregone conclusion.

Alas, that is not the order of things in the Indian judicial system. Aside from systemic challenges and the gamut of dirty tricks we could expect from Sushil, we would have to contend with a less-than-favourable provision of the Indian Evidence Act 1872.

The Act, which governs the admissibility of evidence in Indian courts of law, was originally passed by the Imperial Legislative Council during the British Raj. It has remained in force – substantially unchanged – since. A particular bugbear for the police is Section 25 of the Act which states, 'No confession made to a police officer shall be proved as against a person accused of any offence.'

Essentially, this means an accused can confess to his heart's desire in the police station – even before the commissioner of police – but this, in itself, cannot be presented as evidence of guilt before the court.

The intention of this provision was ostensibly to nullify the effect of police obtaining false confessions by coercion or third degree, or falsely claiming that they had received a confession from a suspect. How useful this provision is in restraining corrupt police personnel from incriminating innocent people is a moot point, though. A corrupt officer could just resort to other chicanery, such as doctoring evidence, to obtain a conviction.

For the honest, hardworking cop, Section 25 of the Indian Evidence Act 1872 is a handicap, especially when confronted with a cunning offender such as Sushil Sharma. To have a criminal freely confess to the police and then escape conviction may seem like a gross miscarriage of justice. But the investigating team knew this could very well happen with Sushil, despite his fulsome confessions to Niranjan, me, other interrogators, and even to Commissioner Nikhil Kumar.

This is not to say that we were legally hamstrung in our questioning of Sharma. Section 27 of the Act gives clear, if qualified, powers to the police to gather admissible evidence from a suspect. It states that 'when any fact is deposed to as discovered in consequence of information received from a person accused of any offence, in the custody of a police officer … may be proved.' If Sushil provided any information during questioning which led us to material facts or evidence, these and his information could be used to prove his guilt in court.

In short, we still had our work cut out for us. We would have to carefully prove our case with the evidence at hand. And we would have to persuade Sushil to tell us of, and lead us to, material evidence so that his statements would be admissible in court. We knew, too, that we must be exacting with the charge sheet.

Indeed, every facet of the case demanded exactitude. First, the physical evidence and forensic analysis of it needed to be carefully compiled and taken stock of, so that the charge sheet could be drafted. Our team was under as much internal pressure to finalise the charge sheet as from politicians and bureaucrats.

The investigators worked painstakingly to take stock of all the exhibits collected during the investigation. There were samples and evidence from the scene of crime at the Mandir Marg flat and the Bagiya Barbeque restaurant, from the cars and the many places where Sharma had stayed; and there were his possessions – including his pistol. All the recovered or seized exhibits were dutifully sealed, carefully preserved, listed and catalogued in accordance with procedure. The investigating team deposited the exhibits with CFSL by 17 July. The results of CFSL's analyses were available within ten days. We received four separate reports from the head of each relevant discipline – ballistics, serology and biology, physics and handwriting.

C.M. Patel, the SSO (serology) at CFSL Delhi, who conducted the laboratory analysis of the blood samples and bloodstained exhibits, reported that the blood sample collected from the remains of Naina Sahni was of group 'B'.

Tests conducted by the serological experts revealed that the blood found on different articles recovered from various exhibits and sites – from apartment 8/2A, DIZ Area, Mandir Marg, from the Bagiya, Keshav Kumar's clothes, the dickey of Sushil's car – was all human blood of 'B' group: the same blood group as Ravi Naina Sahni's.

Blood of the 'B' type was also detected on samples taken from the burnt pieces of bone (recovered from ashes in the tandoor); the black polythene sheet (used for covering and dragging the body into the Bagiya), the white kurta and pyjama (recovered from Gujarat Bhavan), a cloth from the bathroom of the apartment, a carpet, a chatai, a bullet head taken from the apartment, and a bullet head recovered from the body. C.M. Patel reported that samples lifted from a shelf at the Bagiya, the ash from the tandoor and the kurta recovered from Rangpuri did not yield positive indications for human blood.

The SSO (biology) at CFSL, Dr G.D. Gupta, conducted a microscopic examination of the hair samples recovered from Sushil's car and the carpet at the Mandir Marg apartment, and concluded that they were all human hair – although those from the car belonged to Sharma himself, and not Naina.

Dr Rajender Singh, SSO (physics), CFSL conducted laboratory examinations on the black polythene sheet recovered from near the tandoor. He stated that the unusual tear marks on the sheet could very well have resulted from dragging.

It was SSO and ballistics expert Roop Singh who conducted the examination on the revolver and four live cartridges recovered from Sushil at the Pai Vihar Hotel in Bangalore. These were tested along with the discharged bullet lead found in the bedroom of the Mandir Marg flat, the two bullets excised from the head and neck of the charred body, the five fired revolver cartridges recovered from the bedroom of the apartment and the plywood piece from the window. SSO Roop Singh had recovered the bullet lead and five spent cartridges from Naina and Sushil's apartment on 5 July.

Roop Singh stated that the .32 calibre Arminius revolver was in working order and concluded that it had discharged rounds. He further stated that the three fired bullets had been discharged from the revolver in question; the five cartridge cases had been fired from the same revolver, and the four other live cartridges were live ammunition for the pistol. He further stated that the hole in the plywood piece could have been caused by the .32 calibre bullet lead recovered from the room.

Significantly, Roop Singh noted that the bore of the pistol had been tampered with, in a futile attempt to thwart its identification as the murder weapon.

The air-pistol seized by the police from the Mandir Marg bedroom was declared to be not a firearm by ballistics. It had not been used in the commission of the murder.

Assistant Director (Documents) A.K. Gupta, the handwriting and documents expert at the Forensic Science Laboratory (FSL) Delhi, conducted an examination on the torn letter which had been retrieved from the wastepaper basket in the Mandir Marg flat. The letter was reconstructed using cellophane tape. It was composed in Hindi and English, and addressed to Sushil. A.K. Gupta compared it with the admitted writings of Naina Sahni contained in an exercise book. He opined that the person who had written in the exercise book had also written the letter, which was substantially in Hindi. He could not draw any conclusions on the English portion of the letter, as there was no available admitted sample of Naina's writing in English.

There were thus no surprises for the investigating team in CFSL's forensic examination of the evidence. Their report was unequivocal and damning. Every finding matched our crime scene reconstruction and confirmed that Sushil had indeed murdered his wife Naina Sahni at their Mandir Marg apartment, then taken her body to the Bagiya for disposal. There really was no other conclusion any reasonable person could reach.

⚖

While there was as little doubt regarding the identity of the charred corpse found at the Bagiya as there was of Sushil's guilt, we needed to ensure that the forensic evidence was watertight. Naina Sahni's family's disavowal of the body had left at least a perception of uncertainty in the matter. This, and the high-profile nature of the case, warranted that we apply a whole gamut of scientific techniques to put the matter to rest. We could hardly proceed with a murder trial with the public still questioning the victim's identity.

R.A. Mashelkar was then the director general of the Council of Scientific and Industrial Research (CSIR) and secretary to the Government of India in its Ministry of Science and Technology. I telephoned him from Commissioner Nikhil Kumar's office, somewhat exasperated by Naina's parents' refusal to identify her remains, and asked for his help in arranging DNA (deoxyribonucleic acid) fingerprinting. Dr Mashelkar proved to be as gentlemanly as he was erudite, and he promised to extend every assistance to our investigation.

We needed expert guidance in the matter. DNA fingerprinting or profiling is commonly applied by law and enforcement agencies in the twenty-first century, but the technology was not readily available to us at the time of the tandoor murder. The concept of DNA evidence was still quite new, having featured in criminal forensic analysis for less than a decade.

DNA fingerprinting had been first applied in the trial of a certain Colin Pitchfork in Leicestershire, England, by its inventor Dr Alec Jeffreys. Pitchfork was convicted and sentenced to life imprisonment for two instances of rape and murder on 22 January 1988, after his DNA matched evidence found on both victims. Significantly, the DNA fingerprinting exonerated the prime suspect, a local seventeen-year-old youth with learning difficulties, who had confessed to one of the killings during interrogation.

At the time of the tandoor murder, DNA evidence was playing a crucial role in one of the most publicised murder trials of the century. On 6 July 1995 – the day before Sushil Sharma's futile attempt to manipulate the judiciary in Madras – the prosecution rested in the *People of the State of California v. Orenthal James Simpson*. Much of the prosecution's case against O.J. Simpson hinged on DNA evidence, which strongly suggested Simpson had murdered his former wife and her friend.

Simpson's acquittal three months after the discovery of the charred corpse at the Bagiya owed much to tardiness in the handling of DNA specimens. About 100 million people in the US and across the world stopped to watch or listen to the verdict being announced on 3 October 1995.

The tandoor murder was as sensational as the O.J. Simpson trial, at least on the subcontinent. While the prosecution's case would not be predicated on DNA fingerprinting as in the O.J. Simpson case, we were determined that the analysis should be meticulous. For this, we needed the most eminent expert in the field. Dr Mashelkar obliged by helping us engage Dr Lalji Singh, a DNA expert and scientist at the Centre for Cellular and Molecular Biology (CCMB) in Hyderabad, for the DNA fingerprinting.

Dr Lalji Singh, who would receive the Padma Shri in 2004,

had applied DNA fingerprinting in numerous high-profile cases, including the May 1991 assassination of former Prime Minister Rajiv Gandhi. A few months after his work in the tandoor murder case, he would apply his science to the grim mess left after the suicide bombing assassination of Punjab Chief Minister Beant Singh on 31 August 1995. The following year, he would analyse specimens for the Priyadarshini Mattoo murder case in Delhi, which we shall get to later.

Dr Singh first advised the investigating team of the legal requirements and procedures to be adopted while collecting samples. We ensured that these were assiduously followed.

He then set to work almost immediately. On 6 July, he took a flight to Delhi and visited the mortuary. There, he lifted samples of tissue from the thigh muscle and pieces of ribs and radius or ulna (forearm bones) of the charred remains. These were suitably preserved in separate containers, kept in an ice box and dispatched to the CCMB laboratory.

We approached Naina's parents again and managed to convince them that this test would conclusively determine whether the body was Naina's. They relented without much fuss, and their blood samples were obtained for testing.

Before commencing the DNA fingerprinting, CCMB required certificates from the relevant court authorising the laboratory to undertake testing. Identification forms of the individuals involved in the case had to be submitted to the court, too. Niranjan saw to it that these legal requirements were promptly complied with, so as to not delay the tests.

Dr Lalji Singh conducted DNA fingerprinting analysis on the tissues and bones from the charred corpse, and on the blood samples of Harbhajan Singh and Jaswant Kaur, Naina Sahni's parents. Not to leave anything to chance, he visited Delhi again on 13 July and after conferring with DCP Aditya Arya, Naina's parents were once again prevailed upon to provide blood samples. In the presence of Dr Lalji Singh, Dr Naveen Jain took fresh blood samples from Harbhajan Singh and Jaswant Kaur at Ram Manohar Lohia Hospital on Baba Kharak Singh Marg. These samples were then carried personally by Dr Lalji Singh to his Hyderabad laboratory for testing.

After the debacle of Dr Sarangi's botched autopsy and leaks to the media, Dr Lalji Singh's efficiency and professionalism were refreshing. While he was in the process of conducting the tests, he was hounded mercilessly by the national press in Hyderabad. But he steadfastly resisted all pressure to divulge his findings. An *Indian Express* article lamented that 'No amount of persuasion could get a word out of him'.[113]

Just as he kept the blood specimens with him to ensure the chain of evidence remained unbroken, he personally carried his DNA analysis report to Delhi to guarantee its security. Only two copies of the report were made: one for Delhi Police and one which was to be kept at CCMB. With the report in hand, Dr Lalji Singh took an evening flight to the capital on Sunday, 23 July. DCP Aditya Arya and a security detail were at the VIP gate of Indira Gandhi International Airport to meet him. They hurried Dr Singh past reporters to a waiting car, which took him and Aditya to Delhi Police Headquarters. There, the three of us met in my office.

Dr Singh's report, twenty-five pages of bound text supported by three photographs, was impressive, to say the least. It gave the DNA fingerprint of tissues of the charred body, similar prints of Naina's parents, bands of DNA mixes of body tissues and blood samples of the parents, a molecular weight mark and the print of the DNA of an unrelated person as a control.

In short, when the DNA profile in the track of samples from the charred remains was compared with the tracks of samples of Naina's parents, it was clear that every band present in the track from the remains was accounted for in Harbhajan Singh or Jaswant Kaur's tracks. This led inevitably to the conclusion that the deceased was the biological child of Harbhajan Singh and Jaswant Kaur.

This conclusion was further substantiated by using variable

number tandem repeat (VNTR) analysis. In his report, Dr Lalji Singh declared that the charred remains of the human torso were indeed those of the biological child of this couple. While the world's population is somewhere in the order of 6×10^9, Dr Lalji stated unambiguously that the margin of possible error in the DNA test was 1 in 1×10^{23}.

Of course, we had no intention of relying on the DNA evidence alone. Acceptance of DNA evidence in court was less certain in the mid-1990s than it is now, and we anticipated some difficulties in court as a result of Dr Sarangi's blunder in the first autopsy. The last thing we needed was the defence playing on a judge's scepticism of a fairly new science to frustrate or delay the case. We had thus taken a belt and braces approach in ordering a skull–photograph superimposition test on the corpse, while the DNA fingerprinting analysis was underway.

The skull–photograph superimposition technique is an old and common means of identifying unknown, decomposed corpses. It was first used in a criminal trial in Lancaster, England, in 1935. Dr Buck Ruxton, a respected local physician, was convicted of killing his wife and maid, and was later executed for his crimes. The case against Ruxton relied substantially on skull–photograph superimposition to identify the victims' dismembered corpses, which Ruxton had dumped many miles from his home.

The regular use of skull–photograph superimposition in the days before DNA fingerprinting was due, in no small measure, to the ease with which a facial photograph could be obtained from a victim's family. The technique is generally of greater value in ruling out a match between a skull and a facial photograph than it is in definitively identifying remains.

Thus the technique by itself may not have established beyond question that the remains were those of Naina Sahni. If it produced a match, however – as we were convinced it would – it would serve to corroborate the DNA fingerprinting, thus establishing the identity of the corpse beyond any suggestion of doubt.

Niranjan had requested Dr Sarangi to preserve the skull for this test in the notes submitted at the first autopsy. Dr Sarangi had complied with the request. Although detached, the skull remained with the rest of the body after the second post-mortem.

On 17 July, Niranjan met Dr G.D. Gupta at CFSL and took him to the morgue. Dr Gupta sealed the skull in a container in accordance with procedure required for prosecution, and they headed with it to AIIMS in Ansari Nagar.

The media had, meanwhile, whipped themselves into a frenzy over the movement of the burnt cadaver. Some papers reported that the 'body has gone missing'. The national news channel Doordarshan went so far as to inform its viewers that the body had been moved to AIIMS for a third post-mortem. I quickly dismissed this as mere speculation.

We were careful not to share with the media the forensic pathologist's act of severing the skull from the torso of the cadaver, for fear of provoking even more public commotion. I did not, however, conceal our plans to conduct a skull–photograph superimposition test.

Nevertheless, reporters somehow learned of the head's separation from the body. In the coming days, the media was awash with ghoulish copy such as 'forensic experts have decapitated Naina Sahni's body and placed the head in a jar full of hydrogen peroxide'.[114] On 17 July, the day of the skull–photograph superimposition test, photographers and reporters thronged the routes to AIIMS for pictures or glimpses of the burnt remains. And newshounds badgered every police contact for a tip-off or clue regarding the whereabouts of the corpse.

I wasn't spared, either. NDTV's Maya Mirchandani, who was then a junior reporter, spent the whole day on the road with her camera team in her quest to capture some footage of the body or skull being brought to AIIMS. Frantic for a scoop, she inundated me with telephone calls throughout the day, pleading for some information to give her an edge over competing channels. I could not oblige her. We were already plagued by media interference in the case, and I could not afford to fuel it.

At AIIMS, Dr Gupta subjected the skull to a skull–photograph superimposition test under the supervision of Dr T.D. Dogra, the chief of forensics there. Dr Gupta's job was ostensibly simple but exacting. With this technique, the facial photograph of the suspected victim is enlarged to the size of the skull or the skull's X-ray, to facilitate matching of the outline and contours of the skull bone structure. The forensic scientist then takes several anthropometric measurements of both to ascertain whether the skull and photograph match. It is essential here to take into account the thickness of tissues at any given point of the facial anatomy.

No one in the investigating team was surprised when Dr Gupta stated that the skull of the burnt cadaver perfectly matched the photographs of Ravi Naina Sahni.

With unassailable DNA evidence that the body was that of a biological child of Harbhajan Singh and Jaswant Kaur, a matching skull–photograph superimposition and Matloob Karim's positive identification, the issue of the burnt cadaver's identification was settled. Not even the most creative of defence counsel could argue otherwise – or so one would think.

It was now time to contemplate disposing of Naina's mortal remains. But here the police continued to be stumped by the dogged resistance of Naina's loved ones. Her parents and members of her immediate family would simply not receive Naina's body, let alone give her a decent funeral. Neither would Sushil accept his wife's body, despite his melodramatic act at the mortuary. The cunning strategist that he was, he knew this would serve to weaken his defence in court.

While Naina's mother may have been ready to accept her daughter's remains, she was constrained in the matter by the rest of her family. Jaswant Kaur had shed the most tears on seeing the state of the Mandir Marg apartment and when the family had viewed Naina's body in the morgue. I had learnt from Niranjan that Naina's brothers, however, had taken a firm stand against Naina.[115] She had made lifestyle and marital choices on her own which were not to her family's liking, and they had more or less forsaken her, it seemed.

Whatever the motives of Naina's family may have been, they had certainly left the police in a quandary. The last thing we wanted was to be forced to cremate Naina's remains as we would an unclaimed corpse. It would have been the final travesty after the slew of indignities her body had suffered in life and death. This defenceless woman had been murdered and her corpse desecrated by Sushil and Keshav's ghastly attempt to dispose of it. She had then been publicly slandered, simply so that news outlets could sell copy and surely, many of the peccadilloes ascribed to her were imagined. She did not deserve the loveless, desultory finale of a police cremation.

Many public bodies and NGOs – a consortium of eleven women's organisations, Rotary Clubs, Lion Clubs – and some individuals now kindly stepped in with offers to dispose of Naina's body with traditional Sikh rites. Even the 'bandit queen' and feminist anti-heroine Phoolan Devi forwarded an offer through Eklavya Sena, her organisation for downtrodden women. She spoke for most of Delhi, if not the rest of the country, when she said, 'it is unfortunate that Ms Sahni's remains are still to be claimed by her relatives'.[116]

Incidentally, the bandit queen, who was to enter national politics the following year, lived a few doors down from me on 44 Ashoka Road. She was gunned down outside her home six years later, on 25 July 2001. Mixing crime and politics can be deadly business.

Although the offers for arranging a funeral were well-meant, it hardly seemed fitting that Naina's last rites should be conducted by strangers. Commissioner Nikhil Kumar and I deemed it imperative that her immediate family be somehow persuaded to acknowledge and accept her remains. She deserved at least this – and a proper funeral attended by her kith and kin. So, amidst the rigours of the investigation and our struggle to stay ahead of a volatile and creative media, we did not give up hope. We made numerous public and private efforts to convince Naina's family members to do the right thing.

Commissioner Nikhil Kumar first broached the issue publicly at his press briefing on 14 July. He told the assembled media personnel that Naina's parents were still being persuaded to claim the body, as 'we have been highly sensitive on this issue, and would prefer the body to be disposed of in a traditional manner'.[117] He then told the media that 'he would be saddened if the body were cremated by the police as an unclaimed one'.[118] We hoped these diplomatic public statements would reach Naina's near and dear ones.

The women's groups were also doing their part. The group of organisations that had offered to conduct the last rites for Naina contacted her parents to inform them of their decision.[119] One can only imagine the fraught communications they had – the moral pressure on Naina's family must have been enormous.

Privately, we continued to make overtures to the family. When Nikhil and I felt the matter had dragged on long enough, DCP Aditya Arya contacted Naina's elder sister Surjit and brother-in-law S.P. Singh in Kerala. After a marathon telephone conversation on 29 July, Surjit and her husband finally agreed to accept Naina's body on behalf of the family.[120] They travelled from Kochi to the capital, and ensured that proper arrangements were made for her cremation. Naina would finally receive a send-off as a daughter, sister and cousin.

15

Ravi Naina Sahni

It is often said that the victim of a murder is forgotten, overlooked as much as obliterated by the crime. This may well have been a merciful fate compared to the gossip and horrific images associated with Naina Sahni after her killing. Dissected and laid bare by the media, her life and purported 'sins' titillated and scandalised the public – and guaranteed sales and TRPs.

At least Naina's cremation was honourably conducted. One month after her gruesome murder, on the afternoon of Wednesday, 2 August 1995, Aditya and Niranjan accompanied Naina's parents from their Patel Nagar residence in a police vehicle. After some formalities, her uncle and brother-in-law collected Naina's skull from AIIMS, then the charred remains of her torso from the Punchkuian Road mortuary. They drove to the electric crematorium at Vijay Ghat, which is located beside Salimgarh Fort and the Red Fort, on the banks of the Yamuna. There, Naina's mortal remains were cremated. A remembrance service was held at the family's local gurudwara afterwards.

Naina's farewell was attended by almost as many media personnel as mourners. A sizeable police presence ensured order and as much dignity as could be expected for the event. Braving sombre skies and a drizzle, Naina's extended family had waited at the ghat from 4 p.m.; the press, always quick to react, had plenty of time to congregate beforehand. The newspaper reports immediately following the event were awash with photographs.

Naina's remains had been wrapped in a polythene sheet, then shrouded in a white cloth. This was draped with a red and gold veil, covered with marigolds and sprinkled with rose petals, as is the custom, before the cremation. Mourners chanted aloud: '*Jo bole so nihal, satsri akal!* (Whosoever utters this phrase shall be happy, shall be fulfilled: Eternal is the great, timeless Lord!)'. Devotional songs filled the air, accompanied by the background murmuring of the gurubani.

Naina's father seemed utterly overcome by these happenings. When he stood beside his daughter's body, it seemed that only willpower kept his frail body upright. Naina's mother was less restrained in her grief, sobbing, '*Mere Naina nu mere ton le jaa rahe ne* (My Naina is being taken from me)!' She lay beside Naina's shrouded remains and wept, occasionally pulling her headscarf away from her face. She could not restrain herself from railing at the press, too, and had to be consoled by Naina's sister, who gently held her hand across her mother's mouth.

With all the proper rites performed, Naina's mortal remains were consigned to flames at 6.35 p.m., just as the last of the muted daylight faded over Delhi's west.

Afterwards, at the gurudwara, Naina's family made their first public statements about her. Her mother spoke fondly and positively of Naina, and the family released a three-page résumé of her life, which they distributed to reporters. It had some pointed words for the media.

Entitled 'The True Story', the résumé described Naina as 'a well-educated, charming, good mannered and self-respecting girl, who wanted to stand on her own feet. She didn't want to be a burden on the meagre resources of her family.' The document proudly noted Naina's achievements, which were not inconsiderable, and the major events of her life:

Ravi Naina was born on 13 April 1966, daughter to Harbhajan

Singh and Jaswant Kaur. She graduated from Shyama Prasad Mukherjee College of Delhi University in 1986 and joined the Delhi Flying Club for a student pilot license. She finally got her private pilot license from the United Kingdom.

The résumé further claimed that 'Rajiv Gandhi had assured her funds from the NSUI to train for a commercial pilot.'[121]

The document did not shy away from speaking of Naina's relationship with Sushil Sharma, which Naina's family portrayed as a marriage of love:

> Naina had to stop at the second rung of the ladder of her political career [as the general secretary of DPYC] because she fell in love with Sushil Sharma. His pre-condition to marriage was that Naina should stop all her political activities and forget about her political aspirations. She agreed.
>
> After marriage she went to stay with Sushil at the Mandir Marg flat. Sushil had been living there even before the marriage. The house was not a love nest or lovers' hideout, as the press had made it out to be.
>
> As a dutiful housewife and daughter-in-law, Naina was like any other ordinary Indian wife. She had put her political career and ambitions behind her. Her parents-in-law whenever they called her parents spoke well of her good nature. She used to fast on karva-chowth in the traditional way. And whenever she visited her own parents, she always came accompanied by husband Sushil. Both of them always looked happy and contented.

Amarjit Singh, Naina's uncle, quite justifiably asserted to reporters that her 'image has been tarnished beyond repair by the media, which indulged in mudslinging. You should give the "true story" and try to do justice to her.'[122]

Naturally, 'The True Story' was silent on Naina's relationship with Matloob Karim, about which many details had already appeared in the media.

Talking about the murdered woman, M.S. Bitta was now quoted in the media as having said that he had never known Naina.

'However, all those who came in contact with her say that she was a decent girl,' he told reporters. 'I am really astounded how anyone could murder a girl in such a brutal manner.' Several other Youth Congress leaders confirmed that Naina was a trained pilot who had run a successful boutique selling ready-made garments.

Naina's relationship with Sushil began more than a decade before her murder at his hands. She was an active worker of the NSUI in 1983-84, when she was introduced to Sushil Sharma by a friend who later worked as a senior correspondent for a Delhi-based newspaper. In 1986, when Sharma became the president of the NSUI, he nominated her to the post of the state general secretary. Naina was appointed DPYC general secretary soon after Sushil assumed office as its president.

The Times of India quoted Matloob Karim, who said he had known Naina since 1984.[123] They were recommended for appointment to the city unit of the NSUI, he said, by Mukul Wasnik, who was in 1995 the Minister of State for Youth Affairs and Sports. They served on the committee of the DPYC during Sushil's tenure as president between October 1989 and January 1995. Naina was general secretary and Matloob the organising secretary of the DPYC.

According to reports in *The Times of India* and *The Patriot*, Naina lived with Matloob Karim for about six years, between 1984 and 1990.[124] It appears Naina had nurtured hopes of tying the knot with Matloob, but when she came to know that Matloob was married – he married Naaz Gul in December 1988, according to his own statement – she moved out.[125] In any case, there were strong objections from her family to the match. The two had parted on a cordial note, though, with the understanding that they would remain friends.

Matloob Karim described the demise of their romantic relationship a little differently, but was consistent with the *Hindustan Times* report in claiming that they remained close: 'I withdrew quietly and married in my own community. But we promised each other friendship.' Matloob and Naina remained constantly in touch and he visited her at her Mandir Marg home, probably without Sushil's knowledge. He helped her out during her most troubled times. She confided more to him about the woes of her marital life than to anyone else.

According to Matloob, Sushil and Naina's marriage was solemnised at the Birla Mandir in May 1992, in the presence of only her family members. He said Naina's aunt, whom Sushil had helped in a land dispute, had convinced Naina to marry him.[126] Matloob also revealed that within the first few months of the marriage, Naina had called him, complaining about Sushil's abusive behaviour and violence. He would beat her, Matloob said, after drinking alcohol in the evenings. He would lock her in when he left the house. It seems that Naina, a free, lively woman, had become a prisoner of her marriage, in her own home. Her business activities and work as an office-bearer of the DPYC ceased almost completely.

That matters between Naina and Sushil were fraught was borne out by the contents of what seemed to be her last letter to Sushil. It was pieced together from the bits found in a wastepaper basket in their flat, at the first police inspection. A poignant lamentation emerged when the pieces were taped together; and it was of a relationship that had floundered:

> Sushil, I know you hate me. You cannot accept me, so do not waste your time. Take care of yourself and forgive me. Leave me to my fate. We cannot continue like this because I cannot win your confidence even by killing myself. Take away whatever you have to. Don't misunderstand me. Do not let your life be spoiled. I know I do not deserve you. Leave me and make the best from your life. But do not say anything to my family. They are innocent. If you want to, you can punish me.

Considering Naina's fate, the note, especially its final sentence, can only evoke pathos in the reader. But it was more like the statement of a self-negating wife, blaming herself for the failure of the relationship, than an invitation for Sushil to harm her. In view of Sushil's alcohol-fuelled bouts of domestic violence and obstinate refusal to publicly acknowledge their marriage, it seems Naina was being unduly hard on herself.

Ram Niwas Dubey, Sushil's peon and cook through almost the entire duration of Sushil and Naina's relationship, disclosed that Naina regularly pressed Sushil to make their marriage public. Sometimes Sushil would assure her that he would do so after he became an MP or an MLA. Often, however, he brutally silenced her with threats and beatings.

After his violent turns against Naina, Sushil would ask Dubey to have prescriptions for pain medication filled for her. Dubey further revealed that Sushil was suspicious of Naina and kept a hawk-eyed watch on her activities. He did not allow even Dubey to be with her in the Mandir Marg apartment when he was not present. He also made every effort to ensure that Dubey chaperoned Naina whenever she left the apartment.

This suspicious and controlling behaviour was confirmed by Geeta, a friend who assisted Naina in the boutique. She revealed that Sushil was cagey about his relationship with Naina. Once, when she visited their Gole Market flat, Naina had asked her to leave, as Sushil did not like her to meet anyone there.

Naina was most troubled, it seems, after discovering Sushil's ongoing affair with Ila Jhunjhunwala, a rather assertive woman living in South Delhi. It seemed Sushil had met Ila in the late 1970s, and shared a long-term relationship with her before Naina came into his life.[127] Upon discovering the affair, Naina contacted Ila, who apparently revealed Sushil's secretive, womanising ways to her. Naina then decided not to take Sushil's beatings any more without retaliating, and her demands that he make their marriage public became more insistent.[128]

Naina and Sushil's relationship was already disintegrating. This, it seems, was its tipping point.

The revelation of Ila's bit part in the tandoor drama led to a media frenzy. The press speculated that Sushil had fathered Ila's son Kaustav and that Ila, the estranged wife of a rich Calcutta businessman, had bankrolled Sushil's political activities.[129] One article even claimed Ila had been lured by Sushil's promise of a parliamentary ticket.[130] This prompted Ila's visit to Commissioner Nikhil Kumar, accompanied by her husband. She complained bitterly to him that she had been unnecessarily and wrongly maligned.

Doubtless, Ila suffered merely because snippets of her alleged relationship with Sushil made riveting tabloid copy – not that these could compare with the juicy titbits of Naina's love life.[131]

Naina was perhaps looking for love in all the wrong places. She seems to have been drawn to powerful men, most of whom were unlikely to have looked beyond her vivaciousness and beauty. How much of this can be ascribed to personal ambition and how much to her search for a like-minded soul, one can only speculate.

During our search of Sushil and Naina's apartment at Mandir Marg, we came across a photograph of a young, starry-eyed Naina in the company of Rajiv Gandhi, apparently taken during his years in power. Naina seems to have enjoyed more than a passing acquaintance with Gandhi.[132] In the photograph, she seems transfixed by the prime minister, and he quite engaged with her. It is a strange coincidence that within a decade they would each suffer a violent, highly publicised death – indeed, the most sensational of their generation.

Naina purportedly managed to secure a promise of support from Gandhi for her training as a pilot, which is remarkable.[133] It gives as strong an indication of the power of her charm as it does of her penchant for commanding attention.

In death, Naina was derided as a Congress moll which, aside from being uncharitable, gave little credit to her abilities.[134] The media's report that she had had liaisons with two government ministers could not be easily refuted: government ministers will no more incriminate themselves than the dead defend scurrilous accusations. Naina thus stood condemned in the court of public opinion.

Clearly, Naina was a victim of society's hypocrisy as much as she was of Sushil's. Her interests and exploits – swimming, flying, politics and business – would all have appeared quite appropriate, even laudable, for a man of her generation. Similarly, her outgoing behaviour, romantic dalliances, late nights and consumption of alcohol would barely have attracted censure for a Delhi man in politics. A generation later, many parents would indulge far greater excesses in their children, both boys and girls. Naina, however, faced her family's disapproval and desertion, her husband's violence – and, ultimately, a sordid death.

On the other hand, her husband's antics appeared to have been largely tolerated by society until the murder. He seemed content to philander and pursue his ambitions, while trying to brutally contain his wife's gregarious nature and deny her the emotional security she craved.

Naina grew up in a middle-class environment – not far removed socially, it seems, from Sushil Sharma's fairly humble origins. A neighbour volunteered that perhaps her parents were not on good terms; she was raised, it appears, in a tense atmosphere, and thus grew to be outspoken and headstrong.

These characteristics came to the fore when she entered Shyama Prasad Mukherjee College, and promptly took to student politics. The only political link in her household was her maternal grandmother, a Congress supporter. In those years, Naina's rather modern, liberated lifestyle clashed with the conservative values of her family. Her cousin Tejinder recalled, 'Once when I visited their place, Naina was coming home late. Her elder brother was very disturbed.'

But familial objections apparently did little to dampen her adventurous nature. A neighbour explained, 'Bored with politics, she learnt gliding and did well at swimming. Naina went on to join the Safdarjung Flying Club and secured a private pilot's license.'

'Her parents were never in favour of her flying,' said Matloob. A commercial pilot's licence eluded her in any case: Naina could never log enough flight hours. She turned her attention then to designing garments. Naina started by buying a Maruti car with her family's help, then drove around looking for samples and designs. She engaged dealers at her home and used some space offered by her cousin Tejinder in Kirti Nagar to start a boutique named Reeva.

The boutique did well, attracting a loyal following of customers, including the family of Delhi Chief Minister Madan Lal Khurana. 'She had a good sense of design,' said Inderjit Kaur, one of her patrons. Inderjit spoke well of her public relations prowess. 'She threw kitty parties. We all knew her.' Neeru, another frequent visitor to Reeva, said, 'She was polite and had a nice sense of colour and design.' Naina shut down the boutique after two years in business when she married Sharma. 'She said after marriage she did not like to continue with the boutique,' said Tejinder.

A marriage outside her community – Naina was Sikh and Sushil a Hindu Brahmin – widened the gulf between Naina and her family. 'No one from my uncle's family liked [the marriage],' recalled Tejinder. Naina's family did not seem to have noticed problems in her marriage or, at least, did not acknowledge any. Perhaps her parents saw Sushil as her best prospect after her 'scandalous' relationship with Matloob Karim.

In any event, Naina's family seem to have been all too willing to take Sushil's part. Matloob alleged that Naina's brothers joined Sushil in beating her after one particularly ugly domestic dispute.[135] It may very well be that Naina concealed her troubles from her immediate family, knowing that she would receive little sympathy from them. Their absence of outrage at her murder bears this out. One can only speculate that, driven to distraction by her lifestyle and behaviour, they considered her a lost cause, long before she was murdered.

Sadly, Naina fared little better with Sushil's family. Whenever there was an issue between Sushil and Naina, Sushil would have his parents deliver a telephonic admonishment, telling her to behave properly and listen to their son. There was no one to support her, it appears, apart from Matloob Karim.

Naina seems to have endured her abusive marriage as many women do, in silence. According to her sister Surjit Kaur, 'By her look, one could hardly make out she was in trouble.' Surjit knew Sushil quite well, as he and Naina had stayed with her and her husband in Cochin once. She last met Naina at a gurudwara six weeks before the murder.

Another of Naina's friends said it was difficult to understand her. Just two months before her death, she was discussing a recipe she wanted published in a newspaper. She seemed enthusiastic, happily pointing out Sushil's likes and dislikes to her friend. Most people in Naina's circle of friends had no inkling she was suffering domestic violence.

But Naina told some of her friends in the Congress about her travails. According to Mukesh Sharma, an acquaintance, 'She wanted to escape and sought help. She met us on Friday, two days before she was reportedly murdered, in Palika Bazaar, and was very restless. She said she wanted to run away, but feared Sushil would get to her if she remained in India. So, she wanted to go abroad.'

Matloob Karim cast some light on Naina's aspirations in her final days. 'If she had her way,' he said, 'Naina Sahni would have been designing and selling garments in Australia. Or maybe, piloting aircraft for a living. Short of that, she hoped her name would figure in newspapers in the credit-line for spicy recipes'.

Instead of delicious dishes, her name came to be associated with a gut-wrenching murder, a disgusting attempt to cover it up, gossip and political scandal. 'Political ambition was the hallmark of [Naina's] character, and that probably led to her death,' said her schoolmate Shanoo. 'She was sweet and lively.'

16

Hanging the Man

While Sushil's interrogation had yielded a good deal of evidence in addition to what we already had, our success in court was far from assured. The greatest difficulty the prosecution faced was the lack of eyewitnesses to Sushil's crime. The case against him was strong, but entirely circumstantial. Nobody had seen him murder Ravi Naina Sahni; only Keshav had closely witnessed his activities immediately after the killing. And Keshav seemed paralysed by a potent mix of fear and misplaced loyalty; he obstinately rebuffed every overture and request to turn approver.[136]

Indeed, he seemed to be caught between opposing fears: his fear of Sushil, along with loyalty to his former boss, was greater than his fear of the police and incarceration. At the remand hearing on 12 July, he had gloomily told Magistrate Dharam Raj Singh that the police 'haven't hit me yet'. Days later, when officers from the investigating team visited Tihar Jail, he had spoken of his concerns for his family's safety. The officers then assured him they would take steps to protect them.

It appears Sushil had taken it upon himself to wage a campaign of intimidation against Keshav's family from his high-security cell. The onslaught of telephone calls with implied threats, unexpected visits from intimidating men and ominous messages through friends and associates seemed to have had their effect. Keshav's brother and wife spoke with Niranjan expressing concern for their safety.

As concerned for his family's welfare as for his own, Keshav was not the least inclined to assist the police any more than he had in the immediate aftermath of the discovery at the Bagiya.

In the first few weeks after his arrest, Keshav's advocate S.K. Duggal had apparently had some stern words with him. On 13 July, when Duggal was granted five minutes in court for a legal conference with Keshav, he was overheard telling him bluntly, 'I can save you only if you tell everything to the police.' Keshav was shocked. 'You mean everything?'[137]

It would be rare for lawyers in other countries to proffer such advice. But with the protections afforded Keshav under Section 25 of the Indian Evidence Act, disclosing his knowledge of the crime could hardly have compromised his defence – especially with the preponderance of evidence against him. And Duggal knew, given his bleak prospects of acquittal, that it was the only way Keshav could hope to save himself. In no uncertain terms, he told Keshav he was facing a lengthy stint in prison for his crime, and he had little choice but to turn approver if he wanted to reduce his sentence.

Keshav vacillated, then expressed his willingness to cooperate with the prosecution.

Nothing in the murder investigation remained secret for long. Sushil quickly got wind of this development, and somehow issued a slew of dire warnings to Keshav from his prison cell. Nor was he content to rely on threats alone. Despite their being in different wards of the jail, he also managed to give Keshav a chilling demonstration of his power.

After eating his usual prison fare of roti and dal for lunch one afternoon, Keshav returned to his cell feeling nauseated. He lay down on the concrete floor and, in no time, fell asleep. At first, his fellow inmates thought he was merely unwell and resting, but when they could not rouse him, they quickly alerted the jail wardens. Keshav was breathing slowly, and nothing they did could wake him up. He remained unconscious for more than two days.

He was, it is almost certain now, drugged by one of Sushil's confederates inside the ward, but there was no indication of who had committed this sinister act. At the time, Keshav was detained in a ward with some hardened criminals such as Shorab, who was infamous for having kidnapped and murdered several young girls. Sushil had very likely found some means of bribing one of these inmates to slip a dangerous dose of tranquilisers into Keshav's food or drink.

This was vintage Sushil. Without overt violence, he had managed to neutralise his adversary; cow him into submission, even. Although Keshav was transferred to another ward in the jail, he promptly resiled from turning approver.

Some of Keshav's woes were noted in public, and some he kept to himself or conveyed quietly to the police. At one of his first court hearings after he was remanded to judicial custody on 13 July, he had expressed fear for his life. The court responded by ordering that he be given special protection in Tihar Jail. It was implied that the danger was from Sushil.

With Sushil's manipulations, there was little hope of getting Keshav to turn approver, at least not immediately. By morally distancing himself from his crime, Keshav did us no great favour either. He had rationalised that he had only been following Sushil's orders on 2 July and therefore had done nothing gravely wrong; something akin to the Nuremberg defence. We knew that only time, or a loosening of Sushil's grip of fear, could cause him to change tack.

Keshav had, however, made significant disclosures during his interrogation. One seemingly innocuous detail he told investigating officers would lead to a significant breakthrough in the case. While revealing titbits that led his interrogators to the Mandir Marg apartment, Keshav had mentioned that on the day of the murder, Sushil had spent time with an IAS officer from Gujarat, whose name was D.K. Rao.

At the time, this information had appeared fairly insignificant, and Keshav himself would not have known the importance of it. But every lead in the case was being followed up rigorously, however irrelevant it appeared, and all of Keshav's disclosures were being verified.

While the drama in Madras and Bangalore had yet to unfold and our attention was largely focused on tracking down the fugitive Sushil, a police party went over to Gujarat Bhavan on 9 July to make enquiries about D.K. Rao.

A surprise awaited us there. The police was informed by the staff at Gujarat Bhavan that D. Kishore Rao, a 1980 batch IAS officer of the Gujarat cadre, had indeed stayed at the Bhavan earlier in the month. Further questioning revealed that his friend Sushil Sharma had shared Rao's room. It was soon established that Sushil's visit to the Bhavan coincided with Kunju's ghastly discovery at the Bagiya.

Curiously, we found no corresponding entry in the visitor's register, though the staff informed us that Sharma had continued to occupy the room after D.K. Rao had left for Gujarat. Instead, we found the name Jai Prakash alongside that of D.K. Rao. Witnesses who had seen Sushil Sharma at Gujarat Bhavan on the night of the murder were questioned further, and their statements recorded.

Sushil's connection with D.K. Rao on the night of the murder was a crucial breakthrough, and investigating officers immediately set their sights on the IAS officer. Inquiries soon established he was a deputy secretary of the government of Gujarat, with a rather chequered bureaucratic career. A team of two assistant commissioners of police promptly took a flight to Ahmedabad to meet Rao and summon him to Delhi for further questioning.

At first blush, Rao appeared to be a prime suspect as an accessory after the fact of murder, simply for having accommodated Sushil in his room at Gujarat Bhavan after the crime. Given the testimony of the Gujarat Bhavan staff, Rao was in no position to deny having met Sushil that night. There were serious questions, too, as to why this high-level public servant had not seen fit to inform the police of

Sushil's stay at the Bhavan. He could hardly claim ignorance about the murder and Sushil's alleged involvement in it: Sushil's photograph and coverage of the case had been plastered across the front pages of national dailies and televised for more than a week by then.

Doubtless, Rao had much explaining to do. The thrust of our questioning would be to determine whether he had knowingly harboured the absconding Sharma – and whether he had concealed or destroyed material evidence of Naina Sahni's murder.

Unsurprisingly, Rao protested his innocence when confronted. He maintained he had quite unwittingly become involved in the chain of events after Naina Sahni's murder. He was, he said, a victim of Sushil's manipulation. But while he claimed to have afforded hospitality to Sushil in good faith in the early hours of 3 July, he could offer no adequate explanation for failing to report Sushil's presence at Gujarat Bhavan to the police. Nor was there any valid reason for his withholding some critical information on the case, which he would eventually reveal.

This was not the first time Devarapalli Kishore Rao had found himself in a tight spot, and it would, by no means, be the last.[138] It emerged that Rao had cultivated Sushil Sharma a few years earlier when he was facing serious allegations of misconduct as deputy chairman of the Visakhapatnam Port Trust.[139]

Journalists were quick to seize on these earlier alleged improprieties when news of D.K. Rao's association with the murder came to public attention. *The Statesman* reported that Sushil had bailed him out of an earlier difficulty involving charges of financial bungling.[140] *The Pioneer* was less reserved, claiming that Rao first came in contact with Sushil – known in the corridors of power as 'the quick fix man'– while facing corruption charges.[141]

Involvement in the tandoor murder was to be the most publicised low for D.K. Rao in a career that oscillated between dizzying success and bitter controversy. While Rao's career itself was of little interest to us, his status as an IAS officer was, we felt, a factor which could play to our advantage.

The Indian Administrative Service is the elite of India's bureaucracy and selection to its ranks is a much-vaunted honour. Rao must have been painfully aware that his association with the tandoor murder placed his career in jeopardy. Charges of malfeasance still hovered over him from his time at the Visakhapatnam Port Trust, despite Sushil pulling strings for him. He could hardly afford to indulge in the kind of shenanigans that hostile witnesses are prone to, such as unexplained lapses of memory, mysterious illnesses, temporarily impaired eyesight and sudden disappearances. Forty-year-old Rao was compelled by circumstance, if not honour, to cooperate with our investigation.

He was questioned at Parliament Street police station, mostly by Niranjan. Commissioner Nikhil Kumar subjected Rao to his own, firm brand of questioning too, which may have been unnerving for him. Rao came across as a hail-fellow-well-met kind of man, despite his nervousness and obvious anxiety over his predicament. He was, in any event, the epitome of cooperation.

Rao told investigators he had attended a three-week training course at the Lal Bahadur Shastri National Academy of Administration in Mussoorie in June. He had arrived in Delhi on 26 June, he said, and stayed in Gujarat Bhavan till the early morning of 3 July, when he took his return flight to Ahmedabad. He confirmed that he had been in touch with Sushil during his stay in Delhi for personal reasons. And he confirmed Sushil's nocturnal visit to his room in the early hours of 3 July. He recounted to the police the events of that morning, describing in detail Sushil's uneasy state and strange behaviour.

Rao's interrogation also revealed a crucial conversation he had with Sushil on the day following his early morning visit to Gujarat Bhavan. He told investigating officers that on 4 July he had received a telephone call from Sushil, who said he was in Bombay. Sushil, Rao said, requested him to ask Ashok Gandhi, a mutual contact in Bombay, to call him, as he needed some urgent help. When Gandhi did not call, Sushil telephoned Rao again, at 4 p.m. Rao told investigating officers that in the course of the conversation, Sushil confessed to him that he had shot his wife dead. Rao apparently then advised Sushil to turn himself in to the police and asked him not to call him again.

Even after these valuable disclosures, the investigating team took a rather jaundiced view of D.K. Rao's claims of innocence. While he apparently had no direct role in aiding Sushil's getaway, and may well have had no knowledge of the murder until after he returned to Gujarat, our doubts over his conduct remained.

As a diligent citizen and an upright member of the elite Indian Administrative Service, Rao should have known it was his bounden duty to approach the police and share his knowledge of the case – especially after Sushil had confessed to him. Instead, he withheld vital information from the investigation until he was confronted by investigators in Ahmedabad. Suspicions about his behaviour lingered in the press too, and later, the judiciary. *The Indian Express* headline, 'Why did not Rao inform the Police himself?'asked a question for which the man seemed to have no satisfactory answer.[142]

Still, we were in no real hurry to throw the book at him. Rao's testimony as a witness was more useful to us than his prosecution as an offender. Our team was preoccupied, too, with building the case against Sharma, who we knew to be guilty. Pursuing D.K. Rao would only distract us from our primary goal, which was to achieve a conviction against a murderer.

We were conscious though, of the immense value of the extra judicial confession by Sushil, and took the precaution of requesting Rao to make a statement under Section 164 of the Criminal Procedure Code. This is a voluntary statement made and sworn to before a magistrate, which is admissible as evidence in a criminal trial. D.K. Rao made his statement before a link magistrate,[143] behind closed doors, at Patiala House on Thursday, 20 July. While such sworn statements are sometimes recanted in court, we felt confident that Rao would stand by his deposition and give truthful testimony on the stand. He had little choice if he wished to emerge unscathed from the imbroglio. At least, that is what we thought.

Rao was spared the relentless media attention that anyone remotely involved with Sushil or the tandoor murder endured in those months. *The Tribune* alleged that the police had adopted 'double standards' in its treatment of him. It noted that we had arrested Jai Prakash Pehlwan, Ram Prakash Sachdeva and Rishi Raj Rathi for aiding and abetting Sushil's flight from Delhi, yet we merely questioned D.K. Rao.[144] The paper could not have known that Rao had apparently extended hospitality to Sushil without any knowledge of the murder, or that he was making every effort to assist the investigation.

The media and some prominent public figures remained unconvinced of Rao's innocence. And reporters did not have to look far for evidence to undermine his credibility. *The Indian Express* reported Delhi BJP General Secretary Nand Kishore Garg's demand that Rao be immediately suspended from duty.[145] According to a report that appeared the following month in *The Sunday Times*, Rao was no stranger to suspension. He had apparently been suspended by the Central government while with the Visakhapatnam Port Trust, for abuse of his position and 'conduct unbecoming' of an IAS officer. He had, it seems, improperly allowed officers under investigation for embezzlement to retire from government service, thus escaping punishment.[146]

With his reputation and career in the firing line, Rao mounted his own, spirited public defence, and this also found column space in the newspapers. While admitting that Sushil Sharma spent the night at Gujarat Bhavan on 3 July, he claimed that he had been used by Sushil: 'The man knew hundreds of people in the city to whom he could have gone the night when he allegedly killed his wife, but remembered only my name …' Rao claimed he had no inkling that Sushil had allegedly killed Naina Sahni, and that he had only come to know about this later from newspaper reports. He emphatically declared he was an innocent victim of circumstances, and was being made a scapegoat.[147]

Rao seemed less keen to publicly defend himself against allegations of corruption. It seems he had been issued a showcause notice by the Gujarat government four months earlier, on fifteen of nineteen charges levelled against him. The charges, it emerged, involved more than mere 'bungling'. The *Hindustan Times* reported that Rao had been accused of misappropriating ₹40 lakh and sent back to the Gujarat IAS cadre from his Visakhapatnam posting because he had 'become "a law and order problem"'.[148]

Sushil's backroom dealings on his behalf with Union Minister for Surface Transport Jagdish Tytler had apparently led the minister to stall Rao's prosecution for a year.[149] As the depth of his involvement with him became clear, Tytler's claim that Sushil was 'a psychopath' seemed altogether too glib and self-serving for anyone, least of all Delhi Police, to take seriously.[150] As for Rao, this controversy and others, quite apart from the tandoor murder, would haunt him for the remainder of his bureaucratic career.

There was another, less controversial, witness who emerged as a result of Keshav's questioning: Sushil and Naina's cook, Ram Niwas Dubey. Probing for information on Dubey, we learned he had worked for Sushil between 1989 and 1995, when he returned to his village to get married, three months before Naina was killed. Dubey was tracked down in his village Belaur, near the town of Arrah in the Bhojpur district of Bihar. He was brought to Delhi for questioning. Dubey's testimony was formalised, as was Rao's, in a sworn statement under Section 164 of the Criminal Procedure Code.

Dubey told investigators that he had started working for Sushil as a peon-cum-domestic-servant on a salary of ₹500 per month at 4 Bhai Veer Singh Marg, where Sushil lived before he moved to Mandir Marg. When Sushil became president of the DPYC and occupied no. 2 Talkatora Road, Dubey was asked to work at the office as well. Later, in 1992, when Naina Sahni became general secretary of the DPYC, she started visiting Sushil at the Talkatora Road office and also his Bhai Veer Singh Marg house. It was Sushil who introduced Naina to Dubey.

When Sushil moved to apartment 8/2A in Sector-II off Mandir Marg, Naina's visits became more frequent. One day, Naina told Dubey that Sushil had put sindoor on her forehead and married her in front of the 'mata' in the puja room at the house. From that time, Sushil and Naina lived together as husband and wife.

Ram Niwas Dubey's account of Sushil and Naina's marital relationship reflected the dark trajectory of young love descending into tragedy, of a marriage blighted by jealousy and damaged beyond repair by violence. There were no great revelations in his statement. But it was material for our prosecution, because it painted a picture of a man giving free rein to the darker side of his nature – and it established a clear motive for murder.

Perhaps because he was never involved in the murder beyond working for the perpetrator and cooking for the victim, Ram Niwas Dubey was spared the media blitz that Rao would weather. But while Rao was adroitly extricating himself from his legal predicament, I found myself facing difficulties of my own.

Among the headlines in prominent newspapers, the day after we brought Sushil from Bangalore, were some which highlighted one of my statements from the previous day. Within its four-column coverage on the tandoor case, *The Statesman* had carried a bold headline: 'Enough evidence to hang Sushil: Pereira.' The *Hindustan Times* headline was almost identical: 'Enough proof to hang Sushil, says Pereira.' Other papers emphasised this statement in their coverage. *The Pioneer* even issued a flier: 'We have enough evidence to hang him: Pereira.'

At least *The Statesman* quoted my statement correctly: '"The police have sufficient evidence to hang Sushil Sharma," Mr Maxwell Pereira said. "There is enough evidence to hang him; however, every soul is innocent unless proven guilty in a court of law."'

My words were truthful and, as events would transpire, correct. The furore surrounding my statement would confirm, nonetheless, that the blunt truth can bring you a great deal of trouble in public life. In the following year, I would be forced to spend several hours defending myself in court for making a statement of fact, which, in its context, carried little weight and harmed nobody.

Even as Sushil was produced before Magistrate Dharam Raj Singh on 12 July, a lawyer practising in the superior courts of Delhi was making noises about the issue. Dr Janak Raj Jai of Gole Market, ostensibly also the self-styled secretary general of the All India Lawyers and Intellectuals Forum, informed the media that he would address an open letter to me. He was, he said, intent on voicing his distress over my statement that 'we have enough evidence to hang (Sharma)'.

Jai claimed that since the matter was sub judice, it was not open to a police officer to pre-empt the court's decision. He described the statement as 'a gross interference in the process of law and judicial discretion, and demanded [a] public apology from Mr Pereira and asked him to wash his hands from [sic] the case forthwith.'

My statement was an off-the-cuff response to Ananthanarayanan's claim that Delhi Police had scant evidence against his client. I had made it outside the Hoskote District Court complex, in reply to questions from one of the assembled horde of reporters. Doubtless, it was lacking in subtlety and, in a similar situation again, I would certainly choose my words more carefully.

Any Indian advocate would know that law enforcement and the judiciary have quite separate functions. Most citizens would be aware, too, that a police officer cannot legally pronounce judgement against an alleged offender. That is a function of the court. I was an additional commissioner of police and I had not pronounced judgement against Sushil Sharma anyway. I had simply indicated, using a fairly blunt idiom, that Delhi Police had plenty of evidence against him.

This should have been reassuring to most people. The public would have doubtless wanted to know that the police wouldn't issue a nationwide alert and pursue a suspect across the country based on mere suspicion.

The learned Dr Jai seemed to have conveniently overlooked the second part of my statement, which was not mentioned by most media outlets: 'Every soul is innocent unless proven guilty in a court of law.' Clearly, I was not pre-empting the court's decision.

At any rate, a police officer must be guided by evidence. And there was a plethora of unambiguous evidence that indicated Sushil Sharma had murdered Naina Sahni: Constable Kunju witnessing him at the Bagiya, the security guards' testimony, the blood and bullets at the apartment – and the body itself. Conveying this fact to the media was reasonable and warranted in light of his advocate's bluster, and legitimate public interest in the case.

Perhaps Dr Jai was overreacting to the media reports. He may well have hankered after the national spotlight, too, just as had another doctor, Dr Sarangi, a few days earlier. Whatever his motives, he filed a PIL writ in the Delhi High Court on the issue, making the Union and the state governments, Delhi's lieutenant governor, Commissioner Nikhil Kumar and me respondents.[151]

In his application to the court, Dr Jai prayed for the issue of a writ of mandamus to restrain me from issuing statements such as the one reported on 12 July which, he claimed, amounted to the misuse of legal powers. He asserted that the statement was shocking and contemptuous; it 'gave wrong signals in the minds of the general public'. It usurped the function and prerogative of the court, he claimed, and was in gross violation of Articles 14 and 21 of the Constitution.

Dr Jai argued that 'to hang', 'to give life sentence' or 'to acquit' was the domain of the relevant court and not the police. He asked the High Court to examine whether it had the power to interfere in the event of mala fide, arbitrary use of powers by an investigating agency. He further requested the court to involve the chairman of the Bar Council of Delhi, and the presidents of both the Supreme Court and the Delhi High Court bar associations, to assist the court in framing guidelines for future investigations of such sensational cases as the tandoor murder. He also prayed for an order from the court to remove me from the case.

Justices A.B. Saharya and M.S.A. Siddiqui admitted the PIL

application on Thursday, 27 July. While the then standing counsel (criminal) in the High Court, S.K. Aggarwal, assisted by N.K. Handa, the additional standing counsel (criminal), put in appearances on behalf of all the respondents, Dr Jai appeared for himself. The justices held that the 'tenor of the petition raises a question of general public importance viz. whether it is proper for police authorities to make public declaration[s] in respect of matters under investigation in a criminal case'. Mercifully, they rejected Dr Jai's plea to make the chairman of the Bar Council of Delhi and the president of the Supreme Court Bar Association – completely uninvolved parties – respondents in the case.

As the main respondent, I was livid at this turn of events. The investigating team was ready to submit the charge sheet in perhaps the most prominent murder case in at least a generation. And I would be distracted by a frivolous legal case which, aside from giving the plaintiff his fifteen minutes of fame, could benefit no one.

I had no intention of being caught in the wings of Dr Jai's sideshow, however. I lost no time in seeking further guidance, outside the government framework. My friend and financial advisor Pramod Gupta took me to meet former Chief Justice of India K.N. Singh, and ACP Renganathan, who had earlier handled a theft case at the eminent jurist Soli Sorabji's house, introduced me to him. Both these men backed me to the hilt. Under Sorabji's guidance, his junior, Gandhi, assisted me in drafting my reply affidavit. In the meantime, Gurdial Singh, my Rotary Club president, spoke to Abhishek Manu Singhvi an equally influential legal luminary of the time, who, after proffering his own inputs, filed the affidavit on my behalf in the High Court through Joy Basu, his then junior.

I submitted to the court that the petitioner had no locus standi to file this PIL application by virtue of his being a secretary general of the so-called All India Lawyers and Intellectuals Forum. He was not, my reply affidavit argued, a person aggrieved; and no public interest lay in interfering in the criminal proceedings against Sushil Sharma. Further, my affidavit argued that, if entertained,

Dr Jai's writ could impede the discharge of duties under Indian criminal law.

While contesting Dr Jai's locus standi in the matter, my reply affidavit firmly refuted the substance of his allegations. It pointed out the ridiculousness of his suggestion that by giving the press statement, I had assumed the function or prerogative of the courts. In no way was my statement a verdict, anyhow: it referred only to the quantum and quality of evidence. I had, in any event, qualified my fairly robust assertion about the evidence against Sushil by emphasising his inalienable right to a trial. And I had made my statement, the affidavit noted, without malice.

My advocates had done their work thoroughly. They quoted precedent, which dictated that as far as possible courts should not entertain cases of individual wrong or injury by actions of a third party as PIL cases. Since the statement upon which the writ petition was based had a bearing only on Sushil Sharma, it should be dismissed. My reply affidavit pointed out that Sushil Sharma was quite entitled to approach the honourable court himself for relief if he felt aggrieved – which he did, anyway, in the following months.

After a year of adjournments and delays, Dr Janak Raj Jai's much publicised PIL, case no. W.P. (Crl) 417/95, fizzled out, a damp squib. By then, the case had been palmed off to the bench of Justices Arun Kumar and N.G. Nandi, who dismissed it with the observation, 'we do not feel that any useful purpose will be served in keeping this petition pending.'

It was as if common sense had prevailed – far too late, of course, and well after the plaintiff had his fill of media attention. The honourable justices felt there was such little substance in the case that they did not deign to even make a summary decision on its merits. The writ was essentially thrown out of court.

I must confess I was disappointed. If the material in Dr Jai's writ was so lacking in importance or value that it did not warrant a decision to justify its dismissal, surely it should not have been entertained in the first place. I had mustered my resources and prepared myself and our team of legal eagles for a serious brawl. But after all the clamour, it was over before the bell rang to start the first round.

The issue had, by this time, already been sidestepped once by the High Court. Taking a cue from Dr Jai, Sushil had moved the High Court a few weeks after Dr Jai's writ was lodged, in a bid to have his trial postponed or discharged. Sushil's writ alleged that a 'parallel public trial had been held against him'[152] in the media, and he could not therefore expect a fair trial. He made particular mention of my comment at Hoskote, and requested that contempt proceedings be initiated against me and others publishing such news items that 'coloured public opinion and arouse[d] public passions against him'.[153] He rather preposterously suggested that he could not expect a fair trial because our investigation had been 'rushed'.

In her judgement, issued on 1 May 1996, Justice Usha Mehra did not consider any arguments that I should be charged with contempt of court because 'the matter is sub judiced in Criminal Writ Petition no. 417/95'. That is, Dr Jai's earlier writ was still pending at the time of her judgement, and it was only proper for the presiding judges in Dr Jai's case to decide the matter. She could not deliver a 'parallel judgement' on the issue.

More's the pity that Justice Usha Mehra was constrained not to decide the matter regarding my statement. Her judgement on Sushil's writ was meticulously considered, if somewhat long-winded, as court judgements tend to be. In any case, she left it open for Sushil to have contempt proceedings against me revived before the trial court, should Dr Rai's petition be withdrawn.

There were plenty of other contentions in Sushil's application for Justice Mehra to consider. He had mentioned in his writ the more explosive headlines such as 'Sushil, Naina charge sheet reveals a love triangle' and 'DNA tests leave no room for doubt'. He had also exhibited photographs of women protestors demanding that the police hand him over to the public for justice, and evidence of students holding 'chhatra adalat (students' courts) for hanging

Sushil'. He also referred to a prominent political figure felicitating Head Constable Kunju, Home Guard Chander Pal and Anaro Devi for their roles in uncovering the murder. He alleged that these articles and events had prejudiced the public against him, such that he could not expect a fair trial.

The two events referred to in Sushil's application to the court were probably motivated by politics as much as by righteous indignation over the murder. The ABVP had held a rally at Delhi University on Monday, 24 July 1995. After passing through various colleges, the procession held a students' court at Kranti Chowk. The 'court' condemned the Congress for exploiting young women and criminalising politics, and called for the public hanging of Sushil and the Congress culture.

Another event was held a few weeks later, on 19 August. The Janata Dal party's Sixth Convention of National Union of Backward Classes, Scheduled Castes, Scheduled Tribes and Minorities was inaugurated by Anaro Devi, who had raised the alarm outside the Bagiya on 2 July. She and Head Constable Kunju were presented at the inauguration ceremony with a shawl and a trophy and ₹25,000 each, while Home Guard Chander Pal received ₹11,000.

Justice Mehra deliberated whether these and the police briefings to the media, including the supposedly leaked details of the DNA report, could prejudice the trial. She further considered if the relevant media outlets were guilty of contempt of court with their reportage of the case.

In disposing of Sushil's petition to the court, Justice Mehra stated:

> So far as the question of postponement or suspension of trial, to my mind, it is neither sustainable in law nor on facts ... [The] media's attraction to this case and contributing to the building up of public interest in no way establishes that the case would not be decided on its merits ... A judge dealing with the case is supposed to be neutral ... To my mind, the apprehension of the petitioner that he would not get a fair trial is perfunctory and without foundation ... As regards demonstrations by women's

organisations or students, that also cannot mean interference in the administration of justice nor can it in any manner hamper the proceedings [or] amount to denial of a fair trial to the petitioner.[154]

I should mention here that trials in India are decided by judges and not juries as they are in many other countries. This has been the case since the legal furore following a Bombay jury acquitting Commander K.M. Nanavati of murder in 1959, in a majority verdict of 8–1. An upstanding naval officer, Nanavati had shot dead his friend Prem Ahuja after discovering he was having an affair with his British-born wife Sylvia. Reservations over the verdict in the legal fraternity led to a retrial and conviction. In the aftermath of the case, trials by jury were abandoned in favour of trials before a judge.

There were parallels between the Nanavati case and the tandoor murder, just as there were aspects in which the two cases differed sharply. There were allegations of press interference in both. But while the press coverage of the tandoor murder was uniformly negative towards Sharma, a press campaign of support for Nanavati almost undoubtedly influenced the jury's decision in his favour. The Bombay daily *Blitz* ran a public campaign for Nanavati and even published a mercy petition, when his conviction at retrial was confirmed in the Supreme Court.

Both the Nanavati case and the tandoor murder were crimes of passion and evoked powerful public responses. The general public was most sympathetic towards Nanavati, there were even rallies to support him. Public gatherings in the wake of the tandoor murder, however, could very easily have turned into lynch mobs against Sushil Sharma.

Kawas Manekshaw Nanavati was a respected man who had served his country faithfully in the navy and defence establishment, and his conduct before the killing was unimpeachable. Sushil Sharma, in contrast, was a Congress party fixer, prone to dishonesty and needless violence. There seemed no end to revelations of his misdeeds in the press. People could empathise with Nanavati's plight as the distraught, wronged husband whose shock at his friend's betrayal had goaded him to kill. They felt nothing but disgust, however, at Sushil's murder of his wife – and his craven attempt to conceal the crime.

Perhaps the biggest difference between the cases lay in the manner in which the offenders conducted themselves after their crimes. Many were impressed by Nanavati's prompt confession to his provost officer (head of naval police) and surrender to John Lobo of the Bombay Police. This, and the heartbreak that he faced in the hours preceding the murder, moved public opinion in his favour. After serving three years of his life sentence, Nanavati was pardoned by Vijaya Lakshmi Pandit, governor of Maharashtra and sister of Prime Minister Jawaharlal Nehru.

In the case of Sushil, however, the strength of public opinion meant he could not be forgiven or forgotten, let alone formally pardoned for his crime. Where K.M. Nanavati had stood upright and firm and squarely faced the consequences of his action, Sushil had made a shameful, repulsive attempt to destroy evidence of his guilt. He had also become a fugitive from justice for several days. We could never imagine in the weeks after the murder just how long he would continue to run.

17

Let the Games Begin

Despite a brief show of contrition from Sushil, we were under no illusion that his prosecution would be straightforward. He had already shown himself to be an exasperatingly cunning adversary. This, and his almost manic inconsistency, did not augur well for our case.

It was as if we were dealing with two different men: On the night we brought Sushil back to Delhi, he had grovelled before us and Commissioner Nikhil Kumar, begging forgiveness for his crime. The next afternoon in court, he was the showman extraordinaire, playing to the crowd and the media, blaming the murder on a political conspiracy – trying to settle old scores by blackening the name of his political foe. Anyone who could switch off his feelings of guilt and manipulate a situation so masterfully was sure to never submit willingly to justice. We knew we were in for a serious fight.

Julio Ribeiro, a retired veteran cop and the doyen of Mumbai Police, was well aware of the challenges we faced in seeking justice for Ravi Naina Sahni. The biggest of these, he knew, involved delays and witness-tampering. He wrote about these aspects of the case just as we were submitting the charge sheet:

> It is to be fervently hoped that the people will continue to take interest in the course of [the tandoor murder's] investigation and also its prosecution in a court of law. If, like most other crimes

of this magnitude, the accused are released on bail and the case comes up for hearing years later, it will be a travesty of justice.

Delay in trying such offenders gives them opportunities to suborn witnesses. Even straightforward witnesses tend to forget details after a lapse of time. The people should be vigilant. They should raise their voices against any manipulation.[155]

'Justice delayed is justice denied' has become almost a cliché. But that doesn't detract from its truth. We knew that the more protracted the proceedings were against Sharma, the greater the benefit to him, for a variety of reasons. We were especially concerned about delays giving Sushil's lawyers and confederates time to weaken the case against him, one way or another, which is what Julio Ribeiro had warned against.

From the outset, the tandoor murder caused panic in the Congress government. Party heavyweights sensed, correctly as it would turn out, that it had the potential to bring the government to its knees. Even when the party understood that Sushil would not seek to damage its prospects any further, the nervousness in its ranks remained. Leaders were anxious for court proceedings to demonstrate that Sushil was not being assisted by the party. They probably hoped for a speedy, uncomplicated trial leading to a guilty verdict, so they could put the matter to rest.

The first step in a criminal prosecution in India is the compilation of the charge sheet, which is also the final stage of the police's investigation of a case. A charge sheet is a formal document of accusation, which is submitted to the court by law enforcement agencies defined as such in Section 173 of the Criminal Procedure Code of India. It most often includes the FIR, the list of accused and a summary of the evidence along with a list of witnesses, as well as the charges and specific provisions of the Indian Penal Code the alleged offender has breached.

The prosecution of any case relies on a properly drafted charge sheet. Framing the charge sheet in Sushil's case would be especially painstaking: it had to be meticulous, unambiguous and complete, its assertions clearly supported by the attached documentation. There could be no lacuna in the case that Sushil's advocates could use to his advantage during his trial. Although theoretically the charge sheet could be amended during the trial by prosecutors, this would only serve to undermine the case. So we really had only one opportunity to make our case before the matter went to trial – and we had to do it right.

Minister of State for Home Affairs Rajesh Pilot had urged us to file the charge sheet before the monsoon session of Parliament. Though this was onerous, it was politically shrewd. With the charge sheet filed, Pilot could forestall any uncomfortable questions from the Opposition in Parliament. His simple rejoinder to any rumblings on the floor of the House would be that the matter was sub judice: it was for the courts to decide. Also, a well-drafted charge sheet submitted in a timely manner would reassure Parliament and the public. It would demonstrate clearly that the police were serious in their pursuit of Naina Sahni's killer.

The minister had set us quite a task, given that the monsoon session of Parliament was to begin on 31 July, less than a month from the day of the murder. This was nowhere close to the time it usually takes for the police to gather all the evidence and frame a charge sheet.

Apart from the political pressure to expedite the preparation of the charge sheet, we had our own, very practical reasons to do so. In cases of non-bailable offences such as murder, a charge sheet must be filed within ninety days of the registration of the FIR, or the alleged offender may be compulsorily released on bail.

This time limit can pose serious problems for the police. It is often a struggle to file the charge sheet within ninety days, for cases of a nature and complexity similar to the tandoor murder. Gathering evidence, waiting for forensic reports, liaising with the prosecutor – all of this can take time. If the charge sheet is not filed within ninety days of the filing of the FIR, it can effectively endanger the whole prosecution in a serious case. An alleged offender out of judicial remand and on the streets can get up to all kinds of mischief: most often, bribing or threatening witnesses or seeking to tamper with evidence.

Naturally, there was never any thought of filing the charge sheet later than was absolutely necessary. But it was a Herculean task to gather all the loose ends of the case together in just a few weeks. We knew we would need a particularly dedicated team of police officers and prosecutors to accomplish it. We were painfully aware, too, that we could not rely only on the public prosecutors available to us.

Sharma would undoubtedly use his money and influence to hire the most formidable criminal advocates in the capital, who would trounce the average public prosecutor in fairly short order. We would have to recruit some of Delhi's finest legal minds to counter Sushil's defence team, in addition to the cream of Delhi's Directorate of Prosecution. These luminaries would have to be involved in the preparation of the charge sheet, supervised by the seniormost police officer assigned to the case.

In the normal course of events, the duty of supervising the charge sheet's preparation would have fallen to me. However, I was the public face of the murder investigation. I needed to tackle the inevitable daily intrigues and distractions in the media, the home ministry probes and queries from the courts – all of which had become a hallmark of this case. There were almost daily press briefings, too. Along with this, I had to attend to numerous written reports and continually brief the commissioner, lest he be caught on the backfoot by media inquiries. Commissioner Nikhil Kumar could see I not only had my hands full with the investigation, I was juggling several roles.

The architect of the charge sheet, it was decided then, would be Additional Commissioner (Crime) Ramashray Tiwari. Assigning Tiwari this crucial duty was a masterstroke on the commissioner's part. A thoroughgoing professional and hands-on field officer of the old school, Punditji, as he was called, was widely respected for his sheer intelligence. His keen eye for detail and readiness to pit his mind against the best or the worst he encountered in his job was legendary in Delhi Police; he could overcome any obstacle a criminal mind could conceive.

I had witnessed Ramashray Tiwari in action at close quarters, having had the privilege of working with him as his junior and later as a colleague for more than a decade by the time of the tandoor murder. I was relieved to know that the critical matter of preparing the charge sheet was in his competent hands. I was glad, too, to have DCP Aditya Arya's help in coordinating the team.

Tiwari and I sifted through the names of likely candidates for the prosecution team with Nikhil Kumar. Each member of the team, we agreed, must be utterly incorruptible and fearless. Sushil was particularly adept at backroom manipulation and we could not afford to have any team member who was susceptible to inducement or vulnerable to threats. Neither must a team member be swayed by political considerations, or prejudiced in any way.

We quickly settled on Amritpal Ahluwalia for special state prosecutor. Aside from being a man of integrity, Ahluwalia boasted a truly impressive resume. He had been the legal advisor and prosecutor in the Indira Gandhi assassination case and was counsel for the Jain Commission of inquiry into the Rajiv Gandhi assassination, which was going on at the time. Among the many famous criminal cases he handled in his career spanning four decades was the Vidya Jain murder case in 1973. Thankfully, we were able to come to an agreement on his fee, which was no small achievement given the government's tight-fistedness in such matters.

Not to be left out of such a high-profile case, the Director of Prosecution, P.C. Mishra, lost no time in volunteering his services. K.D. Bharadwaj, the senior prosecutor for New Delhi District, who had represented the state in the case till Ahluwalia's appointment, would continue to be involved in the prosecution. Raman Kumar was chosen as the assistant prosecutor.

Raman's time with the team was to be remarkably short. As we were about to set to the task of preparing the charge sheet, he gave a television interview about the case. After Dr Sarangi's frolic in the limelight, we were in no mood for such nonsense, which could only compromise the prosecution. Raman Kumar was immediately transferred. In response to media queries about his removal from the case, Director of Prosecution P.C. Mishra said he had 'simply been transferred and this has nothing to do with the tandoor murder case'.[156] It had everything to do with the case – at least, for speaking out of turn about it.

With Raman Kumar replaced by his senior Pankaj Sanghi, we were ready to get down to business. The team drafting the charge sheet would be best accommodated, we felt, in a venue away from the public eye and the hustle and bustle of a police station or a government office. For this purpose, Tiwari and his team took up two adjoining rooms in Hotel Centre Point which, as the name suggests, was located centrally, near Connaught Place.

This was convenient for everyone: it was almost exactly equidistant between Delhi Police Headquarters and Connaught Place police station. It was most important to keep this venue secret from the media, ever on the lookout for a new lead or titbit of gossip about the case. To this end, only the seniormost officers of Delhi Police and the prosecution team were made aware of the arrangement. That way, with the cooperation of the hotel management, the team could remain undisturbed as they worked.

While the hotel itself was utterly incongruous with law enforcement, it could easily have been the setting for an Agatha Christie-style whodunit. The place was a converted Lutyens-style mansion, a former home from the dying decades of the British Raj. It was comfortable, with the kind of well-worn, old-world ambience that is becoming increasingly rare. Although it had been spruced up nicely and was perhaps a three-star hotel at the time, it was not a flashy, premier establishment that attracted attention. It was the last place anyone would expect to find a hand-picked team of police and prosecutors mapping out a murder prosecution.

I visited the ground-floor rooms of Hotel Centre Point

whenever I could, to keep abreast of progress on the charge sheet. I would invariably find the team members deep in discussion, with notepads in hand and cups of half-drunk tea and plates of biscuits on the table before them. The two desks which had been placed to one side were smothered by haphazardly piled papers and law books. The team members, facing one another with their chairs in a roughly circular arrangement, would be so engrossed in their discussions that I would refrain from disturbing them. Mostly I would listen, and perhaps add a thought here and there or pose the occasional question.

For more than ten days, the investigators deliberated under the watchful eyes of Ramashray Tiwari. He was assisted by the senior crime branch sleuths he had brought along. ACP V. Renganathan, who had made a dash to Madras on 8 July to counter Sushil's anticipatory bail, was in the south of the country, confirming Sushil's movements during the manhunt. He and other teams of police in the north continued to brief the team drafting the charge sheet.

Renganathan had managed to make some seizures of various items from advocate Ananthanarayanan's Shenoy Nagar residence. Among these were Sushil's ModiLuft ticket and boarding pass counterfoil for his Jaipur-Bombay flight and his Bombay-Madras Jet Airways ticket. Sushil had also left with his advocate a free meal coupon from Tirupati, dated 5 July, two packets of prasad from the temple there, a handkerchief, a picture of Goddess Durga, a fountain pen and some prescription drugs. These items would become exhibits, physical evidence in the case.

Some of the exhibits would confirm Sushil's movements while he was on the run. It seems he had kept them with the purpose of shoring up his alibi. Perhaps the most telling item recovered from Ananthanarayanan's house was Sushil's medication: a half-used strip with four tablets of the drug Alprazolam. Alprazolam, or Xanax, is a mood-stabilising tranquiliser often used to treat panic disorders. Its presence suggested that Sushil was probably dependent on prescription drugs.

With all the information before them from across the country, our team of elite legal minds put together the charge sheet. Each piece of evidence was cited carefully to support the prosecution account of events. The exercise was completed with astounding swiftness, and the charge sheet, or challan, in the case was ready by 27 July 1995.

Delhi Police filed the charge sheet the very next day, on Friday, 28 July, which was within twenty-six days of the commission of the crime and the registration of the FIR. This was a record of sorts: Never had a charge sheet in a Delhi murder case been submitted to court in such a short time. The charge sheet, a nineteen-page document in Hindi, was filed before Link Magistrate V.K. Maheshwari at the Patiala House court complex.

More than 100 documents comprised the attachments to the charge sheet, including a list of ninety-nine witnesses and their statements. Two of these were of D.K. Rao and Matloob Karim, both of which had been recorded before magistrates under Section 164 of the Criminal Procedure Code.

The challan narrative named former DPYC president Sushil Sharma as the prime accused and four other persons as co-accused in the case. The charge sheet summarised the facts of the case and listed the material evidence – physical, forensic and oral – adduced against them.

Sushil Sharma was booked under sections 302 (murder), 201 (destruction of evidence) and 34 (crimes committed with another) of the Indian Penal Code. Keshav Kumar was charged with destroying evidence along with Sharma under Section 201, and for helping him flee the scene of the crime. Both Sushil and Keshav were also booked for criminal conspiracy, an offence punishable under Section 120B of the Indian Penal Code. The other three accused – Jai Prakash Pehlwan, Rishi Raj Rathi and Ram Prakash Sachdeva – were charged with helping Sharma to destroy evidence under Section 201, and with harbouring Sushil and assisting and facilitating his escape from the capital.

The same day, Commissioner Nikhil Kumar addressed a press

conference. He stated that despite the phenomenal speed with which the challan had been prepared, the police were constrained to submit it to the court two days after Sharma was sent to judicial custody. This, he explained, was owing to delays in the scientific aspects of the investigation.

The commissioner briefed the press on the contents of the charge sheet, detailing the prosecution's account of Naina Sahni's murder and outlining our investigation of it. He confirmed that the police charge sheet stated Sushil Sharma had killed Naina Sahni as he believed she was continuing an affair with her fellow Congress supporter Matloob Karim.

The commissioner stressed, too, that investigations had not revealed any indication of anyone helping Sushil financially to evade arrest. There was no question of the police indicting any other politician in the charge sheet – or even D.K. Rao, the Gujarat cadre IAS officer, who would be made a prosecution witness.

Significantly, the media, which had been speculating on this score, made it a point to report the next day that no major political leader's name figured in the charge sheet.

⚖️

While we were compiling the charge sheet, Sushil was preparing a crack legal defence team. After the initial shock of incarceration, when he isolated himself with hours of quiet prayer, he began to reach out to his fellow inmates. He spent a lot of time inquiring about the best criminal lawyers and their fees, a subject that was to become quite a preoccupation for him.

Indeed, now that his interrogation was over, he had nothing more pressing to occupy his time with than weighing his options and plotting his next move. He was a past master at both these.

Reports filtered out of Tihar Jail that Sushil had cultivated two contractors – one who supplied milk and milk products to the jail, and the other, vegetables – and they helped him, it seems, to mobilise his resources. The adverse publicity from the case had naturally led most of his associates, especially those affiliated with the Congress, to quickly distance themselves from him. Many, however, feigned loyalty to him, probably on account of the havoc he might wreak on them otherwise. Some, it appears, may have secretly helped him out of fear.

Sushil's intention of countering the prosecution had become apparent when he appeared before Metropolitan Magistrate Dharam Raj Singh on 12 July. There he had gestured to the assembled advocates, urging them to come forward to defend him. On Saturday, 22 July, when he was again produced before the metropolitan magistrate, he signed more vakalatnamas, engaging a staggering seven lawyers to plead his case. He engaged R.P. Tyagi, Pradip Chaudhury, S.P. Sharma, Manohar Lal, Lalit Kumar and O.P. Sharma, along with Rohit Minocha.

Sushil's advocates were of the more adventurous breed, and a couple of them had known him for some time. Pradip Chaudhury was apparently the president of Dayal Singh College students' union when Sushil was the president at Satyavati College. Lalit Kumar, a Stephanian, had worked with Pradip from the beginning of their careers. The duo had handled the cases of a number of dreaded gangsters, many of whom like Jitendra Pahal, Narain alias Babboo Tyagi, Sunil Tyagi and Gopal Thakur died later in encounters.[157]

Sushil's crimes appeared even more egregious to the public than those of most gangsters; not even Sushil's lawyers could escape the ignominy of their association with the tandoor murder. Stung by Sushil's desperate attempts to implicate him in the murder, his arch-enemy Maninderjeet Singh Bitta lashed out, and Bitta's words hit at Minocha. He declared in a Zee TV interview that any lawyer representing Sushil was a 'darinda' (monster).

It was an ill-considered statement that would have been better made privately. It is a little harsh to judge advocates by their clients, anyway. Making a handsome profit from defending monsters in court doesn't necessarily turn the lawyers into monsters. Minocha, at any rate, was most unimpressed with Bitta's libellous bluster. After collecting the video and audio recordings of the interview, he informed the press on 21 July that he had lodged a complaint with the Delhi Bar Council. He asked the council to take action against Bitta on his behalf.

Minocha also appeared offended by Sushil, who was busily taking on eager new recruits. He emphasised in interviews that he alone had come forward in Sushil's darkest hour and it was only now that others were offering him their services. The clear implication was that the advocates were taking advantage of Sushil's situation. Minocha had known Sushil since his college days and had represented him before the murder. 'What can I say when everybody is showing interest. There is nothing I can do,' he said.

His resentment was to boil over publicly at least once. Though he seemed fairly philosophical about the arrangement when talking to the media, on 29 July, Minocha and R.P. Tyagi engaged in a spat in court over who would present Sushil's case.

They shouldn't have bothered. There were to be more advocates on Sushil's defence team in the coming days, and neither of them would land the plum job of representing their infamous client at the trial.

Writing in *The Times of India*, Sreerupa Mitra Chaudhury speculated that 'The intense desperation with which Sushil Sharma … is seeking to escape the prosecution dragnet is evident from the posse of lawyers which he has engaged.'[158] She reported that in addition to as many as ten lawyers from various courts already representing him, he was also seeking to engage the city's most prominent criminal lawyer, I.U. Khan. Khan had long been in the public eye, having appeared in high-profile cases such as the Vidya Jain murder case in 1973 and the diamond merchants' kidnapping in 1991. He would not, however, confirm to Ms Chaudhury whether he had been engaged by Sushil.

Perhaps Sushil was trying to outdo O.J. Simpson, whose team of ten high-profile lawyers were effectively undermining the prosecution murder case against Simpson at the time. Minocha was quick to suggest, at any rate, that a sizeable team of lawyers was not at all unusual in such a case.

A more pertinent matter for conjecture was how Sushil was managing to pay for the services of his eminent lawyers. Obviously, they couldn't all be volunteering their services free of charge. His visible sources of revenue had been relatively modest, and his family members didn't have any discernible capacity to mobilise such costly legal support for him.

It was a mystery, too, how Keshav Kumar was paying for his legal defence. We could only speculate about the means by which a man without formal employment and dependent on a meagre salary as Sushil's restaurant manager, could afford first-class legal representation. It was only reasonable to surmise that Sushil was somehow arranging this too – with the obvious understanding that Keshav would support his case.

Keshav's advocate S.K. Duggal set the tone for the kind of preposterous court submissions we would hear in the course of the trial. On Wednesday, 19 July, at the first of Keshav's countless bail hearings, Duggal made some fairly outlandish claims. The tenor of these was that Keshav was an innocent dupe wrongly accused of destruction of evidence.

He said Keshav had told him that on 2 July Sushil had arrived at the Bagiya Barbeque restaurant with a sack and told him it contained old political posters and banners, and asked him to burn it. It was only after the sack was alight that Keshav became aware that there was a body inside it. Duggal managed to make this statement with due conviction and a straight face before Additional Sessions Judge B.S. Chaudhury. He made a contradictory claim at Keshav's next hearing that the body had been kept on the tandoor in Keshav's absence. He claimed Keshav was a 'victim of circumstance.'

Doubtless, Keshav was facing a very different battle from Sushil's. His sole aim was to be granted bail so that he could be reunited with his wife and three children. All his judicial efforts were to this end, and aside from making some fairly ridiculous claims in court, he made little trouble. The prosecution stoutly resisted his pleas for bail, knowing he would very likely become a cat's paw for Sushil should he be released.

In contrast, the prosecution's battle with Sushil was to be waged on many fronts, as we would soon see. Represented by no less than five advocates in Metropolitan Magistrate Dharam Raj Singh's court on 26 July, he began his manoeuvring. Predictably, he began by retracting his confession, claiming that he had been forced to sign blank pages, which later formed the confession. He also denied identifying Naina Sahni's body. He then requested that he be accommodated in a more relaxed, 'B'-class jail facility and provided suitable security, as he feared an attempt on his life. Magistrate Dharam Raj Singh ordered that Sushil be given extra security, but little else.

A few days earlier, we'd had a foretaste of the more sinister tactics Sushil would employ during the trial. He was often kept in a lockup at the Tilak Marg police station while he was on police remand, and especially on days when he had court hearings. Matloob Karim would regularly visit the station to assist the investigation, providing information on Naina and Sushil's relationship and activities during this time. On Saturday, 22 July, when Matloob Karim and his friend and Youth Congress activist Mukesh Sharma were at the station, Sushil made a brazen attempt to intimidate Matloob.[159]

Through the bars of his cell, Sushil spoke to Mukesh Sharma, as he stood near the SHO's room.

'Tell Matloob to keep off the case, for I am not going to be here forever. Otherwise, I will settle everything the day I come out,' he said in his chillingly calculated manner.

Mukesh reported the incident to the police immediately and Matloob was provided with round-the-clock security.

We knew Sushil still had considerable support outside the jail – and not necessarily of the political kind. At each of his court hearings, a group of well-built, tough-looking characters – obviously wrestlers –

would be present. No witness for the prosecution could escape their subtle and not-so-subtle eyeballing, and no one could miss their intimidating presence outside the court and in the public gallery.

Waging psychological warfare against witnesses was just one of the myriad ways in which Sushil would attempt to disrupt his trial. He would just as easily manipulate judicial procedures and play on the court's indulgence of lawyer's arguments and requests. All this seriously jeopardised the proper functioning of the court, and also of the prosecution.

It seemed not even the police were immune to Sushil's machinations as the court battles began in earnest. Inspector Niranjan Singh was relaxing with his family one Sunday night at home, when the telephone rang. When his wife answered, an unknown man politely asked to speak with Inspector Niranjan Singh. When Niranjan came to the telephone and greeted the caller, the man calmly said, 'We know your son is studying engineering in Pune.' The line then went dead. There was no overt threat – but the implication was clear.

18

Trials and Intrigues

Anyone in judicial custody or remand in India is required under the Criminal Procedure Code to be produced before the court every fifteen days, for judicial custody to be reviewed. The magistrate usually extends the remand for 'undertrials' as a matter of course, as did Magistrate Dharam Raj Singh with Sushil and Keshav. Given that magistrates are extremely busy and courts are inundated with cases, this can sometimes mean that offenders' remands are extended without proper consideration of their circumstances. If a prisoner on remand cannot afford to engage an advocate or post bail, he may languish for years waiting for his trial.

In some cases, an alleged offender's incarceration in remand far exceeds a fitting penalty for his alleged offense. This disturbing prospect loomed large for Keshav Kumar as the trial plodded on in the court.

None of this was to be an issue for Sushil Sharma. As an alleged murderer in a high-profile case, he knew he could not expect to be granted bail. Backed by the Delhi Bar's finest, his regular remand hearings were an opportunity to grandstand and keep the prosecution on the back foot with false allegations and meritless arguments.

Sharma seemed to have adopted a strategy of attack as his best defence. And he didn't confine his court action to the regular, scheduled court hearings. He began on 17 July, with Rohit Minocha moving an application in the metropolitan magistrates' court, seeking the provision of special privileges for Sushil: newspapers, toiletry items and a fan. Minocha had earlier complained to reporters that his client 'had developed dark rings around his eyes and was generally looking pale'.[160] He alleged that Sushil was being 'tortured' by the police to make confessions, by withholding basic amenities. The application was denied.[161]

Minocha and Sushil were making a concerted effort to portray him as a victim of police excesses, which was far from the truth. Sushil whipped up his own drama at his second remand hearing on 22 July. When prosecutor K.D. Bharadwaj was submitting arguments in support of custody, Sushil could not contain himself. He flourished a packet of tablets and said he might go 'mad' from the effects of the medication he had been given. He declared that he had 'neither eaten nor slept properly during the last ten days of my custody'.[162]

Granted, a police interrogation is no picnic for an alleged murderer. Sushil must surely have been feeling the pressure of the intense questioning he was subjected to. We would see in the coming months, however, that his claims of being wronged were not merely the indignant outbursts of a man accustomed to getting his own way. They were part of a cunning strategy to delay and frustrate the prosecution and divert our energies from other tasks. And while his accusations took on a somewhat paranoid character in the coming months, they were no less effective in making our work as difficult as possible.

On 9 August, again at Patiala House, Sushil and Keshav came face to face for the first time since Sushil had fled the Bagiya and left Keshav to deal with the police. With the cooperation of the jail authorities, the police had managed to keep them apart till then, to lessen the opportunities for collusion. Upon their request, the magistrate gave permission for the pair to confer.

The atmosphere in the courtroom was alive with tension as the two huddled together behind the dock. Their expressions told of roiling emotions: Sushil was intense; Keshav seemed accusatory at times – and the faces of both betrayed their apprehension. They talked in hushed voices for around ten minutes.

It was reported the following day that Sushil told Keshav, '*Tu beqasoor hai. Mere chalte tu case mein phas gaya* (You are innocent. You have been dragged into the case because of me)'.[163] It was, one would think, the very least Sushil could say to Keshav.

Beyond that, heaven knows what they discussed. Sushil and Keshav shared a strange relationship, and an inscrutable chemistry. At least for now, there was no shift in Keshav's stance in the case; he was still in thrall to his former boss and friend.

In the months that followed, Sushil's legal team would contest every court decision they could, and issue a number of proceedings to head off the trial. Sushil went so far as to appeal to the Supreme Court that he be granted bail, despite there being no reasonable grounds for it, nor hope that his appeal would succeed.

He could slow the courts, but he could not halt his prosecution. On 15 September, Principal District Judge S.P. Sabharwal referred the case under Section 194 of the Criminal Procedure Code to New Delhi Additional Sessions Judge S.L. Khanna. Judge Khanna held a preliminary hearing on 25 September.

Sushil had by now engaged I.U. Khan to head his defence team. A master of court intrigues, Khan was unabashed in his attempts to prevent the trial from commencing, causing delays and seeking adjournments on the flimsiest of pretexts. A case in point was his request for time to have the court documents translated into Urdu, which was granted on 5 October. The learned I.U. Khan and his team were, of course, more than proficient in Hindi and English.

Then there were other delays, the likes of which we would see throughout the trial. Later that month, on 26 October, an adjournment was given when lawyers suspended work to condole the death of a colleague. Adjournments would be granted for far less pressing reasons as the trial proceeded.

Around this time, Sushil opened another legal front in a bid to head off the prosecution. On 22 September, he approached the Supreme

Court of India[164] in its original jurisdiction through advocates D.N. Goburdan and K.K. Luthra. He sought transfer of the trial under Section 406 of the Criminal Procedure Code to a jurisdiction outside Delhi. Sushil submitted that the trial should be conducted away from jurisdictions ruled by political parties hostile to him. He alleged bias on the part of Delhi Police, too, stating that the police hierarchy wished to get the 'petitioner [Sushil] hanged' through a media trial, which was an obvious reference to my statement at Hoskote.

Around this time, Sushil inducted another legal luminary, K.G. Bhagat, a former additional solicitor general of India, into his legal team. Bhagat would now lead his defence, assisted by I.U. Khan, O.P. Sharma and others.

The process of hearing charges began on 16 October in the Additional District and Sessions Court of S.L. Khanna. By now, the police think-tank monitoring the trial had decided to streamline the prosecution. It was better, we knew, to focus our campaign in court; we were already battling some of the nation's shrewdest legal minds in three different courts. Accordingly, the prosecution decided not to pursue the charges against Rishi Raj Rathi, Jai Prakash Pehlwan and R.P. Sachdeva. Their testimony would instead be used to bolster the prosecution's case. On 19 October, the defence pressed the court to treat these men as prosecution witnesses alongside D.K. Rao.

On 20 October, after many fierce legal arguments, the Supreme Court rejected Sushil's plea that his trial be conducted away from Delhi. At this stage, it must have become clear to Sushil that his efforts to scuttle the prosecution were failing, and his tactics became more desperate.

He alleged, in the Additional District and Sessions Court on 8 November, that he was being threatened in jail by DCP Aditya Arya. Standing in his politician's white kurta – which had become something of a uniform for him at the trial – he addressed the court from the dock, visibly shaken, his voice thick with emotion. 'Why are so many policemen here? ... He [Aditya Arya] is pestering my father and he is here today with all his armed men to further threaten me,' he said.[165] With timing and drama that would have made a theatre artist proud, Sushil then went on to elaborate that DCP Aditya Arya had been threatening to falsely incriminate his father; to frame him in sham cases.

Sushil was speaking in support of his advocates I.U. Khan and O.P. Sharma's application to debar Delhi Police officials from the court proceedings. His counsel further submitted to the court that he was being kept in solitary confinement, and was not allowed to talk to other inmates at Tihar Jail. Judge S.L. Khanna instructed Sushil's counsel to prepare a submission detailing specific instances of his being 'terrorised'.

Sushil's application was pure gamesmanship, not to mention utter hypocrisy. He thought nothing of standing over witnesses via intermediaries – as we had already seen, and would see more of, as events unfolded in the court of trial. He felt entitled to have a band of goondas present, supporting him at the hearings. These were probably the same men who paid visits to witnesses to suborn or frighten them. He felt quite justified, though, in objecting to having policemen in the courtroom, some of whom were witnesses, on grounds that their presence intimidated him.

Perhaps emboldened by the judge's instructions that he produce a detailed submission of the instances where he had been 'terrorised', Sushil's accusations would become even more outrageous. He made an application before the court on 29 November, alleging that Aditya Arya had made an attempt to 'eliminate' him on 15 November.[166]

Sushil had been produced before Magistrate P.D. Gupta of Tis Hazari court complex that day, in relation to charges of rioting, which had been pending against him since 1990. His counsel submitted that on the way back to Tihar Jail, the police van he was travelling in was stopped on a deserted stretch of road on the New Delhi Ridge (a reserve forest located on the western flank of New Delhi). Sushil was forced from the vehicle, he claimed, as a few police officers spread out along the road and into the treeline. DCP Aditya Arya and other officials then arrived and threatened Sushil with dire consequences, he said, because they had failed to convince Keshav Kumar to turn approver. Their original design to kill him in an encounter was thwarted, he alleged, only because a few people had gathered in the area.

The story was complete fantasy and mildly ridiculous. The court, however, was duty-bound to take the allegations seriously. Aditya Arya was summoned on 13 December. In his written submission to the court, Aditya vigorously denied the allegations against him, and stated they were 'false, mala fide and concocted with some ulterior motives'. Nevertheless, the magistrate ordered that the van driver be summoned to the court and the record of the escort for the van and the PCR wireless messages be produced before the court on 3 January.

I knew before perusing the evidence that Sushil's story was utterly implausible. Delhi Police had every reason to keep him alive, not least so he could be convicted of murder. Perhaps, as the papers and some Opposition leaders suggested, there were some prominent figures who would have been happily rid of him. But they would have found no sympathy within Delhi Police. For Sushil to have been murdered while in our care would have been a complete humiliation; an unmitigated catastrophe.

The then-65,000-strong[167] Delhi Police force already had enough public relations issues without counting Sushil. There was lingering public resentment over the death of three people earlier in the year when police had fired on a mob in Ashok Vihar – one of the episodes that would eventually provide a pretext for K. Padmanabhaiah to replace Commissioner Nikhil Kumar. Moreover, corruption was being extensively reported by the mid-nineties, and the statistics were sobering. Later that year, the media also played up the fact that a total of 164 police personnel were being investigated by the vigilance department of the police in 138 cases, including 6 of rape, 4 of murder and 23 under the Prevention of Corruption Act.[168]

If any good came of the tandoor murder, it was the boosting of public confidence in Delhi Police. From Constable Kunju's superb work to start with and all the way to the end, Delhi Police showed neither fear nor favour in pursuing Naina Sahni's murderer. And, for the most part, our actions met with the strong approval of Delhiites – we enjoyed an unusual surge in public support. No one involved in the case – least of all Aditya Arya – could have wished for a staged encounter to put an end to this public faith and botch up the most followed murder prosecution in decades.

At any rate, Sushil's attempted incrimination of Aditya in itself strained credulity. The direct involvement of any deputy commissioner of police in a staged encounter would have been highly unusual – not even the most corrupt senior officer would wish to dirty his hands thus – and DCP Aditya Arya was an officer of the highest moral and professional calibre. Most Indian police officers would have found the story laughable – and perhaps we would have laughed too, had we not been compelled to defend ourselves against it.

At least one of the assertions Sushil's advocates made in court on 29 November had substance. O.P. Wadhwa made mention of Delhi Chief Minister Madan Lal Khurana's statements that his party would make much of the tandoor murder in the coming elections. Khurana apparently went so far as to declare that the case would be a 'central plank' of the BJP campaign in the Lok Sabha polls.[169] This, as events would show, was perhaps the most truthful and accurate of any of Sushil's submissions in the murder proceedings.

Two days before this special hearing dealing with Sushil's allegations, on 11 December, K.G. Bhagat had unsuccessfully urged the additional sessions judge to discharge Sushil. The circumstances, Bhagat contended, were not conducive to holding a trial. He criticised the police and the media harshly, saying both had sensationalised the case. He then sought an adjournment until late January 1996, because in the interim he would be busy in the Supreme Court, he said, and also out of station.

The judge granted his request in deference to his eminence, and posted the case for hearing on 23 January. Neither K.G. Bhagat nor anyone else had any inkling that this would be his last appearance in the case.

Eleven days later, on 22 December, K.G. Bhagat suffered a massive heart attack and passed away. His loss was a serious blow for Sushil's defence, but Sushil was the kind of man to see opportunity in any adversity. Bhagat's death prompted perhaps the most ludicrous and bizarre of his claims in court.

Back before Additional Sessions Judge S.L. Khanna on 2 January 1996, Sushil made the grotesque declaration that his murdered wife, Ravi Naina Sahni, was actually alive. He went on to claim that 'The police does not want this fact to come before the court.'[170] He said his deceased former counsel was set to place evidence before the court about Naina's miraculous survival on 23 December, the day after he died.

Anyone with an ounce of sense knew that finding Naina Sahni alive was as likely as Subhas Chandra Bose and Elvis Presley holding a joint press conference in Delhi to announce their return to public life. Given the veritable mountain of forensic evidence that the investigating team had amassed, everyone knew the charred cadaver found at the Bagiya was that of Ravi Naina Sahni. Sushil's outlandish claim made for excellent tabloid copy, and led many to question his sanity. It also wasted court time, which seems to have been the intention of this disgraceful ploy in the first place.

Sushil made the controversial suggestion, too, that K.G. Bhagat's death may have been related to the threats he had received for accepting his brief. He alleged that Bhagat had only succumbed to a heart attack after a 'heated argument' with a 'threatener'.[171] I.U. Khan, who had resumed his earlier place at the head of Sushil's legal team after Bhagat's death, went on the offensive too, claiming that Sushil had been kept in solitary confinement in Tihar Jail. He alleged collusion between Delhi Police and jail officials in this and that Sushil was being 'tortured' for making his complaint against DCP Aditya Arya. In his petition, he stated that keeping Sushil in solitary confinement was a breach of his fundamental rights.

Sessions Judge S.L. Khanna fixed the next hearing for 8 January and told the prosecution to file a reply to Sushil's petition.

Back in court on 8 January, Tihar Jail Superintendent Tarsem Kumar denied Sharma had been kept in solitary confinement. He also assured the court that Sushil would be afforded the very best medical treatment at nearby hospitals, whenever this was advised by the medical officer. He was being kept in the high security ward purely for his safety. Extra security had been ordered for him by Magistrate Dharam Raj Singh on 26 July.

The high security section of Tihar Jail was no hotel: Prisoners slept on the concrete floor of the cells and the food was hardly restaurant quality. But accommodating Sushil there and keeping him away from other inmates was the only way his safety could be assured, short of constructing a special VIP cell for him. This did not stop I.U. Khan from complaining that Sushil had been housed with some of Delhi's most dreaded criminals.

At the same hearing, Sessions Judge S.L. Khanna began to show signs of judicial frustration. He noted that due to numerous adjournments, five months had elapsed, and only the issue of charges had been argued. He somewhat ingenuously asked Sushil's counsel I.U. Khan not to seek further adjournments, and that he cooperate in allowing the trial to proceed.

On 11 January, however, I.U. Khan was back in his usual fine form, levelling wild and sensational allegations. He declared before the court that efforts were being made to render Sushil insane so he would not be able to disclose any details about VIPs during his trial. This, he said, was the reason for the Tihar Jail authorities keeping him in the high security section, where he could not talk with anyone. '[The authorities] want him to lose his mental balance,' he said, 'which amounts to serious interference in a fair trial.'[172]

There was, of course, no mention of unnecessary delays, false allegations and gratuitous complaints from the defendant – not to mention witness-tampering. We were to continually encounter these and other disruptions as the proceedings continued.

In court on 18 January, Judge S.L. Khanna's patience was beginning to fray. In deciding on Sushil's complaints regarding his treatment in prison, he gave vent to his frustration at the wild allegations. In his sixteen-page order, he stated that Sushil 'makes a mountain of an ant hill' and 'smells conspiracy in every move made by any authority and apprehends danger to his life.'[173] While directing the jail superintendent to house Sushil in a well-lit cell with drinking water and electricity, he noted that Sushil had not been deprived of his rights in jail. Judge Khanna stated that the only difference between the high security ward and the ward in which he had been kept initially, was the ward's level of security, and that it was guarded by Tamil Nadu Special Police personnel.

On the morning of 23 January, Bhagat's replacement, Senior Advocate R.K. Anand, accompanied by advocates I.U. Khan and Abdul Samat, called on the judge to inform him of his appointment as senior counsel for Sushil. He said he would need at least a month to study the documents relating to the case. At this stage, Sushil's earlier plea that all records from Doordarshan, Zee TV, Star TV and Jain TV be called for, was considered by the judge. Inspector Niranjan Singh submitted to the court that 'The right to know has come to be well recognised as a perfect right in this era and the media is doing its duty.' The plea was rightly disposed of. It was, after all, just another desperate tactic of a desperate man.

Sushil's selection of R.K. Anand to replace K.G. Bhagat clearly evinced his determination to fight the case. Ram Kumar Anand was a greatly respected, high-profile lawyer, whose celebrated career included successfully defending three consecutive prime ministers of India. He was affiliated to the Congress party and would be elected to the Rajya Sabha in 2000, as a Congress member from the state of Jharkhand. He had earlier failed in his attempt to win a seat from Haryana. Later, he made an abortive bid on a Congress ticket for the Lok Sabha seat of South Delhi in the 2004 general elections. In more recent times, he unsuccessfully contested the 2014 elections for the Faridabad constituency, as an Indian National Lok Dal

(INLD) candidate. One can only speculate that Anand's services were secured for Sushil through his political connections.

While R.K. Anand and I.U. Khan made a formidable team in the tandoor murder defence, it seems their fates were also connected in another way. More than a decade later, their careers would be marred by a television sting operation. Video evidence against them led to criminal charges. On 21 August 2008, the Delhi High Court found both of them guilty of obstructing the administration of justice.

The charges related to a famous hit-and-run case later known as the 1999 Delhi hit-and-run case or the BMW hit-and-run case, in which I.U. Khan was the public prosecutor and R.K. Anand the defence lawyer. Incredibly, the video evidence suggested both had attempted to bribe a witness in favour of the main defendant in the case, Sanjeev Nanda. Nanda was the grandson of the retired admiral and chief of naval staff, S.M. Nanda.[174]

Sanjeev Nanda had mowed down seven people, including three policemen, with his BMW at a police checkpoint on Lodhi Road, early on the morning of 10 January 1999. He had then fled the scene in his car along with some friends. Evidence suggested the BMW had been travelling at speeds in the vicinity of 130 km per hour. Six of the seven victims of the accident perished.

The conviction against I.U. Khan in this sordid episode was later overturned in the Supreme Court, but the court noted he had behaved improperly. R.K. Anand was not so lucky, though he escaped a jail term.

All this lay more than a decade ahead for Anand and Khan. At the time of the tandoor murder case, they were practising law with all the confidence and verve of two senior advocates at the top of their profession. For the prosecution, this meant contending with cunning legal posturing, endless arguments on procedural issues and a range of tactics designed to stymie the trial.

R.K. Anand would not disappoint Sharma. When he first appeared before Sessions Judge S.L. Khanna's court on 6 February, he let fly a salvo of arguments against the case, the police and the media. He questioned police motives, saying the police had 'fixed' Sushil and then collected evidence. He raised questions about the identity of the two men Constable Kunju had seen in the Bagiya at the time of his discovery and accused journalists of virtually holding a parallel trial in the case.

Bizarrely, R.K. Anand also questioned the whereabouts of Naina Sahni's body, asking why the magistrate's permission had not been sought for its disposal. This prompted an angry riposte from Special Public Prosecutor A.P. Ahluwalia. Anand then went on to allege that various politicians' statements had affected the investigation, adding that an additional commissioner would not usually leave the state to apprehend a suspect. He was, of course, referring to my trip to Bangalore to bring Sushil back to Delhi.

Some further comments R.K. Anand made – about the politicisation of the case – were closer to the truth. 'The [BJP Opposition] want to make it an issue during the coming elections. The Congress wants to be rid of [Sushil]. And the Janata Dal has even awarded some witnesses.'[175]

Sushil's new advocate topped off his entry into the fray with a petition to initiate contempt proceedings against various newspapers. This was for publishing articles allegedly prejudicial to his client receiving a fair trial. The petition took up arguments made by his predecessor Bhagat, who had maintained that there was a hostile atmosphere against Sushil which would hamper a fair trial for him. R.K. Anand quoted US guidelines for acceptable press coverage before and during trials.

In America, verdicts are usually handed down by a jury and trial judges and prosecutors sometimes hold elected offices. They do not shun publicity, and it appears they cannot afford to ignore public opinion. In certain high-profile cases, publicity and extensive press coverage may thus sometimes influence the course of justice.

In India, though, judges alone decide cases, for reasons discussed earlier, and judges, being legal professionals, are far less likely to be swayed by adverse media coverage than juries. Moreover, judges in

India do not contest elections for higher courts but are elevated to their posts by a panel of senior judges. They are thus less likely to be influenced by public opinion than their American counterparts.

Judge S.L. Khanna seemed none too impressed with R.K. Anand's fairly speculative argument citing foreign reporting practice, and summarily dismissed his petition on 8 February.

Anand and Khan were far from finished. They simply took their pleas to the High Court, where they hoped for a more sympathetic hearing. On 20 February, they argued their petition before Justice Usha Mehra. Ultimately, they would fare little better with Justice Mehra than with Judge Khanna. But they managed to use this action to delay the continuing court discussion on the charges against Sushil. When the additional sessions judge would not brook any further delay, the defence team simply changed tactics.

Judge S.L. Khanna posted the case to 4 March, so the court could conclude arguments on the matter of Sushil receiving a fair trial, which Senior Advocate K.G. Bhagat had raised before his unexpected demise. R.K. Anand then told the court that he was simply unable to proceed. He was unprepared, he said, having been instructed by Sushil not to argue the matter before the High Court decided on the writ. With months of toing-and-froing having passed, Judge S.L. Khanna stood firm with 4 March as the next hearing date.

When the day arrived, we would see that Sushil and his advocates had other ideas about the matter, and they had no qualms about orchestrating the situation to suit their needs. First, assisting defence advocate O.P. Sharma made a prayer for an adjournment. The court promptly denied the request. At this point, the lock-up[176] supervisor informed the court that Sushil had 'fainted' in the lock-up and had been moved to Ram Manohar Lohia Hospital. Judge S.L. Khanna ordered that he be brought back to the court after a check-up and treatment, and directed that the court reconvene at 3 p.m.

When Sushil was not produced at 3 p.m., the lock-up supervisor was asked to make inquiries at the hospital about his condition. The matter was taken up again at 3.30 p.m., when the court was told that

Sushil was being administered glucose intravenously, and was only likely to be discharged after 4.30 p.m. The court adjourned the case to 6 March. It was an exercise which could only have been planned by Sushil with his advocates' connivance.

It did not finish there. On 6 March, while all the other defendants appeared, the lock-up supervisor informed the court that Sushil had been admitted to Bara Hindu Rao Hospital. With this, the case was adjourned again.

On 8 March, Sushil took centre stage and addressed the court himself. He told Judge Khanna that his counsel was busy in the High Court, where his criminal writ was being heard in the afternoon. The court adjourned the trial to 18 March 'in the interest of justice'.

Sushil's junior advocate I.D. Rana made an application for adjournment again on 18 March, because 'arguments in the criminal writ petition are continuing in the High Court'. Despite the prosecution vehemently opposing the application, the case was adjourned to 27 March.

Sushil made a further application for adjournment on 27 March on grounds that orders on the writ petition in the High Court had been reserved. The court recorded that it was convinced now of the dilatory tactics of the accused, especially since the High Court had not stayed the proceedings in the lower court. The trial court ruled that as no arguments had been presented, it was taken that the charges framed against Sushil were conceded. The court now asked the prosecution to file its own submissions on the issue on 29 March.

On 29 March, yet another application was moved on behalf of Sushil, alleging that the police investigation was incomplete 'because the identity of the second person near the tandoor in the prosecution story has not been established'. It presented a statement I had allegedly made to the media – that two persons were accosted by the police at the Bagiya on 2 July.

The court held that it was not its job to reinvigorate the investigation, and that it was for the prosecution to ensure it had a foolproof case. Judge S.L Khanna saw through the application as yet another tactic to justify an adjournment and prolong the trial. He recorded that 'the accused cannot thus be allowed to circumvent the law by moving such frivolous applications'.

Judge Khanna did, however, allow Sushil's counsel to present arguments against the charges – despite having already ruled on the issue. I.U. Khan now challenged the charges against Sushil with a theatrical court performance that would make O.J. Simpson's winning defence seem bland. The scenarios Khan presented were far-fetched, to put it mildly, and at times verged on surreal. His long-winded oration would carry over to a hearing on 18 April and continue on 2 May.

Khan declared the tandoor murder a 'blind murder': There was not an iota of evidence to link the accused to the killing, he maintained, as there was neither an eyewitness nor a motive for the crime. He stated that even Naina's parents had no complaint against Sushil and believed in his innocence.[177] Khan submitted that Sushil was a man of simple habits, a vegetarian and a teetotaller. Naina was fun-loving, given to drinking and partying.

He then presented alternate scenarios in the hope that the charges might be undermined. First, he turned his attention to the torn letter that investigating officers had retrieved from the wastepaper basket in the Mandir Marg apartment on 4 July. He said that 'each and every word' of the letter indicated that Naina had committed suicide. He further asserted that it had been written in her husband's absence on 2 July, because 'one cleans the house every day … Had it been written some other day, then one would not have found the torn pieces there.'[178]

I.U. Khan very cleverly used the prosecution's own evidence to bolster his argument. He quoted Matloob, whom he described as a 'villain', swearing in his deposition that Naina was depressed and crying on the evening of 2 July. He then seized on the prosecution's claim that Naina had been feeling 'suffocated' by her marriage: 'What more is required for a woman to commit suicide – suffocation, tension and a licensed weapon available in her house?'[179] Never mind that suicide would have been physically impossible, given Naina's two grievous gunshot injuries, either of which would have killed or incapacitated her.

Far more believable was Khan's second scenario. Khan suggested that Naina had been carrying on an affair with Matloob, even after her marriage to Sushil, and this had upset Sushil. 'No husband will accept a wife who has an extramarital affair,' Khan said. He added that Naina had even gone to Bombay accompanied by Matloob and was planning to migrate to Australia. A sensitive man, Sushil may have overreacted to such developments.

On that fateful day, he said, Sushil and Naina had a heated argument about her affair with Matloob and her trip to Bombay. There was a scuffle, during which Naina might have sustained firearm injuries leading to her death. Blaming the victim, Khan said, 'Sometimes a crime is committed because of the situation created by the other party.'

This second scenario was a crafty submission: It relied on the very evidence upon which the prosecution account of events stood. While Khan here conceded homicide, it was manslaughter, or non-culpable homicide, which engenders very different treatment and penalties under the law.

Additional Sessions Judge S.L. Khanna adjourned the case to 2 May, when he would hear the prosecution submissions in response to I.U. Khan's arguments against the charges proceeding to trial. May began badly for Sushil's case, with Justice Usha Mehra dismissing his petition to the High Court on the first day of the month. Judge Khanna heard the prosecution counsel A.P. Ahluwalia's often scathing responses to I.U. Khan's arguments on 2 May. A week later, he predictably made his order that the charges proceed to trial. On 9 June, the charges were confirmed, and the first trial hearing was set for 9 July.

The trial was transferred to the court of Additional Sessions Judge G.P. Thareja, then after a few hearings, back to Additional Sessions Judge S.L. Khanna on 25 July. Sushil's counsel objected –

probably because Sushil felt he would get a more sympathetic hearing from Thareja – and it finally rested back in Judge G.P. Thareja's court.

The new presiding judge G.P. Thareja was one of the last of a long string of colourful characters to play a major role in the case. Hailing from Kanpur, Uttar Pradesh, he was an experienced judge, having joined the Delhi Judicial Service in 1972. Thareja was diminutive in stature and soft-spoken in private. But when he sat at the bench, he underwent something of a transformation, becoming altogether larger in demeanour and expression. While he was regarded as an unconventional jurist, his earnest approach to his duties and his integrity were renowned in the legal fraternity.

Be that as it may, Gyan Prakash Thareja struck me as the kind of man who took himself rather too seriously. The manner in which he went about his work – recording his thoughts meticulously and sermonising – suggested a desire to be remembered as extraordinary. He was equally apt to air his views with a flourish which, as events would demonstrate, bordered on impetuousness. His disapproval of Ahluwalia's appointment to the case would trouble the prosecution too.

As it turned out, Additional Sessions Judge Gyan Prakash Thareja would get a lot of public attention, but perhaps not in the way he might have wished. Before he could render a judgement in the tandoor case, his decision in another high-profile murder case would provoke a public uproar and inspire speeches in the Lok Sabha, calling for justice. This well-meaning, thoughtful judge would eventually be called out by the Superior Court for 'mauling' justice with a 'perverse' decision.

More on that later.

From the very outset, the new judge showed he meant business. When he took up the case on 8 July, counsel I.U. Khan immediately presented with a new delaying tactic, and Thareja quickly proved his mettle.

In March that very year, Khan said, the Supreme Court had

directed the constitution of ten Additional Sessions Courts exclusively for trying 880 murder cases. These cases were to be tried within six months. He claimed that the tandoor murder case was not among those 880 listed for a speedy trial. He pointed out that in many of those cases, the alleged offenders had been languishing in jail for many years, but their trials were being overlooked. Why, he asked, was preference being given to the tandoor murder case and not to these other pending cases?

Thareja gave short shrift to Khan on this fairly transparent attempt to delay Sushil's trial. He informed him, nonetheless, that the convenience of counsel was always taken into consideration in fixing court dates. He asked for the counsel's cooperation, as officers of the court, to assist in the administration of speedy justice. Finally, conceding something to their wishes, he fixed the next hearing for 9 August. Thareja then directed that proceedings should continue and started examining witnesses.

On 9 August, the hearing was due to commence in the morning, but Judge Thareja felt compelled to postpone the hearing until the afternoon for the convenience of the defence counsel. When the case was taken up again at 2 p.m., Special Public Prosecutor Ahluwalia brought to the notice of the court Sushil's attempts to intimidate and influence witnesses.

It must be said that neither the police nor the prosecution expected anything less from Sushil Sharma. As much as bribery, intimidation had been his stock-in-trade as a political fixer long before the murder. In India, attempting to suborn or intimidate witnesses is de rigueur for a certain class of offender. We would have been utterly dumbfounded had Sushil meekly submitted himself to his fate and run an honest, ethical defence in court.

19

Wheels of Justice

After more than a year of legal wrangling and with the trial hardly having begun, the nonsense in court, and outside it, continued. Sushil kept plotting from inside Tihar Jail's high-security Ward 5 cell. While much of what he threw at the prosecution was anticipated, some of his manoeuvres were especially inventive.

For instance, just as the trial got underway, he launched an audacious argument that would have been unlikely to gain traction in most judges' courts. On 9 August, he moved an application for appointment of a defence counsel at the State's expense, on grounds of his inability to afford his own counsel. His parents, he submitted, were extremely poor, and expenses for his father's medical treatment had depleted the family's resources. His incarceration and efforts to defend himself against false charges had impoverished him too, and this necessitated that the court appoint a defence counsel for him.

Nobody was the least convinced by Sushil's claims. But it was the sheer effrontery of his demand that galled. Sushil refused to be represented by anyone from the court's list of amici curiae.[180] Instead, he submitted to the court the names of three senior advocates – Rajinder Singh, a senior counsel from Jabalpur, B.L. Kalra and K.K. Sood, both counsels from Delhi – and asked to be represented by any of these advocates at government expense. He should, he argued, only be represented by an advocate of equal standing to the special public prosecutor.

It was a bold-faced appeal for 'fairness' which did not have the backing of legal precedent and seemed all but destined to fail. Special Public Prosecutor Ahluwalia was scandalised and argued passionately against Sushil's plea. Strangely though, after a string of setbacks, Sushil found a sympathetic ear in Judge Thareja. Instead of summarily dismissing this arrogant and rather hopeful submission as most other judges would have, Thareja gave it his in-principle agreement.

Astoundingly, Sushil would be represented by the advocate of his choice, K.K. Sood, who would receive the same rate of remuneration as the special public prosecutor. This followed months of deliberation, during which Thareja probed the special public prosecutor's appointment, K.K. Sood unsuccessfully postured for a junior to assist him, and the court heard arguments over Sushil's financial status.

Judge Thareja was more than accommodating in this matter, even indulgent. His decision was made despite the government tendering evidence that Sushil was the owner of a plot of land in Gurgaon. In reply, Sushil had claimed, rather too conveniently, that he had sold the land to one of his friends, Supreme Court advocate Suhail Siddiqui of Chaman Ganj, Kanpur. The money from the sale, he said, had been invested in his hotel business. He was yet to help his friend transfer the plot to his name. Sushil, it must be said, always had a glib reply or explanation for any unfavourable truth.

In the meantime, on 21 August, the Supreme Court had handed down an order in which Sushil's request for transfer of the case out of Delhi was dismissed. The apex court observed that 'the learned trial court, which is master of the orderly conduct of the court proceedings, shall take all such measures as are necessary to enforce conditions for free and fair functioning of the court.'

A year and a half after the crime, there had been seventy-six hearing dates in the trial court alone, and only two witnesses had given evidence in court. Worse, the next few months were to be taken up with some fairly ritualised dithering over files. It began when K.K. Sood asked to be provided with fresh copies of the case papers.

Judge Thareja initially denied his request, on the basis that Sushil's former counsel Khan had already been provided the court documents. But after I.U. Khan's office failed to provide the files, even after a court order was passed demanding that he surrender them to Sood, Thareja relented. This small, practical issue took up a number of court appearances and consumed three months – half the time allotted for a full murder trial in a fast-track court.

The delays continued, throughout. Countless times, the court adjourned to the afternoon or to another date simply because advocate K.K. Sood failed to appear. Sometimes, he would send his junior to convey his inability to attend. Other times, he would just play truant. The court staff, other counsel, witnesses – everyone would be sent home, because this one man had failed to attend the hearing. All the while, Judge Thareja would tut-tut on the court record about delays, yet take no action to bring the errant counsel into line.

He would not, however, be quite so accommodating with Special Public Prosecutor Ahluwalia, who was, in comparison, the epitome of diligence. Sometime in the next year, Ahluwalia told the court that he would not be available between 6 April and 24 April, as he had to travel to Bahrain for compelling reasons. He asked for an adjournment of proceedings until he returned. Judge Thareja was obdurate in his rejection of Ahluwalia's request and insisted on posting the case on those very days when he knew he would be absent. He almost laughably observed that 'It is necessary ultimately to write where the delay lies in the judicial process.' Indeed.

Other adjournments would be given for far less compelling reasons than absent counsel. Numerous strikes by the Delhi Bar Association would play their part in delaying the case. There were also the usual other difficulties, such as witnesses legitimately failing to attend due to illness. That there were witnesses who failed to attend court without any plausible reason is another matter. But more on that later.

Sometimes, it must be said, it was hard to comprehend why the court adjourned a hearing at all. On 4 September 1997, no one was examined, even though one witness was summoned and was waiting in court. The court was convened, with court staff, the judge, advocates and a witness – all bar the witness at State expense – when it decided not to do its duty for the day. Judge Thareja did not feel the need to justify this folly, other than to record that 'no other witness is present today as it was supposed [sic] that this witness was likely to take time …'.[181] Perhaps the Delhi Bar had a social engagement that day.

Plain disorganisation was to take its toll on the judicial process too. On 8 June, in the absence of K.K. Sood, Judge Thareja decided to let counsel for Ram Prakash and Rishi Raj cross-examine K.K. Tuli, the general manager of Ashok Yatri Niwas. Both promptly declined, as they had no questions for him. Sood's junior then told the court that Sood would cross-examine witnesses only on the next fixed court date, which was 9 June. The court recorded that 'judicial time has been wasted for nothing'. Clearly, a brief discussion between the ahlmad[182] and counsel beforehand would have averted this situation.

Sharma never gave up his extracurricular legal battles, however fruitless they seemed, and this, too, inevitably delayed proceedings. On 29 March 1997, he moved an interim bail application in the Delhi High Court, which was quickly declined by Justice J.K. Mehra.

The following months, at least, would see our star witness depose. After Nisha and Philip, the performers at the Bagiya, Head Constable Abdul Nazeer Kunju gave evidence, followed by Home Guard Chander Pal, Anaro Devi the vegetable vendor, K.K. Tuli and Head Constable Majid Khan.

Of all the witnesses, Kunju's testimony was crucial for the case. If the defence managed to undermine his statement made on the night of the crime, the prosecution would face grave difficulties, despite the mass of circumstantial evidence against Sharma.

Kunju's time in the Additional Sessions Court was to be a marathon – and he did not just face pressure from the counsel. Shockingly, Sushil attempted to bribe him at his first court appearance.[183]

Kunju had already withstood a great deal of pressure from Sushil – indirectly, at least. He had shrugged off a number of death threats and ignored the shady-looking characters who got on the bus with him when he was on his way to work. A calm, unflappable man, Kunju took all these moves in his stride, even if they it unnerved his family.

Nonetheless, when he was waiting outside the courtroom on the morning of 8 April 1997, he was flabbergasted when Sushil approached him as he was being led into the court.

'I'll give you ten lakhs if you change your statement. Say you saw Matloob there,' Sushil said, calmly and pointedly.[184]

'My statement is in the FIR. I won't change it,' Kunju replied.

It is hard to imagine that Sushil truly thought Kunju would succumb to his boldfaced approach. Perhaps he just wanted to enjoy Kunju's reaction and throw him off balance. But he would see little for his effort.

Head Constable Abdul Nazeer Kunju deposed clearly and did not waver in the face of intense cross-examination, despite the defence counsel's concerted efforts to overawe and discredit him and pick holes in his deposition. He paid little heed to the menacing stares Sushil's thugs in the gallery cast at him throughout. Although we knew Kunju to be unshakeable, we were as relieved as he was when his cross-examination was over. Kunju managed to hold firm on the witness stand for no less than forty-five appearances, through the grilling of eight defence counsels.

The witnesses who followed Kunju managed to hold firm too. But with their testimony, we began to see some of Sushil's more sinister behaviour, which would feature throughout the trial.

Sushil was among the more flamboyant criminals I have encountered, and he knew how to put on a show. His outfit, his manner in the courtroom and his gestures were part of a disturbing, carefully stage-managed performance during the trial. It seemed to have its effect.

He was almost invariably dressed in a white kurta pyjama, which in itself was significant. For most Indians, a white kurta pyjama may be homewear, but in public life it is the garb of a leader – an intimidating garment. By wearing it, Sushil was declaring that despite being in the dock, he was still powerful, and still considered himself a leader. Witnesses could only have felt unnerved by his confident presentation in the courtroom.

Then there were the mind games and other antics. Sushil would make use of calculated gestures and drama in an attempt to dominate the courtroom – although he was the criminal in the dock. Before the judge arrived, he would stare balefully at the ahlmad and stenographer and any witness present. On the way to the dock, he would walk slowly and deliberately past the seated court staff, trailing his hand along the bench in front of them. If there was a file there, he would sometimes flip it in front of them.

For law enforcement professionals, enduring such shenanigans is routine. Apart from overt violence, this is the usual manner in which most criminals hold sway, exert their control over people. But while the police become inured to all manner of mind games and intimidation, for lay prosecution witnesses it is quite another matter. The court environment itself is intimidating, and they face a grilling by the defence counsel, who will often try, by any means, to demoralise them on the stand. Contending with the mind games of a criminal on top of such tribulations can make court appearances a truly harrowing experience.

One of Sushil's trademark gestures was to place his hand in his kurta pocket in sight of a witness, folding his three fingers into his palm and holding his index finger straight and thumb erect in the shape of a pistol. He would then gaze intently at the witness, pressing his hand out against the garment so the shape of his hand was clearly visible.

It sounds puerile, a stunt befitting a bullying schoolboy. But for the witnesses, the message was clear: with this simple gesture, Sushil was signalling his murderous intent towards them. It was all the more alarming because they suspected he had already killed with a pistol – while wearing a similar outfit.

Sushil would, of course, have denied that he was even making such a gesture. Had he been questioned, he would doubtless have maintained that he simply had his hand in his pocket.

Sushil's background machinations were to have their effect on witnesses, as we would soon discover. But more worrying still was the court's pitiful functioning. It seemed that the system just couldn't get out of its own way to conduct a trial with any semblance of efficiency.

More than two years after the commission of the tandoor murder, only a handful of the ninety-nine witnesses had deposed. The defence had made every effort to delay and frustrate the trial at every juncture, and the defendant had proved himself litigious in the extreme. The wheels of justice were turning slowly, at times exceedingly slowly.

20

On With the Motley

Keshav Kumar had done a deal with the devil, and the devil for him was Sushil Sharma. From the moment he committed to helping his boss's desperate attempt to rid himself of Naina Sahni's body, Keshav's fate was bound to Sushil's. And the legal wrangling and courtroom grandstanding Sushil indulged in was doing nothing for Keshav. As the murder trial limped past its second year, every month wasted in pointless legal arguments and posturing was another month Keshav would have to spend in Tihar Jail.

It hardly bears mention that Keshav and Sushil's interests had diverged long ago; indeed, immediately after the grisly discovery at the Bagiya on 2 July 1995. As the drama unfolded, their interests only became more starkly opposed.

Keshav, of course, was facing far less serious charges than Sushil, The charge against him of criminal conspiracy and destroying evidence may have attracted as little as a two- or three-year jail sentence. Sushil, however, was running from a judgement that could very well see him swing from the gallows.

Sushil knew, just as Julio Ribeiro had pointed out, that people forget details with the passage of time and tend to lose interest in a case. He must have felt his best chance of achieving an acquittal lay in impeding the trial's progress. That way, prosecution witnesses might make mistakes on the stand to his advantage.

He may have surmised, too, that failing an acquittal, public outrage over the murder would wane over time, and his sentence might be less harsh. Also, a prolonged trial offered more opportunities for him to approach, suborn and turn witnesses hostile.

In contrast, after a couple of years on remand, guilt or innocence mattered little for Keshav. Notwithstanding the conspiracy charge, he had by August 1997 served a fitting jail sentence for his crime at the Bagiya. But while the court dithered and Sushil and his lawyers ran amok, there was very little he could do except come to terms with his incarceration.

After the drugging episode, Keshav was not content to trust his safety to the police and prison officials. From criminal intelligence sources within the jail, we got wind that before long, he sought the protection of a don in the jail: the feared Uttar Pradesh mafia leader, Om Prakash 'Babloo' Srivastava.

Babloo Srivastava was notorious for kidnapping and extortion, and had once been Mumbai kingpin Dawood Ibrahim's right-hand man. Wanted in connection with numerous crimes, Srivastava fled India, but was captured in Singapore. With his Nepalese citizenship of convenience revoked, he was sent back to India to face trial in 1995. At the time of writing, Babloo was in Bareilly Central Jail, serving a life sentence. He has remained criminally active in prison, even reportedly running a kidnapping and extortion racket from within the prison's walls.[185] While there is no indication of Keshav's involvement in Srivastava's racket – which largely involved Babloo's contacts outside jail – gossip abounded that Keshav had become one of this gangster's most trusted men on the inside.

Srivastava's protection would undoubtedly have given Keshav some peace of mind and comfort in the unforgiving jail environment. Srivastava reportedly warned Sushil off Keshav, telling him that Keshav was now his man and to stop threatening him. Under the don's aegis, Keshav was relatively safe in jail, but getting out of jail was another matter entirely. To regain his freedom, Keshav could only hope for bail or a speedy trial, both of which were elusive.

Much hinged on the charge of conspiracy, and Keshav's advocates waged a valiant campaign in court against it. They knew that having the charge for this non-bailable offence dropped was Keshav's best hope of being granted bail.

On 3 August 1995, before Additional Sessions Judge B.S. Choudhury, Keshav's counsel S.K. Duggal argued that the evidence did not support a charge of conspiracy under Section 120B of the Indian Penal Code. The most he could be charged with, Duggal contended, was destruction of evidence under Section 201 of the Indian Penal Code – and this was a bailable offence.

Special Public Prosecutor Ahluwalia held firm in arguing that Keshav was 'an accessory to the crime and not merely involved in the destruction of evidence.'[186] He emphasised Keshav's long discussion with Sushil in the latter's car outside the Bagiya, before the pair had constructed their makeshift funeral pyre. He also submitted that anyone who joined a conspiracy was a party to that conspiracy, regardless of the point at which he joined it.

In response, Duggal railed passionately against the very existence of a conspiracy between Sushil and Keshav. Based on the prosecution's own version of events, he declared, there had been no such conspiracy. If there had been a conspiracy, why would Sushil have taken Naina Sahni's body to the ITO bridge to dump it in the Yamuna before going to the Bagiya? He made a plea for equal treatment for his client and Rishi Raj Rathi, Jai Prakash Pehlwan and Ram Prakash Sachdeva. These three were also facing charges of destroying evidence under Section 201 of the Indian Penal Code. They, Duggal pointed out, had been released on bail.

Never mind that Rathi, Pehlwan and Sachdeva had not hoisted the body of their murdered friend's wife onto a restaurant tandoor and helped burn it with a pile of waste. Or that they hadn't been so obliging as to scurry off to a nearby shop to buy butter with which to ignite the ghastly inferno. Be that as it may, although we felt the case against Keshav for attempting to destroy evidence was almost unassailable, we were far less certain of the conspiracy charge.

S.K. Duggal had earlier claimed Keshav was a 'victim of circumstance'. While some of his other statements were truly risible, such as Keshav not being aware he was burning a corpse, there was perhaps some truth in this one. A combination of the need for him to be tried for conspiracy alongside Sushil, Sushil's scheming and extravagant defence and the court's inefficiency meant Keshav Kumar would suffer an unduly harsh punishment for his crime.

Not that Keshav sat idle through it all. His primary strategy to regain his freedom was to pursue bail applications and he did so prodigiously. His first was denied on 4 August 1995 by Additional Sessions Judge B.S. Choudhury. He filed another application in November, in which he submitted that his daughter was seriously ill, requiring his presence at his home. The application was rejected by Judge S.L. Khanna on 30 November 1995.

Keshav simply would not give up. He made plea after plea for bail, in the Additional Sessions Court, the Delhi High Court and the Supreme Court of India. He submitted before them that he be released for the duration of the trial. At other times, he asked to be granted temporary release to attend a family member's death anniversary ceremony or a wedding or to see his children for one hour. All but one plea he made for temporary release, however, were denied.

The court relented briefly and in dramatic circumstances, very early on. Just as we were pursuing Sushil in Bangalore on 10 July, Keshav was produced before Metropolitan Magistrate Dharam Raj Singh to extend his police remand. In the packed courtroom, a relative carried news to Keshav that capped the worst week of his life. His mother Natho Devi, who had been ailing with terminal cancer in a Noida nursing home, had passed away that morning.

Upon hearing the news, Keshav collapsed, then said, '*Mujhe kya ho gaya! Inhone meri maa ko maar diya, ab mere baap ko marenge. Sushil Sharma, mein tujhe nahin chhodunga. Yeh log mere parivar ko khatam kar denge* (What has happened to me! They have killed my mother. Now they will kill my father. Sushil Sharma, I will not let you get away. These people will destroy my family)'.[187]

Natho Devi's demise had very likely been hastened by the shock of her son's arrest and the magistrate was moved by Keshav's plight. He directed the police to allow Keshav to attend the cremation and perform his mother's last rites at the same cremation ground that three weeks later would see Naina Sahni's farewell. The prosecution had no objection.

Otherwise, Keshav's pleas for bail fell on unsympathetic ears. Some pleas were rejected ostensibly on grounds that he had not given sufficient notice. Others were denied due to his appeals to the High Court on the matter – that it was sub judice and a lower court should not decide an issue being considered in a higher court. One was rejected in consideration of judicial discipline: that the matter had already been rejected in higher courts and should not be contemplated afresh. The tenor of the various presiding officers in all the courts, though, was consistent regarding Keshav's bail: You cannot burn a murdered woman's body on a tandoor in the middle of the nation's capital and expect to get bail.

With his avenues to even the most temporary freedom barred, Keshav began to plead for a speedy trial. This perhaps evinced his state of desperation rather than any confidence that his plea would actually help his cause. Having seen the dawdling pace of business in the Additional Sessions Court, he must have assumed it could not make matters any worse. Nevertheless, Judge Thareja noted his plea on 11 October 1996 in court.

The continuing adjournments and delays showed a speedy trial was as vain a hope for Keshav as making bail. As the trial wore on, he reluctantly made Tihar Jail his home, as Sushil and countless other inmates have since it opened in 1957.

The largest jail complex in the subcontinent, Tihar Jail is located seven kilometres from Chanakyapuri, to the west of New Delhi. It is chronically overcrowded, routinely accommodating well in excess of double its sanctioned capacity of 5,200 prisoners. Corruption is rife, too: International serial killer Charles Sobhraj managed in March 1986 to bribe his way to freedom. Collusion between wardens and prisoners, a thriving trade in contraband and regular gang wars – not to mention a concrete slab for a bed – have made Tihar Jail no easy place for all but the most hardened criminals to survive.

Little wonder Keshav Kumar made so many bids for freedom.

⚖

There are many ways in which a witness can turn hostile, and in thirty-five years in law enforcement, I have seen and heard them all. In India, witnesses turning hostile during trial is far from uncommon. Indeed, it is almost routine. What set the witness-tampering in the tandoor case apart is the scale on which it occurred. Of the ninety-nine witnesses the prosecution listed, eighteen turned hostile.

Of course, many of the witnesses who turned hostile were fairly inconsequential for the prosecution's case: they may, such as the videowala, have simply confirmed a delivery to Naina Sahni on the fateful day. But the fact that Sushil Sharma apparently managed from inside a high-security cell in Tihar Jail to suborn or frighten eighteen witnesses says much of the clout he still wielded. Or at least the clout he wielded over the less savoury elements of society.

One of the first indications in court that witness-tampering would seriously disrupt the trial came in September 1997. On 11 September, no witnesses turned up court, despite summons. The court issued a rather ingenuous admonition that any notice of inability to attend should be made well in advance, so that the court would know when a witness was going to be available for evidence. Judge Thareja directed that a bond of ₹500 be taken from each witness who was served a summons to ensure their attendance.

Sushil must have chuckled at this. Five hundred rupees bought much more in the 1990s than it does now, but it could still hardly inspire anyone to do something against his conscience or better judgement. Sushil would surely have been willing to add a zero or two to that amount so that a witness would not attend court. And evidently, he did just that.

Later in the trial, one particular witness became suddenly and inexplicably unavailable. And just as inexplicably, his impoverished family members suddenly found themselves with sufficient funds to drill a new borewell on their property. Neighbours told police of a group of men from Delhi visiting the family shortly before they sank the well.

On 24 September 1997, both witnesses summoned, Ashok Yatri Niwas hotel guard Mahesh Prasad and security supervisor Rajiv Thakur, failed to appear. The prosecution submitted to the court that Mahesh could not be located in his village. Thakur, who had been served with a summons, also failed to be present in court – despite having furnished a bond of ₹500.

Judge Thareja did not take the matter lightly. He ordered the forfeiture of Thakur's bond and directed that a non-bailable warrant be issued against him. He then issued a notice[188] to Thakur to show cause why a penalty of ₹500 may not be imposed on him for his failure to appear on summons. He criticised the prosecution, too, for the lack of evidence recorded on two consecutive hearings. He then directed that five witnesses be summoned for the next court date against a bond of ₹500 each and fixed the next hearing date for 3 November 1997.

Surely, Judge Thareja's frustration was misdirected, especially seeing that the prosecution had already reported instances of Sushil approaching witnesses at the court complex. Special Public Prosecutor Ahluwalia could hardly be responsible for witnesses turning hostile and the resultant waste of time.

Aside from witnesses ignoring summonses, another troubling sign was the palpable change in the attitude of witnesses who were actually deposing. Anaro Devi had previously been firm and quite prepared to testify, but on the day she was to give evidence, she made a fuss and told the court she was not feeling well. The court recorded that she appeared hale and hearty and directed her to depose. Judge Thareja also deemed it appropriate to record that Anaro gave perfectly rational answers to counsel's questions.

Perhaps Anaro felt intimidated facing Sushil in court. It may well be that threats against her and her family weighed on her as she was about to give evidence in court. Anaro would later tell reporters that after threatening her, Sushil had offered her two lakh rupees to leave Delhi.[189] She and her family received police protection for some two years after the night of the tandoor murder – well after her giving evidence.

In any event, the other witness who had been summoned to give testimony on 3 November, Naginder Nath Gupta, failed to attend court. And hotel guard Mahesh Prasad had, it seemed, simply disappeared. When he finally emerged, late in the trial, it was to make outlandish claims in court, contrary to common sense as well as his own previous statement and the prosecution case.

An unmistakeable pattern was beginning to emerge, but Judge Thareja seemed oblivious to it. Exhibiting incredible naïvety, he recorded that the prosecution did not appear serious about producing its witnesses.

He could not, however, ignore the witness-tampering issue for long. On 13 November, Ahluwalia informed the court that he did not want to record the evidence of witnesses Pradeep Sharma and Jagdish Taneja, as they had been won over by the defence.

The next witness was Matloob Karim, who was made of sterner stuff and determined to give evidence. He was scheduled to begin his testimony on 19 November, but the Delhi Bar passed a resolution to abstain from work that day. Curiously, Sushil assured the court that his counsel would attend despite the resolution and he sought a hearing in the afternoon.

Perhaps Sushil could not contain his anxiety and compelled his advocate to attend so that he could hear his rival's evidence. Matloob's testimony could only be damning, Sushil knew, and much rested on his account of Naina and Sushil's ill-fated relationship. Incidentally, the only other witness who could offer the court much insight into the couple's habits and tribulations was Ram Niwas Dubey, Sushil's peon and cook. We would find Dubey almost as elusive as the hotel guard, Mahesh Prasad.

Matloob giving evidence would turn into a trial in itself. His deposition began on the afternoon of 19 November 1997. His cross-examination was finally completed on 6 May the following year. His testimony consumed nearly six months of court time. A fast-track court should, according to the Supreme Court, have completed the entire trial in the time it took to examine this one witness.

In the intervening period, the trial's progress was impeded by the judge taking leave, Sushil's advocate K.K. Sood's preoccupation with other matters (and Judge Thareja's indulgence), the court failing to convene, and protracted legal arguments.

When the opportunity presented itself, though, Judge Thareja waxed eloquent, relishing his chance to record his thoughts for posterity. On 10 December, he wrote a commentary likening a trial to a 'dark room' where 'light is to be thrown into ... to trace the elements of facts through ocular testimony of witnesses in examination-in-chief, cross-examination and re-examination.'

There were other instances of judicial whimsy. Inexplicably, Judge Thareja granted permission to Jai Prakash Pehlwan to temporarily leave the country.

This kind of indulgence was almost unheard of. Jai Prakash had been charged with a serious crime and despite the prosecution not pursuing the charge, he should certainly not have been allowed to travel overseas. Nonetheless, the pehlwan was allowed to travel to Cairo so that he could participate in the grand prix Ibrahim Mustafa Freestyle and Greco-Roman style Wrestling Tournament. This was subject to his furnishing an undertaking to the court that he would leave the country on 25 April 1998 and return by 5 May. In the interim, his lawyer Khanna would represent him at the hearings.

The progress of the murder trial was practically glacial for the following two years. Sushil and Keshav moved one application after another, even as the evidence of peripheral witnesses was recorded.

The proceedings continued to be marred by a campaign of dirty tricks, quite apart from witness-tampering. Files, exhibits and crucial X-rays seemed to disappear from the court records. I am constrained by libel laws not to apportion blame here. Needless to say, it is an unavoidable truth about the Indian judicial system that such occurrences are all but routine.

The X-rays of Naina Sahni's body are a case in point. When the radiologist was asked to identify the X-ray plates, they were found missing from the court record. When the court ahlmad failed to trace them, Sushil's counsel argued vehemently that no X-ray had been taken and no bullets had been recovered from the body. Naturally, he made mention of Dr Sarangi's abortive post-mortem, which stated that there was no evidence of firearm injuries on Naina Sahni's body. The bullets, he claimed, were planted by the police to frame his client.

The court made it Inspector Niranjan's responsibility to find the X-rays, which was more than a little unfair, given that they had been 'lost' by the court staff. The case record had travelled to several courts: the committal courts of magistrates Dharam Raj Singh and V.K. Maheshwari, then to the Additional Sessions Courts of S.L. Khanna, G.P. Thareja and V.K. Jain, then to the High Court in connection with various petitions and the Supreme Court in bail matters. A search had to be conducted at all these premises. But still, the X-rays could not be traced.

Eventually, the index of papers annexed to the charge sheet was checked, and it revealed clearly that the X-ray plates had been received by the committal court's ahlmad. The judge was apprised of this and, on his further directions, Niranjan managed to locate the X-ray plates in the former courtroom of Additional Sessions Judge S.L. Khanna.

Miscreants acting on Sushil's behest had other, more inventive, ways of disrupting the trial. During Niranjan's cross-examination, he was asked to identify Sushil's briefcase, which had been seized from the Pai Vihar Hotel in Bangalore. Niranjan was taken aback: he could not recognise the briefcase. Another briefcase had been substituted for Sushil's. Niranjan was forced to hastily seek an adjournment to investigate the matter and the ahlmad could only locate the correct briefcase the following day.

Despite all these setbacks, the trial was moving inexorably against Sushil Sharma. In an act that was born of desperation rather than contrition, Keshav finally deposed on 2 November 1998, confessing to his involvement in the burning of Naina Sahni's body. It was a massive blow to Sushil's defence, and prison sources spoke of him losing hope afterwards.

This long-overdue move on Keshav's part would do little for his prospects of freedom, however. Keshav's statement was clear and his final counsel for the trial, V.K. Ohri, had made necessary arrangements with the special public prosecutor for the charge of conspiracy to be dropped. Having heard his repeated pleas of innocence for the preceding years though, Judge Thareja was none too impressed with Keshav's belated admission of guilt. He led Keshav into a judicial trap that the less experienced man could never have seen.

Judge Thareja asked Keshav why he had decided to make a statement admitting to his knowing involvement in burning Naina Sahni's corpse after his earlier claims of innocence. The special public prosecutor had told him, Keshav said frankly, that he would be allowed bail after he made his statement. Judge Thareja immediately ruled the statement inadmissible – at least for the moment– on grounds that it had been induced.

Judge Thareja's decision here seems to have been as much against Special Public Prosecutor Ahluwalia as Keshav, but it was Keshav who suffered. The trial continued its slow grind through the Additional Sessions Court and he remained in Tihar Jail.

The trial's abysmal progress was duly noted by the higher courts, which made at least some effort to ameliorate the situation. On 11 November 1999, while disposing of one of Sushil's numerous writs to superior courts, Justice Cyriac Joseph of the Delhi High Court directed the Sessions Court to conclude the trial within six months.

Passing a court order in India is one thing. Having it executed is another – even when it is a High Court order directing officers of a lower court.

Justice Cyriac Joseph's court order had no effect whatsoever. There was no progress in the trial between November 1999 and March 2000, thanks to 'amicus curiae' K.K. Sood, who frequently did not appear for one reason or the other. In the meantime, Judge Thareja was transferred from Patiala House to Tis Hazari as additional rent controller – something of a demotion, but more on that later – and replaced by Judge V.K. Jain.

Sharma moved a writ in the Delhi High Court on 28 November 1999, pleading that Judge Thareja continue trying his case. His advocate O.P. Sharma submitted a writ the following day for a stay of proceedings in the trial until Sushil's writ was decided. Essentially, Sushil was asking that the higher court transfer the trial to a civil judge with no powers to try criminal matters. One must say, such things only happen in India.

Astonishingly, Sushil's plea was successful. On 17 April, Justice R.C. Chopra of the Delhi High Court passed an order transferring the case from the court of Additional Sessions Judge V.K. Jain at Patiala House to Judge Thareja of the rent control tribunal in Tis Hazari in North Delhi.

Meanwhile, on 7 April 2001, Keshav Kumar had approached the Supreme Court again, through a constitutional writ, no. 1535, alleging that his detention in jail was illegal. He prayed for the quashing of proceedings and the granting of immediate bail. After due application of judicial minds, the apex court refused any relief to Keshav. The petition was disposed of, with yet another direction to expedite the trial.

And so, the case lurched from one hearing to the next, for nearly eight and a half long years.

The statistics of the tandoor murder trial are staggering. By the time Judge G.P. Thareja delivered his verdict, there had been well in excess of 450 court dates. By now an assistant commissioner,

Niranjan Singh had sat through some 370 of them. The court had convened, then adjourned, more than 225 times without transacting any business. Matters pertaining to the trial were listed in the Delhi High Court more than fifty-five times in response to various petitions from Sushil and Keshav. And the pair had approached the Supreme Court no less than seven times.

Despite his contribution to the trial's mind-numbing delays and his courtroom posturing, Judge Thareja showed himself to be exceptionally thorough. The court heard testimony from eighty-five witnesses for the prosecution from the original list of ninety-nine. When the prosecution dropped eighteen witnesses who had turned hostile, Judge Thareja took the unusual step of calling and examining seven of these as witnesses for the court.

There was good reason for the prosecution not calling these witnesses, and this was no better demonstrated than by Mahesh Prasad's disgraceful performance in court. Called to the stand late in the trial, the security guard completely repudiated his earlier statement, contradicted other witnesses and indulged in a flight of fancy that could only have been at Sushil Sharma's behest. He claimed not to have seen Sushil at the Bagiya on 2 July 1995. Instead, he stated he had chased two unknown men from the scene, who, he declared, were responsible for the charred corpse on the tandoor – which, he swore, was that of a man.

What penalty for perjury? None, it seems, in India.

Dr M.P. Sarangi's testimony was equally unhelpful. When he was called before the court from Jamaica in November 2002, he virtually read out his report, sticking cussedly to his widely discredited claims that Naina's body had been mutilated, and that she had died from loss of blood. One wished he had just saved himself the airfare.[190]

At least some of the witnesses' testimony had merit. The first court witnesses Judge Thareja called were Jaswant Kaur and Harbhajan Singh, Naina Sahni's parents. Seven years after their daughter had been brutally murdered, they took the stand in court to give evidence. Both confirmed that Naina had been married to

Sushil. And they had not, they said, heard from their daughter since July 1995.

It was the least Naina's family could have done for her. And the time for it was right too. Naina's mother, Jaswant Kaur, died a few months before the verdict was pronounced.

21

Judgement

Sushil Sharma's final advocate for the trial was P.K. Dham. Dham's appointment came after a hiatus of around fifteen months, which began when K.K. Sood was appointed additional solicitor general on 31 August 2000. Naturally, Sood was denied permission to continue acting for Sushil. A retired judicial officer, P.K. Dham had earlier assisted Sood when he acted for Sushil. He agreed to represent him as amicus curiae in November 2001, after most other advocates approached by the court had declined to take on the case: the early allure of the tandoor murder for Delhi Bar's finest had waned. Sushil, who had earlier been fussy in his choice of counsel, had simply left the matter of his new counsel to the court. He quickly agreed to P.K. Dham representing him.

Sushil would be well represented by Dham, who faced the difficult task of reviewing all the evidence of the preceding six and a half years and summing up the case.

As is quite routine in criminal cases, Sushil made a statement at the conclusion of the prosecution's case under Section 313 of the Criminal Procedure Code. His statement went much further than denying his involvement in Naina Sahni's killing and the burning of her body. He seemed intent on denying almost every aspect of the prosecution's case, even entering the realms of fantasy in doing so.

First, he claimed he was in Tirupati between 1 July and 6 July

1995, and only reached Madras on 7 July. He then stated he had telephoned his family residence in Pitampura from Madras and discovered that ACP Alok Kumar had visited there on 3 July. He alleged Alok Kumar had removed his vehicle, revolver, licence for the revolver and ammunition from his home and left a message for Sushil to telephone him. Sushil claimed that when he telephoned, ACP Alok Kumar told him to obtain anticipatory bail or he would be arrested.

There were but a few threads of truth in Sushil's fabric of lies. He stated that he went to a police station in Madras on 8 July and showed some Delhi Police officers at the station the papers for his bail. They then took him to Bangalore and claimed he was arrested there on 10 July. He admitted that the Maruti car, registration number DL-2CA-1872, belonged to him, but maintained that it was removed by Delhi Police from his residence at Pitampura and moved to Malcha Marg.

Sushil eventually admitted, in response to a question posed to him, that he lived with Naina Sahni in Gole Market. His other statements about Naina were intended to be exculpatory. But they did little for him other than show that he was prepared to deny their relationship, deny his love for his wife and disrespect her memory. His court submissions made a mockery of his show of grief at the mortuary in the days following Naina's death.

Sushil made mention of the help he had given Naina in getting admission to a correspondence course in the mid-1980s and how he had assisted her with her pilot training. He alleged that from 1994 to January 1995, Naina lived in a flat opposite Birla Mandir as a paying guest, and that she had lived apart from her family after a disagreement with her father. She had, he claimed, lived in a flat at Gole Market for some time, and he had visited her there occasionally. He denied he had been married to her and stated that he had not seen her since January 1995: 'She remained busy in her career and I remained involved in politics.'

Sushil's defence was essentially a blanket denial of the prosecution's claims. The defence produced no witnesses, and the defence case was underpinned by legal arguments and an extremely shaky alibi. The work of the counsel, therefore, was largely confined to discrediting witnesses and raising doubts about circumstantial physical evidence. It hardly bears mentioning that there was an abundance of witnesses and evidence connecting Sushil to the murder.

P.K. Dham rose to the challenge before him. He quoted from the pre-Independence English precedent telling the court that in the administering of justice, 'one golden thread is always to be seen that it is the duty of the prosecution to prove the prisoner's guilt …'[191] Dham stated that if evidence could be read to point two different ways, whichever was favourable to the defendant must be adopted. He highlighted the numerous minor discrepancies between the witnesses' accounts in an effort to discredit the prosecution's case and proffered alternative scenarios to the prosecution's version of events.

Although the State's case was strong, Special Public Prosecutor Ahluwalia assiduously rebutted P.K. Dham's arguments. In any case, it would take a sympathetic judge indeed to overlook the sheer preponderance of evidence stacked against Sushil. Judge Thareja had shown himself to be thorough, but seemed to go to great trouble to show that he was being fair to Sushil. It remained to be seen if he would give credence to the faint shadow of doubt P.K. Dham and his predecessors had managed to cast on Sushil's culpability.

⚖

In the years that Sushil and Keshav's trial lingered on the court roster, there was another highly publicised Delhi murder case, and it had a number of parallels with the tandoor murder. It, too, was about a well-connected man brutally killing a woman known to him, and it sparked a similar conflagration of public outrage. The cases also shared a presiding judge: Additional Sessions Judge Gyan Prakash Thareja.

Santosh Singh was tried for the rape and murder of twenty-five-year-old law student Priyadarshini Mattoo on the afternoon of 23 January 1996. The verdict in the case nearly four years later placed the judiciary in the public spotlight, and it was found badly wanting. The furore in the wake of Judge Thareja's decision was undoubtedly the low point of his judicial career.

The Priyadarshini Mattoo murder case began under my jurisdiction, which was, at that time, the Southern Range of Delhi. An FIR had been lodged against Santosh Singh before the murder at Vasant Kunj Police Station, for stalking and harassing the victim; Singh was immediately the prime suspect for her murder. Shortly after the discovery of her body in a bedroom in her home, no. B-10/7098, Vasant Kunj, South Delhi, the South-West District Police arrested Santosh Singh at his home. I later had the case transferred to the CBI.

The controversy over the CBI's handling of the case is beyond the purview of this book. Suffice it to say there were numerous anomalies in the prosecution's case. And unlike the tandoor murder, which set the media hounds off on a frenzy of investigation, crucial circumstances surrounding the Priyadarshini Mattoo murder were never revealed by the press.

There is perhaps no better illustration of the Delhi media's inconsistency than in the contrasting approach it took to the tandoor murder and the Priyadarshini Mattoo case. It seems that while journalists were hell-bent on uncovering the lurid details of Naina Sahni's personal life after her murder, just months later, they seemed at pains to protect Priyadarshini Mattoo's image. Perhaps their appetite for smut had been temporarily sated by their excesses in the tandoor murder reportage. It may also be that it suited the press to accentuate other aspects of the case, such as the alleged interference of senior policemen and bureaucrats.

Whatever the reason, the public heard a bowdlerised account of Priyadarshini Mattoo's tortured relationship with Santosh Singh. The aggravated stalking and harassment she suffered at his hands was given a great deal of media coverage, as were her family's desperate efforts to protect her from him. What was overlooked in the press, and glossed over in the courtroom, was that Priyadarshini Mattoo and Santosh Singh were involved in a deeply troubled love affair and were, it seems, physically intimate.

The relationship was vehemently opposed by Priyadarshini's family, though it appears Singh's parents went so far as to make overtures for a matrimonial alliance at one stage. Priyadarshini was hopelessly caught between her parents' wishes, a new and more promising alliance, and the increasingly irrational Singh.

Nevertheless, the evidence is unequivocal that on the day of her killing, she had invited Singh to her home when he called her from a booth near his university – telephone records confirmed the call. This, despite the FIR she had lodged against Santosh for stalking, and the personal security she had sought and been duly provided by South-West District DCP U.N.B. Rao. Priyadarshini did not inform her personal security officer Head Constable Rajinder Singh from Vasant Kunj police station of her arrangement with Santosh Singh. She took pains to conceal his visit from her domestic help as well, sending him away to buy medicine and then to walk the dog so she could be with Singh at her home in private.

Without prejudice to the case presented to the court by the CBI, and to the best of my knowledge – and that of the other Delhi Police officers who did the spot inspection of the crime scene immediately after the murder and arrested Santosh Singh – the events of that afternoon were somewhat at odds with the findings of the court.

In his early interviews with the police, Santosh Singh maintained that on the afternoon of the killing, he and Priyadarshini had engaged in consensual sex at her apartment. Afterwards, he said, she asked him to write a letter withdrawing the complaint he had lodged with the Delhi University authorities, about her studying for two degrees (LLB and M. Com.) simultaneously, in contravention of the university's rules. A pen and paper were found at the scene, which seemed to corroborate this claim.

Santosh told the police that when he refused, Priyadarshini threatened to lodge a police complaint against him for breaking into her home and raping her. Singh flew into a rage, bashed her with his motorcycle helmet and fists, and then strangled her with the cord of an electric heat convector which was nearby.

Killing a defenceless woman under any circumstances is a heinous crime. But Priyadarshini Mattoo's homicide was not a premeditated act, and Santosh Singh was hardly the crazed sexual predator he was portrayed as in the media.

On the basis of what Santosh Singh told the police after his arrest, he could well have mounted an argument in court for diminished responsibility, had he so wished. And, in my opinion, instead of contesting the basic facts of the case, his lawyers could have presented the history of Singh's deeply troubled relationship with Priyadarshini Mattoo and his mental state at the time of the killing. This may have reduced the charge of murder to manslaughter, or at least lessened the degree of culpability in the eyes of the court. Instead, Singh's lawyers hoped that by discrediting the witnesses' testimony and undermining the physical evidence in the case, they could achieve an acquittal. Indeed, they were successful in this – temporarily, at least.

Judge Thareja's judgement for Santosh Singh in the Priyadarshini Mattoo murder case, which was delivered on 3 December 1999, provoked a public uproar. He would thereafter be spoken of, not as an assiduous, fair-minded judge, but as a man who knowingly acquitted a murderer.

The 449-page judgment itself was as controversial as it was verbose. Thareja lambasted Delhi Police, the CBI and senior scientists at CCMB, Hyderabad, accusing them of tacitly acting on Singh's behalf by withholding evidence. This aspect of the judgement was shocking in itself, but not nearly as shocking as the truly bizarre statement he made in finding Santosh Singh not guilty. Judge Thareja declared that 'Though I know he is the man who committed the crime, I acquit him, giving him the benefit of the doubt'.

This ironical declaration may have been a misplaced expression of the judge's ire at the prosecution, but it was viewed by most people as dereliction of duty – a judge failing to convict a murderer. Of course, had Thareja felt the evidence was poorly presented such that there was reasonable doubt as to Singh's guilt, he could simply have criticised the prosecution, issued pertinent recommendations, declared Singh not guilty, and left it at that. As it transpired, however, his judgement evoked a strong response from all quarters, quickly reaching the floor of the Parliament.

It did not bode well for Judge Thareja's career when President K.R. Narayanan, while addressing a gathering of Supreme Court judges soon after Thareja's infamous statement, said with barely concealed disgust, '... in this country, we have judges who acquit the accused, even when convinced of their involvement in the crime!' Thareja's transfer later that year to the rent control tribunal was confirmation of his ignominy. It was felt that he had been kicked downstairs for his lapse in judgement.

That was not the end of his humiliation, however.

Galvanised by the media hype surrounding the case and the sympathy it generated for the victim and her family, the CBI appealed Thareja's verdict in the Delhi High Court. Santosh Singh was portrayed by the prosecution as a sexual predator, hell bent on having the object of his obsession at any cost, without mention of some relevant facts surrounding the case. The court reversed the acquittal and criticised Judge Thareja unreservedly on 17 October 2006, describing his approach as 'perverse' and stating that Thareja had 'mauled justice ... [and] shocked the judicial conscience of [the] court'.[192]

Singh was sentenced to death on 30 October 2006. The sentence was commuted to life imprisonment by the Supreme Court in October 2010.[193]

Whether this trial and the hurly-burly in its wake affected Judge Thareja's approach in the tandoor murder case can only be a matter of conjecture. It is likely that he did face considerable pressure while delivering his judgement nearly eight and a half years after

Ravi Naina Sahni's murder. Although the High Court judgement overturning his acquittal of Santosh Singh was still ahead of him, Thareja surely anticipated at least some judicial condemnation for his gaffe. And the tandoor murder verdict was likely his last hurrah before retiring from the bench.

Not surprisingly then, the verdict seemed to weigh heavily on Thareja. On the appointed day for the judgement, he postponed it saying, 'Since October 27 was a holiday and the presiding officer is not well, the verdict requires two more days to be studied.' In speaking of the 'presiding officer' and his 'viral fever', he was, in fact, referring to himself in the third person with more than a touch of pompousness.

The pressure on Thareja pales in comparison to what Sushil Sharma must have gone through. Sushil had devoted all his resources and applied his obvious though misplaced intellectual abilities to run away from justice. Nearly eight and a half years of evasion would soon end. He would have to face the court's judgement and there was, he knew, a very real prospect of his receiving the death sentence.

Naturally, the strain was beginning to show on him too. Sushil had been one of the most cheerful and sociable inmates in Tihar Jail during his time in remand. He had taken it upon himself to perform regular pujas for other inmates and participated happily in jail events. His usual gregarious behaviour changed as the verdict loomed. He began to withdraw from the activities in the jail, his bravado deserted him, he began to shun company and spent time in the jail temple, praying.

The delay in delivering the judgement seemed to affect Sushil deeply. In the days before the verdict was to be announced, he trembled with fear as he boarded the jail bus on the way to Tis Hazari. On the day that Judge Thareja postponed giving his verdict, Sushil was visibly distressed. As he was led away from the court, he merely told reporters, 'I have no comment to make.' When a fellow inmate in the bus on the way back to jail advised him to prepare for the worst, he struggled to hold himself together.

For Keshav, the judgement offered quite a different prospect: while Sushil faced it with dread, Keshav was almost hopeful.

⚖

It was just after 2 p.m. on Monday, 3 November 2003. A sizeable detail from the 3rd Battalion of the Delhi Armed Police escorting Sharma and Keshav had halted for a brief photo opportunity just outside the Tis Hazari court complex. Flanked by the officers, Sushil and Keshav posed for the cameras. In just a few minutes, they would hear Judge Thareja's verdict.

Both had put on some weight in the years they had been in Tihar Jail – perhaps the prison food was not so bad, after all. Indeed, Keshav, sporting a full beard, looked radically different from the thin, uptight-looking man he had been eight years earlier. Sushil adopted a showman's stance, but his forced smile only made him look sinister, with his three-day growth of stubble and slicked-back black hair.

The appearance of the pair gave more clues about their feelings. Keshav was dressed almost casually, in a green-and-blue tartan short-sleeved shirt, whereas Sushil wore a formal white shirt, with a pen clipped inside the breast pocket, a saffron-coloured inner garment peeping out at the neck. While both men looked anxious, one could discern some relief on Keshav's face. Sushil's confident expression looked feigned, the dark rings under his eyes a sign of sleepless nights. Keshav was leaning away from Sushil, as if after all the years of suffering for his former boss and friend, he wanted to be free of him. And he had good reason to believe he would soon be.

By this time, everyone had become accustomed, if not inured, to the noise that invariably attached itself to the hearings. The scene that day was reminiscent of the time when we first brought Sushil from Bangalore.

Around 1 p.m., a horde of activists from the glibly named All India Crime Prevention Society gathered outside the Tis Hazari court complex, in anticipation of the 2 p.m. verdict. They were soon joined by a veritable army of women who claimed they were from the All India Federation of Housewives (AIFHW), but were probably Opposition cadres. They joined in chanting anti-Congress and anti-Sushil slogans, beating drums to keep time: 'Tandoori Congress hai hai'.

The AIFHW women had come well prepared. They had brought a mock tandoor in the form of a steel drum, and one woman embarked on a street theatre performance, re-enacting the burning of Naina Sahni's corpse. The 'tandoor' was emblazoned with the word 'khooni' (murderer); the paint dripping down the yellow drum was meant to simulate the flow of blood. Chanting slogans, the women held up placards, along with mirrors, to signify that the Congress should reflect on its criminal culture. Predictably, the tandoor and other props were to make further appearances in the coming days.

The courtroom was crammed with lawyers, reporters, activists and curious members of the public – and that was after some activists had been herded out of the court complex by the police. Judge Thareja postponed the pronouncement of his verdict for an hour, perhaps to allow for some of the hysteria to subside. Sushil was confined in the court lock-up till the hearing began.

The gallery would soon see a different side of Additional Sessions Judge Thareja. Throughout the trial, the judge had catered to Sushil's whims and fancies – be it in acceding to his demand for a highly qualified government-appointed counsel or in granting adjournments. Those assembled would soon understand that for all his indulgence of Sushil and his truant counsel over the preceding years, this judge meant business.

Judge Thareja delivered his verdict with due gravitas before the court: 'Charge under section 302 of the Indian Penal Code against Sushil Sharma for causing the murder of Naina Sahni is proved beyond doubt.[194] Accused Sushil is held guilty and convicted under section 302 of the Indian Penal Code. The charge of criminal conspiracy to cause disappearance of evidence of murder stands proved against both accused Sushil and Keshav. Both accused are guilty and convicted under sections 120B and 201 read with 120B of the Indian Penal Code.'

Judge Thareja exonerated Jai Prakash Pehlwan, Rishi Raj Rathi and Ram Prakash Sachdeva of charges under Section 212 of the Indian Penal Code, observing that the charge of harbouring Sharma had not been established against them. He made no mention of the fact that the prosecution had earlier petitioned the court to not pursue the charges against them.

The written judgement was fairly nondescript and considerably shorter than that in the Priyadarshini Mattoo case. The judge was careful with his words, to shield himself from public disapproval. But amidst the turgid language, some poor grammar, the odd malapropism – he referred to the bench as the 'backside' – Thareja gave diligent consideration to the evidence in the case.

Once Judge Thareja delivered his verdict, his role in the case would be over, aside from the sentencing. But the case seemed to have fired his righteous indignation. He let fly with a volley of stinging criticisms and firm recommendations, as if by his word alone he could right the myriad wrongs of the case.

Judge Thareja was particularly scathing of IAS officer D.K. Rao. He asked the Delhi chief metropolitan magistrate to prosecute him, and requested that the Gujarat chief secretary take appropriate administrative action against the employees of Gujarat Bhavan in Delhi for 'dereliction of duty'.

He then issued an admonishment to senior bureaucrats in general which, given the nexus between politics, bureaucracy and crime in India, was astoundingly naïve: 'IAS officers should ensure that politicians who try to exploit their position as public servants by using extra-constitutional influence are not encouraged in any manner.'

He did not spare the Congress party either, invoking religious imagery to make his point: '*Rajniti ka asli rang kya hai, koi mujh se poochche. Maine rajniti ka sabse ghinona chehra dekha hai. Jiske aage*

Ravan ke dus chehre bedaag hain! (Someone ask me what the true colour of politics is; I have seen it at its horrendous worst. Even the faces of the ten-headed Ravana are flawless in comparison!)'

Thareja also voiced his disapproval of Special Public Prosecutor A.P. Ahluwalia, saying, 'You (Ahluwalia) being specially appointed have not done anything which a normal prosecutor would not have done. The State is acting as if it is in link with the accused. It has created loopholes. Why is the State behaving like this?' As far as the investigating team was concerned, this was just humbug. Heaven knows what precipitated Thareja's vindictive outburst against Ahluwalia. He had run a decent, successful prosecution and deserved credit for his efforts.

Judge Thareja was perhaps more justified in his criticism of Dr Sarangi, who, he declared, had 'obstructed the administration of justice'. He then went further, expressing doubt about the doctor's motives: '… his conduct does not seem to be above board'.[195] Upon hearing of the judgement, the good doctor must have wished he had stayed in Jamaica a year earlier, instead of appearing in court.

In short, Judge Thareja spared nobody. Sushil seemed deeply perturbed by the verdict, but kept his emotions in check. His supporters, who used to stand around eyeballing witnesses, were absent. There was nothing they could do for him now. Sushil remained sombre, with a deadpan expression on his face. '*Mein kuch nahin boloonga* (I won't say anything),' he muttered as he was led away by the police.

The verdict could hardly have come as a surprise to Sharma. Despite his considerable efforts to pervert the course of justice, Kunju and D.K. Rao's testimony, along with Keshav's later admissions, weighed heavily against him. And that was without the virtually unassailable physical evidence linking him to the crime. He must have been terrified at the prospect of the sentencing, which Judge Thareja had postponed till Wednesday, 5 November 2003.

The tandoor murder case was replete with coincidences, quirks of fate and apparent coincidences. One of the latter was another verdict in a murder case against another Congress party functionary named Sharma, the very same day that Sushil and Keshav were convicted on 3 November. Almost simultaneously with Judge Thareja's judgement, in Ghaziabad, Uttar Pradesh, former Congress council candidate Mukesh Sharma was found guilty, along with twelve of his henchmen, of killing political activist and theatre personality Safdar Hashmi.

Hashmi was bludgeoned with iron bars in front of a large audience at his outdoor play on 1 January 1989. Stricken, he was taken to a trade union office by his supporters, in a vain attempt to keep him safe. Hashmi's attackers followed soon afterwards and attacked him again. He died in hospital the following day. A local resident, Ram Bahadur, was shot dead in the same incident.

It was nearly fifteen years later that a judgement was delivered in the Safdar Hashmi case. In the years that the trial had dragged on – with inordinate delays on the part of the defendants, the prosecution and the police – two of the defendants had died. It is worth noting that at the time the verdict was handed down, Uttar Pradesh was governed by the Samajwadi Party – a party then in opposition to the Congress – and it is remarkable that the judgement coincided with that of the tandoor murder. The effect of the combined verdicts could only have been devastating for the Congress.

Of course, the politics of the tandoor murder trial were far from our minds when Thareja pronounced his guilty verdict. To say the investigation team was elated would be an understatement. We were also relieved. After the largest manhunt and the most extensive investigation in memory, and eight and a half years of courtroom intrigues, justice had triumphed. Money, criminal conspiracy and thuggery had been set aside. The system had ultimately done its job, and Naina Sahni's killer would now face due punishment. It was cause for celebration.

I summoned Head Constable Kunju to my office to thank him on behalf of the force for his efforts. Not only had Kunju's dogged policing uncovered the terrible crime in the first instance, his courage since then had been the mainstay of the case. He had been unwavering in the face of Sushil's attempts to bribe and threaten him, and firm against a tag-team onslaught from the various counsels in court.[196] His conduct throughout the saga set an example for his peers and immeasurably boosted the public's perception of the force.

My brief meeting with Kunju was reminiscent of his promotion in Commissioner Nikhil Kumar's office those many years ago, the day after his discovery at the Bagiya. I had little time to spend with him though, as I was inundated with telephone calls, some congratulatory and others, predictably, from my media contacts seeking comments on the verdict. I was also more than a little preoccupied with a minor but disturbing intrigue, which had begun with an invitation from former Delhi Police Commissioner Nikhil Kumar.

Nikhil had retired from Delhi Police in 1997 – pushed out after some political manoeuvring by Home Secretary K. Padmanabhaiah – and was then serving on the National Security Advisory Board. The following year, he would be elected to the fourteenth Lok Sabha. His interest in what he described to the press as the biggest case of his career had not waned with the years or with his change in profession. He was, in his understated manner, overjoyed at the verdict, and invited members of the investigating team to his home on Akbar Road for a celebratory afternoon tea.

Strangely, the then Delhi Police Commissioner R.S. Gupta was none too pleased with Nikhil's tea party, which he seemed to view as a personal affront, or at least a threat. Gupta ordered his officers not to attend which was perplexing, since Nikhil's informal gathering was planned for 5 p.m., outside working hours. Gupta's order signalled his insecurity and petty-mindedness, not to mention a singular lack of generosity. It hardly endeared him to the officers on the investigating team, most of whom – including the star of the investigation, Niranjan – quietly ignored Gupta's order.

I would have liked to go too, but I was by now the joint commissioner of Delhi Police and Commissioner R.S. Gupta's second-in-command insofar as Range policing was concerned. I could not jeopardise our relationship by openly defying him. And I would not attend any such event furtively, as if I should be ashamed. Gupta's petulance rankled, until his retirement three months later. Hopefully his successors were more magnanimous towards him than he was to his team.

At any rate, we had other, more important matters ahead of us.

The courtroom was crammed with spectators from all walks of life on Wednesday afternoon, including reporters and lawyers, and the crowd spilled from the courtroom into the corridor. Outside the Tis Hazari court complex, women from the BJP's Mahila Morcha set the scene with a rowdy demonstration before the 2.30 p.m. hearing. Waving placards and chanting, they demanded that Sushil be hanged. Their anti-Congress slogans were even more strident. The hearing was delayed by twenty-five minutes because Special Public Prosecutor Ahluwalia had difficulty threading his way through the noisy throng outside the court and the shoulder-to-shoulder bodies inside to reach the bar table.

The hearing began with Ahluwalia submitting that Sushil's crime qualified for the 'rarest of rare cases'[197] which, he declared, warranted a death sentence. His arguments didn't get very far before the drama outside and inside the court merged. A group of the Mahila Morcha protesters surged into the court complex, and only the detail of police personnel present there managed to prevent them from storming the courtroom. Nevertheless, their chanting almost drowned out Ahluwalia's arguments. When the spectators and even the lawyers in the courtroom joined the cacophony, Judge Thareja called a halt to the proceedings.

Before adjourning proceedings to the following day at 2 p.m., Thareja set down some ground rules for the hearing. Entry to the courtroom, he ordered, would be restricted to fifteen lawyers and one representative from each newspaper or television channel. He bitterly criticised Delhi Police Commissioner R.S. Gupta, as if he was personally responsible for the commotion. He directed the commissioner to ensure there were no further demonstrations to disrupt the court, until the conclusion of the sentencing.

This was not, of course, the end to the drama. It just became quieter the following day, focused on the counsel's arguments – some of which seemed more than a little strange given the circumstances – and the judge's posturing before handing down the sentences.

Curiously, P.K. Dham declined to argue for his client, on the basis that Sushil had 'full faith' in the court and was ready to accept whatever sentence the court imposed on him. This, from an offender who had dedicated a fortune and prodigious energy to courtroom intrigues and had attempted to obstruct justice for nearly eight and a half years.

It was hard to ascertain whether Sushil had had some kind of epiphany or was simply keeping his powder dry for an appeal. If his past performances were any indication, it would be the latter. It seems prayer had given him some comfort though, as he awaited the court's decision. He had intimated to his fellow prisoners that he trusted his fate to the Almighty and this seemed to be the case – at least for the moment. Keshav, however, had very different prospects, and his counsel made every effort to further arguments in his favour.

Making pleas for leniency was almost a pointless exercise: Keshav had already been incarcerated nearly one and a half years beyond the maximum sentence for his crime. Perhaps his counsel V.K. Ohri wanted to spare him the added pain of an onerous fine. He may also have wished to finish the case with a flourish; the press reports would surely record his valiant efforts on his client's behalf, however futile they may turn out to be.

Whatever his motivation, V.K. Ohri took centre stage on 6 November and made impassioned pleas on his client's behalf. Some of his submissions were mildly ridiculous, just as Keshav's first court submissions had been, when he denied any knowledge of burning Naina Sahni's corpse. Keshav, Ohri asserted, was never the manager of the Bagiya: he was only a senior waiter, and an illiterate one at that. He was the sole breadwinner of a family with children, and he was not in a position to pay a hefty fine for his offence, he stated. Of course, Keshav had not been in any position to be a breadwinner for more than eight years now.

Judge Thareja, who had discarded his earlier, somewhat indulgent and whimsical persona, strutted into the limelight then, to place his moral outrage on record. The 'tandoor is a place for cooking food, not roasting the human soul,' he declared, and Keshav was 'not to be spared' for his crime.

Never mind Keshav's marathon eight-and-a-half years' remand for an offence that would normally attract a sentence of two years or less. Nor that the law dictated that Keshav's remand be considered time served. Thareja was constrained to release him upon sentencing. For all the sound and fury at the 6 November hearing, the only issue of contention was whether the court would issue a fine to Keshav and, if so, the quantum of the fine.

After labouring the point of Keshav's culpability – speaking to the gallery and burnishing his record – Judge Thareja adjourned proceedings to the following day, 3 p.m., for the sentencing.

Just before the appointed time, on Friday, 7 November 2003, Sushil and Keshav were brought to the court in their usual shuttle bus from Tihar Jail, under heavy police guard. The contrast between the pair never seemed greater than when they stood for the customary media photo, with a throng of Delhi Armed Police in khakis as extras, outside the court complex. Sushil wore his trademark white shirt and a haunted look, dark rings etched deep under his eyes. Keshav looked almost nonchalant in comparison, in an inky, long-sleeved shirt. There was a huge disparity, too, in the large contingent of family members awaiting Keshav in the courtroom and Sushil's few supporters. Sushil had only one or two friends in the gallery, along with a cousin who had been by his side throughout the trial.

Judge Thareja had issued specific orders to limit the crowd in the court for the finale, but it seemed to have had little effect. The courtroom was as full as it could be without spectators standing on top of each other's shoulders. Again, the crowd overflowed into the corridor beside the courtroom, and spectators pressed together, necks craned and listening intently. It was a mercy that the last hearings of the trial took place in Delhi's cooler months.

For reasons best known to himself, Judge Thareja delayed convening the court for half an hour, and the tension in the packed room escalated as the minutes ticked by. The drama of the tandoor murder would soon be over, and Judge Thareja would shuffle out of the public gaze, back to the rent control tribunal. The public gaze, it must be said, was truly fierce, and in the final act of the most publicised trial of his career, he would have known that he had to play his role with suitable verve.

When he finally assumed his place at the bench at 3.30 p.m., Judge Thareja quickly got down to business. This was not a case, he said, where the 'accused has committed the crime and, thereafter, left the dead body so that it is properly disposed of according to the customs of the society to which the deceased belong … Profaning the dead body by burning in tandoor of a helpless and hapless woman whom the convict exploited for his own political career is an insult to womanhood … A dead body is respected in this country. Everyone reveres a dead body on its last journey. By burning the dead body, the accused intended that Naina Sahni should go unwept, unsung and unheard.'

Throughout, Sushil's eyes were closed, his lips moving in silent prayer. He asked the constable who was escorting him and holding his hand with intertwined fingers, to release his grip so he could cover his face in supplication. The constable refused, but Sushil continued his entreaties to the Divine.

Nothing could save Sushil from Judge Thareja's sentence now. The court was hushed for his words, the culmination of the trial: '[The] death sentence is [the] only appropriate sentence. For charges of murder, Sushil Sharma shall be hanged by the neck till he is dead.'

Sushil bowed his head in the silence after the sentence was pronounced. His face flushed as he fought back tears and as the gravity of Judge Thareja's sentence registered with the assemblage, he willed upon his features a stoic expression and lifted his head. The buzz of a hundred conversations filled the courtroom. Sushil was soon besieged by reporters. All they could elicit from him after some minutes was the stoic statement: 'I respect the order of the court.' He seemed more or less resigned to his dire fate, gesturing skyward and smiling ironically at talk of an appeal.

The judge had some more punishment in store for Sharma. For his offence under Section 302 (murder) of the Indian Penal Code, he was fined ₹2,000 – a trifling amount for the crime – and for the offence under Section 201 (destruction of evidence) read in conjunction with section 120B (criminal conspiracy) he was awarded a seven-year term of rigorous imprisonment and a fine of ₹10,000. With his stringent sentencing of Sushil, Judge Thareja was finally free of the albatross around his neck: his baffling decision for Santosh Singh nearly four years earlier.

Judge Thareja was equally firm in sentencing Keshav, given the circumstances of his crime and the charges for which he was convicted. He imposed the maximum seven-year jail sentence on him for destruction of evidence, along with a fine of ₹10,000. This set off an immediate frenzy amongst Keshav's numerous siblings – he had five brothers and four sisters – who rallied around him to collect the money so he could be freed immediately.

Keshav himself was elated, but he wished to voice his dissatisfaction about his time in remand to the media persons clustered around him. 'After being in jail for eight years, there is no reason to be happy. I will seek compensation for the extra time spent behind bars,' he said. His brother Lalit interjected, 'We are happy [Keshav] will be released and we will pay the fine right now ... Please ask any further questions to his brother, who is an advocate.'

Still, Keshav spoke briefly to reporters about Sushil. After sidestepping questions about the death sentence his former boss and friend had just received, he claimed, rather unconvincingly, to have only known him for six months before the murder. He also stated that he had not met Sushil even once while they were in jail.

At the end of the sentencing for their two very different crimes arising from the same chain of events, from fates interwoven by their desperate acts on 2 July 1995, the men were finally parted. Keshav could now return to his Uttam Nagar home and his children, while Sushil was back in his Tihar Jail cell as convict number 31, awaiting a hearing in the High Court for confirmation of his death sentence.

The tandoor murder trial was over. The story, though, is far from finished.

22

Aftermath

A few days after his release from Tihar Jail, Keshav Kumar visited me at my office. I was quite taken aback. Rarely had I been willingly visited by a criminal, and never before by one whom I had helped send to jail. I liked a minimum of fussy protocol around me, and allowed easy access for everyone when I was at work, so Keshav had no difficulty in being shown into my office when he presented himself.

His visit was a courtesy call, and he approached me in a cordial manner. He appeared calm, and eager to share his joy at his release. I could not detect the least trace of smugness; Keshav was merely peaceful. Not having much time amidst my heavy schedule, and without really knowing how to react to his unexpected visit, I could only wish him well and tell him to lead his life honestly and without violating any laws.

Later I came to know that I was not the only one Keshav visited. He met all his relatives and friends and almost everyone connected with the case – including the police and those he was close to in the Congress party – just to let everyone know that he was going right back to his life as it was before his incarceration. He would pick up its loose strands, he said, draw them together and move forward. And he did just that. He secured employment with some cable television operators in north-west Delhi and rose in that industry to earn a decent livelihood.

Sushil's prospects after the trial were, of course, decidedly bleaker. In the days after the sentencing, he remained deeply perturbed, and a deathly pallor of fear hung over his features. But he soon came to terms with his fate through prayer, declaring to his fellow inmates, '*Upar-wale ko jo manzoor hai woh hoga* (Whatever the One above decides is fine with me).'

Indeed, incarceration seems to have kindled a spiritual renaissance in Sushil, as it often does with prisoners facing the ultimate punishment. He never forgot his daily prayers – morning and evening – and because of his brahminical upbringing and knowledge of the scriptures and incantations, Hindu inmates would often turn to him for their prayers and rituals. Sushil Sharma became something of a pujari in Tihar Jail.

There is a strange irony in this. In his earlier life, Sushil was a political fixer, the man one would consult to alleviate bureaucratic woes and problems – for a fee, of course. The same man who had killed his wife and burned her body now became one whom other inmates turned to for alleviating their spiritual woes and to seek God's blessings.

Just the same, the wheels of justice continued to turn slowly for Sushil Sharma and he did not trust his fate to God alone. Although he had earlier vowed not to challenge his sentence, Sushil's instinct for self-preservation would ultimately prevail and he took his appeal to the Delhi High Court.

His conviction and sentence were confirmed by the High Court on 19 February 2007.

Sushil was to remain in Tihar Jail no. 2 – where he was, by all accounts, a model prisoner – for several more years before there was any development in his case. His final appeal, which was lodged in 2007 in the Supreme Court, was eventually decided more than eighteen years after Naina Sahni's murder, on 8 October 2013. The Supreme Court bench of P. Sathasivam, Ranjana Prakash Desai and Ranjan Gogoi confirmed Sushil's conviction, but commuted his death sentence to life imprisonment. The justices found that Naina Sahni's murder was 'the outcome of [a] strained personal relationship. It was not an offence against ... society'.[198]

For what it is worth, the Supreme Court judgement was promulgated by a woman, Judge Ranjana Prakash Desai, whereas the earlier High Court decision rejecting his appeal outright had been issued by a bench comprising only men. Besides sparing Sushil from the gallows, the Supreme Court made findings favourable to his release on parole. The judgement noted, 'It is ... not possible in the facts of the case to say that there is no chance of the appellant being reformed and rehabilitated.'[199]

The court based this critical observation on Sushil's unblemished jail record. There were no instances of Sushil indulging in violence or showing aggression towards other prisoners. He had reportedly been a well-behaved inmate and took some interest in teaching other prisoners how to use computers, for which he earned ₹90 per day to spend in the prison canteen. It is hard to say, though, whether his exemplary prison behaviour was a calculated effort to make parole or whether he had actually forsaken his earlier criminal habits.

At any rate, it seems that Sharma adjusted to prison life remarkably well. In recent times, he has spoken in interviews of his disciplined habits in jail, which are a far cry from his reprobate days in politics. He credits his new perspective on life to chanting the Gayatri mantra, which he apparently does religiously for three hours every day.

If his interviews are to be believed, Sushil has dedicated his time to taking courses and developing himself, and he also keeps prodigious notes of his life in jail. Incredibly, he claims to have written the basis of a three-month course for couples planning to get married, which he has done in cognisance of his own mistakes. He says that the 'problem [with marriage] is that when a husband loves the wife, then, because of the physical intimacy, it leads to high expectations. A man should love his children and just respect the wife', and he adds, apparently without irony, 'expectations kill marriage.'[200]

After the Supreme Court's sympathetic decision in 2013, and

more than eighteen years spent in jail, Sushil applied for early release. On Tuesday, 15 September 2015, his application to the Delhi High Court to be freed on parole was successful, and the court passed an order that he be released that day from Tihar Jail.

Unfortunately for Sushil, the director general of prisons had other views on the matter. The Tihar Jail authorities simply ignored the order until Sharma's advocate Sumeet Verma brought the matter to the court's attention on 19 September. Justice Siddharth Mridul of the Delhi High Court responded indignantly, summoning Ajay Chaudhary, the OSD (Officer on Special Duty) to Delhi's lieutenant governor, to explain why the order had not been complied with. He also upbraided the jail authorities for flouting his order. He ruled that until Sushil's plea for early release was decided by the sentence review board and confirmed by the lieutenant governor, he would be unconditionally free on parole.

Sushil was finally released, after twenty years, one month and two days in Tihar Jail. In the first few hours of his freedom, he reportedly took his mother to a temple in north-west Delhi. Although he was technically – and unconditionally – free, he kept a low profile in the following months, staying at his family's Pitampura home. He received few visitors and prayed for hours on end.

Predictably, Sushil was reluctant to engage with the media, but he spoke with at least one reporter in the days after his release. More than two decades after murdering his wife, Sushil issued what was his first, however qualified, public admission of guilt: 'That day is a blur … It happened in a fraction of a second, and that one second has cost me twenty years.'[201] There was no talk, it seems, of Naina Sahni. Sushil apparently did not express any regret for killing her, or for her family's loss.

While time and his long jail sentence had softened the media and the judiciary's stance against Sushil, this wasn't the case with the bureaucracy, it turned out. In January 2016, the sentence review board recommended the rejection of Sushil's plea for early release from prison.

In the Delhi High Court on 22 January 2016, Justice Siddharth Mridul confirmed that Sushil would remain free on parole until the board's recommendation was confirmed by the lieutenant governor. He also made mention of Sushil's right to lodge a petition with the court, challenging the lieutenant governor's order, should he be sent back to prison.

At the time of writing, Sushil Sharma was back in Tihar Jail. It is most likely, though, that he will be released on parole, sooner or later: In any disagreement between the bureaucracy and the judiciary, the latter must prevail. If he is not released in the next few years, his incarceration will run contrary to Tihar Jail practice. The jail has a long-standing policy of not keeping an inmate longer than twenty-five years. And Sharma holds an unenviable record: He has apparently served the longest term in Tihar Jail without parole for a life sentence. His life sentence is thus unlikely to see him die in jail – that is, unless he falls seriously ill in the near future.

I would not be disappointed if the court ultimately decides to release Sushil on parole. Nothing can compensate for a murder, the loss of another human being. More than twenty years of languishing in an overcrowded jail – the best years of a man's life, no less – is no small price to pay, however. Sushil Sharma has undoubtedly suffered for his crime. Some would even say he has paid his debt to society.

Sushil's suffering may seem like that of one man, but the havoc he wreaked on the Congress party affected countless Indians, and immeasurably so. The tandoor murder and the ensuing public furore had far-reaching consequences. It has played no small role in changing the nation's political landscape. Within months of the murder, the political scene would experience a seismic shift, perhaps the most notable since Independence.

In 1995, the Congress party still dominated national politics, and it had held sway for all but a few of the nearly forty-eight years since Independence in 1947. The Congress's various opponents – barring the Janata Party government of 1977–79, which had been brought to power in a backlash against the Emergency – only managed to cling to power for some months at a time before the Congress inevitably swept them from office. Not one prime minister from a party other than the Congress had held power for a full five-year term of the Lok Sabha.

Rather than its opponents winning power, it was the Congress which lost it, and power was generally the Congress's to lose. Access to the reins of power was restricted too. The Congress's rule was dynastic, with members of the Nehru-Gandhi family steering the party and the nation alike. The greater part of the ruling elite until the mid-1990s were associated with the party.

A series of scandals leading up to the tandoor murder, along with the case itself, weighed heavily against the Congress. The electorate began to view 'Gandhi's party', which had strayed far from its roots, with a more critical eye – and it continues to do so. The Congress no longer enjoys the luxury of being the default governing body of the land.

In the absence of empirical data – authoritative polling on specific political issues was almost nonexistent in the mid-1990s – it would be hard to demonstrate a clear causal relationship between the tandoor murder and the subsequent shift in support against the Congress party. Equally, it would be pointless to maintain that the massive negative publicity from the case was not material to this shift – that it had no part in the party's fall from grace.

Certainly, the Congress government of the then prime minister P.V. Narasimha Rao was beset with scandal and corruption, quite apart from its association with Sushil Sharma. But the tandoor murder was its crowning ignominy. The publicity it generated could not have come at a worse time for the Congress. General elections were held nine months after Naina Sahni's murder; the case made regular headlines during the campaign period. And in August 1995, just days after the tandoor murder charge sheet was submitted in court, the sensational Vohra Report, which probed the criminalisation of politics, was released to the Indian Parliament.

The report confirmed what many had known for years: That an

unholy politician–criminal nexus was 'virtually running a parallel government, pushing the state apparatus into irrelevance'.[202] Sushil Sharma's misdeeds that came to light in the aftermath of the tandoor murder gave ample evidence of this nexus. Sharma became the poster boy for organised crime running rampant in the corridors of power, which the Vohra Report, even in its redacted form, laid bare.

Nothing was redacted in the murder reportage. And, by association, the ghastly details of Sharma's crimes ineluctably besmirched his party. The odium that the murder invoked, the naked disgust felt universally in response to the grisly killing of Naina Sahni, became a rallying point for the anti-Congress sentiment that had been brewing for years. Opposition figures, quick to exploit the opportunity, successfully painted Sharma as an archetypal Congress villain. His horrific deeds at the Bagiya and backroom deals in the party were conflated, caricatured even, for devastating anti-Congress propaganda.

Combined with the other scandals the Congress faced at the time, the tandoor murder proved to be disastrous for the party. Opposition parties made good their vow to make the crime a 'central plank' of their campaigns before the general elections were held in April–May 1996. The Congress polled its worst result yet in the elections, and it would not govern again at the Centre for eight years.

Sadly, whether it is the Congress in power or the BJP-led National Democratic Alliance (NDA) government headed by Prime Minister Narendra Modi, the taint of criminality on the Indian Parliament remains. A staggering 186 members of the 543-seat Sixteenth Lok Sabha either have criminal records or face criminal charges. This represents some 34 per cent of the lower house of Parliament, an increase of 4 per cent from the previous Lok Sabha. Of the sixty-six members in the council of ministers, thirty-one have criminal charges pending against them. It is worth noting here that of the alleged offenses of India's wealthy and powerful, only a small fraction find its way into the courts. Politicians are especially adept at silencing witnesses and most police investigations of their crimes yield 'no prosecutable evidence'.

In fact, entrenched criminality within the major parties has only worsened since the tandoor murder, and a resurgence of lumpen, thuggish elements in our political life gives fresh cause for alarm. Intolerance and violence have become widespread, threatening minorities and stifling public discourse. One can only hope that an educated, discerning electorate will demand higher standards of conduct from its representatives in the coming years.

The fallout from the tandoor murder case is a cautionary tale for Indian leaders of all political hues. Few could have believed before this murder that a crime of passion, especially one committed by a man who had never held public office, could have such drastic consequences. Without question, the imbroglio in the wake of Naina Sahni's killing helped bring down India's national government and humbled the country's dominant political party. While crimes of passion continue to take place, as they have since time immemorial, and cases still grind on for years through India's courts, the nation's political scene – it can be said, without hesitation – would never be the same again after the tandoor murder.

Endnotes

1. The author was then an Additional Commissioner of Police, responsible for the New Delhi Range. Delhi, in those days, was divided into three ranges and nine police districts, three in each range.
2. For policing, a district is headed by a DCP. New Delhi is one of the nine districts and is considered the VIP district, as it contains the seat of power and the diplomatic enclave.
3. A tandoor is a large, pot-shaped oven intrinsic to the cuisine of northern India. With a belly diameter as large as three feet, it has burning charcoal at the bottom and a mouth at the top. Almost every restaurant and caterer in the region uses a tandoor.
4. Public Call Office – a telephone booth, usually privately operated, for public use. The mobile network was introduced in Delhi a few weeks after this evening, but it would be years before the mobile phone proliferated.
5. A VIP housing complex for members of Parliament on Janpath, with its rear grounds opening on to Janpath Lane.
6. Throughout my time with Delhi Police, I advocated placing the single word 'Police' on the two sides and bonnet of all police control room vehicles instead of 'PCR'. This was finally done years later when Brijesh Gupta was Commissioner.
7. Staff receiving distress calls in the PCR are often troubled over the fact that many people prefer to telephone the police (100), despite there being an independent emergency number to call the fire

brigade directly (101). Perhaps this is because people are confident of an assured response from the former.
8. Literally a 'record of observations by five people'. A panchnama is a first listing of the evidence and findings that a police officer makes at the scene of a crime. The document has to be signed by the investigating officer and two impartial witnesses.
9. *Prem Shankar Shukla vs Delhi Administration*. 1980, 1980 AIR 1535, 1980 SCR (3) 855.
10. An autonomous public sector undertaking of the government of India under the Ministry of Tourism.
11. The CFSL functions under the Central Bureau of Investigation (CBI), which handles federal crimes and important cases referred to it for investigation. The CFSL also caters to the forensic needs of Delhi Police cases.
12. Written communication.
13. First Information Report (FIR) is a document prepared by police when they receive information about the commission of a cognizable offence.
14. A formal document of accusation, which is submitted to the court by law enforcement agencies in India defined as such in Section 173 of the Criminal Procedure Code of India.
15. Editorial, *The Tribune*, 6 July 1995.
16. Ibid.
17. A cane mat used as a window screen or a floor mat, or even a mattress when made of finer reed.
18. Ram Niwas Dubey, Sushil and Naina's cook and peon, had no such difficulty. He promptly identified the anklets as those of Naina, on 27 July. Ref.: Statement of Ram Niwas Dubey, FIR 486/95, 302/201/212/34 IPC, which was sworn before Metropolitan Magistrate T.S. Kashyap.
19. Sreerupa Mitra Chaudhury, 'Naina's character was maligned', *The Times of India*, 16 January 1996.
20. Naina's family's apparent disavowal of her, or her strained relationship with them, was given much print coverage in the wake of her murder:
    In 'Who will perform the last rites?', *The Pioneer*, 15 July 1995, stated that her father Harbhajan Singh had said, '*Woh meri beti nahin hai* (She is not my daughter)'. The article went on to state that Naina's

brother had said, 'she had left the family about three years ago and therefore, had nothing to do with them.'

In 'Naina's death a result of our sins', *The Statesman*, 15 July 1995, stated that 'Mr Singh recalled on the fateful day before her death, Naina while passing by had wished him and he had replied *'Jaa mar! All dar asyogi to koi baat hoti* (Get lost; you should have come home instead)'.

Sreerupa Mitra Chaudhury, in 'Naina's character was maligned', (*The Times of India*, 16 January 1996), made mention of her mother Jaswant Kaur stating that '... many people wrote that even at home she was loved only by me and not by other members [of her family]. This is not true.' That her mother felt moved to say this to a reporter says much of the damning of the family in the wake of the murder.

The assertion that Naina's brothers had joined Sushil in beating her was published in 'Sushil met Solanki on murder night', *The Pioneer*, 19 July 1995.

21. 'Fresh witnesses "incriminate" Sharma', *The Hindu*, 28 July 1995. 'Sushil was "obsessed" with Naina's "affairs": Police', *The Patriot*, 29 July 1995.
22. 'Sushil, Naina had strained relations', *The Times of India*, 6 July 1995.
23. 'Fresh witnesses "incriminate" Sharma', *The Hindu*, 28 July 1995.

Photograph caption: 'Matloob Karim, who claims to have been the lover of Nainu Sahni ...', *The Pioneer*, 28 July 1995.

'Sushil was "obsessed" with Naina's "affairs": Police', *The Patriot*, 29 July 1995.

'Naina ties with Matloob led to murder', *TheTimes of India*, 29 July 1995.

'Cook's testimony vital in tandoor case', *The Hindu*, 3 August 1995.

24. 'Victim and accused', *The Pioneer*, 29 July 1995.
25. The Nanavati Commission Report, released in February 2005, found 'that there is credible evidence against Shri Jagdish Tytler to the effect that very probably he had a hand in organising attacks on Sikhs in the 1984 riots.' Thousands of Sikhs were bludgeoned, hacked and burned to death in the aftermath of the assassination of Prime Minister Indira Gandhi that year.
26. Archana Jahagirdar, 'Courting Disaster: Deceit and violence

instrumental to ill-fated relationship of Sushil Sharma and Naina Sahni', *India Today,* 31 July 1995.
'Stern action against culprits demanded – Conman to a Congman', *Hindustan Times*, 6 July 1995.
'Who wasn't behind him', *The Pioneer,* 9 July 1995, stated that 'Congress sources said Sharma [had] a dubious record of petty offences such as rioting and misbehaving with women …'
'Polite for some, haughty for others', *The Times of India*, 23 July 1995, made mention of his 'roving eye … [and] extra-marital affairs.'
'Is police adopting double standards?', *The Tribune*, 19 July 1995, stated that 'It is also no secret that Sushil Sharma and Naina Sahni were living like husband and wife and yet both of them were having affairs with whomsoever they liked for political and monetary benefits.'
27. Editorial, *The Indian Express*, 6 July 1995.
28. Editorial, 'Covering up a murder', *The Tribune*, 6 July 1995.
29. The Emergency, a suspension of democratic governance in 1975–77, remains the most controversial period of India's post-Independence history. Prime Minister Indira Gandhi had a state of emergency declared across the nation. She was swept from office in subsequent elections, on 23 March 1977, but managed to regain power in the year-end national elections of 1979.
30. 'Congress rivals blame each other', *The Statesman*, 6 July 1995.
31. 'Latest Census data shows youth surge: Nearly 41% of India's population is below the age of 20', 13 January 2016, http://www.firstpost.com/india/latest-census-data-shows-youth-surge-nearly-41-of-indias-population-is-below-the-age-of-20-2581730.html, accessed 24 January 2018.
32. 'Naina's body shifted to AIIMS', *The Pioneer*, 18 July 1995; 'Victim and accused', *The Pioneer*, 29 July 1995.
33. 'No politician charge sheeted in Naina murder case', *Hindustan Times*, 29 July 1995; 'Sushil Sharma was in Delhi on July 3, says partner', *The Times of India*, 15 July 1995; 'Sushil, 4 others charge sheeted', *The Hindu*, 29 July 1995.
34. 'Naina's body shifted to AIIMS', *The Pioneer*, 18 July 1995.
35. 'Murder mystery deepens: Naina was shot, reveals second autopsy', *The Times of India*, 14 July 1995.

36. Central Forensic Science Laboratory report, no. F-692, 26 July 1995.
37. Board of surgeons constituted vide order no. F.8/70/95-HP-II, Government of NCT of Delhi Home (Police-II) Dept. Delhi.
38. Dr Bharat Singh was for long the head of the police hospital. He conducted hundreds of post-mortems at the Sabzi Mandi mortuary.
39. 'Naina's body sent for 2nd post-mortem', *The Patriot*, 14 July 1995.
40. 'Murder mystery deepens: Naina was shot, reveals second autopsy', *The Times of India*, 14 July 1995.
41. 'Second postmortem report can't be "too conclusive" – DNA sampling "difficult"', *The Statesman*, 14 July 1995.
42. 'Doctors involved in first autopsy may be booked', *The Patriot*, 15 July 1995.
43. Shakti Sharma, 'Naina was shot – First autopsy report may have been done under pressure: Medical board recovers bullets from skull, neck', *The Delhi Midday*, 13 July 1995; 'Naina's body sent for 2nd postmortem', *The Hindu*, 14 July 1995; 'Doctors involved in first autopsy may be booked', *The Patriot*, 15 July 1995.
44. Gautam Roy, 'Action against forensic expert', *The Pioneer*, 1 August 1995.
45. *Dr Murari Prasad Sarangi vs Ministry of Health and Family*, 30 October 2012, Central Information Commission, File no. CIC/LS/A/2012/001908.
46. 'Tandoor murder suspect Sharma granted bail', *The Indian Express*, 8 July 1995.
47. *The Indian Express*, 9 July 1995.
48. Public Interest Litigation.
49. *The Statesman*, 9 July 1995; 'Metro News', *The Indian Express*, 9 July 1995.
50. 'We pass dozens of bail pleas daily: Madras Judge', *The Indian Express*, 9 July 1995.
51. Ibid.
52. 'Bail Extraordinary', editorial, *The Statesman*, 10 July 1995.
53. *The Indian Express*, 17 July 1995.
54. *P.D. Joseph vs Sushil Sharma, the Inspector of Police, Connaught Place Police Station, New Delhi and the Commissioner of Police, Egmore, Madras*, Laws (Mad)-1995-7-112.
55. 'All for the glimpse of a murderer', *Hindustan Times*, 12 July 1995.

56. 'Sushil: Bitta responsible for murder', *Hindustan Times*, 12 July 1995.
57. 'Sushil alleges Bitta is behind conspiracy – Suspect brought to Delhi', *The Times of India*, 12 July 1995.
58. 'Evening News', *Hindustan Times*, 11 July 1995.
59. *Hindustan Times*, 13 July 1995.
60. Somnath Batabyal, Rahul Pandey, 'No stranger to violent ways', *The Pioneer*, 12 July 1995.
61. Vijay Jung Thapa and Archana Jahagirdar, 'Act of barbarism –Scandal and speculation follow former Youth Congress (I) leader Sushil Sharma's arrest in the tandoor murder case', *India Today*, 31 July 1995.
62. Somnath Batabyal, Rahul Pandey, 'No stranger to violent ways', *The Pioneer*, 12 July 1995.
63. Ibid.
64. 'Sushil remand', *Hindustan Times*, 16 August 1995; Sanjay Kaw, 'Police let Sushil turn a proclaimed offender', *The Times of India*, 18 August 1995; 'Sushil Sharma acquitted of beating up DCP's orderly', *The Delhi Midday*, 24 May 1996.
65. Vijay Jung Thapa and Archana Jahagirdar, 'Act of barbarism –Scandal and speculation follow former Youth Congress (I) leader Sushil Sharma's arrest in the tandoor murder case', *India Today*, 31 July 1995.
66. In CRMP 5519/95 of 22 September 1995.
67. Vijay Jung Thapa and Archana Jahagirdar, 'Act of barbarism –Scandal and speculation follow former Youth Congress (I) leader Sushil Sharma's arrest in the tandoor murder case', *India Today*, 31 July 1995.
68. 'Sushil had stoned Vajpayee', *The Times of India*, 14 July 1995.
69. Somnath Batabyal, Rahul Pandey, 'No stranger to violent ways', *The Pioneer*, 12 July 1995.
70. Shailesh Shekhar, 'Sushil had close links with Tejpal', *The Times of India*, 23 July 1995.
71. 'Encounter' is a word that has taken on quite a sinister meaning in India. It describes a purported exchange of fire between police or armed forces with terrorists or gangsters, which usually results in at least one fatality. There is often controversy as to whether an encounter involved a genuine exchange of fire, or was simply a means of covering up an extrajudicial killing.

72. Statement of Ram Niwas Dubey, FIR 486/95, 302/201/212/34 IPC, 27 July 1995.
73. Blackening someone's face, a fairly common tactic in high-profile agitations on the subcontinent, is done with the obvious intention of humiliating and shaming the subject.
74. When a person is charged with a serious offence, and the court believes he has absconded or is concealing himself to avoid an arrest warrant, the court may make a proclamation demanding his appearance within thirty days. If he does not appear, he is deemed a proclaimed offender.
75. Vijay Jung Thapa and Archana Jahagirdar, 'Act of barbarism – Scandal and speculation follow former Youth Congress (I) leader Sushil Sharma's arrest in the tandoor murder case', *India Today*, 31 July 1995; 'Stern action against culprits demanded', *Hindustan Times*, 6 July 1995.
76. 'Sushil's IAS friend is controversial', *Hindustan Times*, 16 July 1995.
77. Vijay Jung Thapa and Archana Jahagirdar, 'Act of barbarism – Scandal and speculation follow former Youth Congress (I) leader Sushil Sharma's arrest in the tandoor murder case', *India Today*, 31 July 1995.
78. 'Silence reigns in Sushil's house', *The Indian Express*, 15 July 1995.
79. 'Sushil's parents avoiding publicity', *The Statesman*, 13 July 1995.
80. 'Silence reigns in Sushil's house', *The Indian Express*, 15 July 1995.
81. Ibid.
82. *Vakalatnama* is an Urdu term for a document empowering a lawyer/advocate to act for his client. This term is widely used in Indian courts, even though it is not defined either in the Power of Attorney Act, 1882, or in the Civil Procedure Code, 1908.
83. 'Crowd bays for blood, Sushil's BP rises', *Hindustan Times*, 16 July 1995.
84. 'Sushil thinks he can get away', *The Times of India*, 20 July 1995.
85. 'More clues add fire to tandoor – Bullets found in Naina's body', *The Indian Express*, 14 July 1995.
86. 'Minister sheltering him: Former TNCC chief', *The Pioneer*, 10 July 1995.
87. 'Sushil alleges Bitta is behind conspiracy: Suspect brought to Delhi', *The Times of India*, 12 July 1995.

88. Ramesh Vinayak, 'Beant assassination: Reconstructing the killing', *India Today*, indiatoday.in, 27 March 2012, accessed on 29 May 2017.
89. 'Sushil met Solanki on murder night', *The Pioneer*, 19 July 1995.
90. 'I will be out on bail in two months: Sushil – Naina case almost solved: Police', *The Pioneer*, 15 July 1995.
91. Janak Singh, 'Sushil allegedly admits murder, says Naina was dating two VIPs', *The Times of India*, 13 July 1995.
92. 'Padmanabhaiah pulls up police officials', *The Statesman*, 23 August 1995.
93. Harish Gupta, 'Another twist to Naina case', *The Tribune*, 25 July 1995.
94. Vijay Thakur, 'Sushil "confesses" to murder of Naina – Police get remand for 10 days: Counsel allowed during interrogation', *The Patriot*, 13 July 1995.
95. 'Is police adopting double standards?', *The Tribune*, 19 July 1995.
96. 'They want Bhagat in the dock', 'Evening News', *Hindustan Times*, 19 July 1995.
97. 'Congress rivals blame each other', *The Statesman*, 6 July 1995.
98. 'They want Bhagat in the dock', 'Evening News', *Hindustan Times*, 19 July 1995.
99. Ibid.
100. Janak Singh, 'Sushil allegedly admits murder, says Naina was dating two VIPs', *The Times of India*, 13 July 1995.
101. Janak Singh, 'Mukul Wasnik, Kalpnath, deny liaison with Naina', *The Times of India*, 14 July 1995.
102. 'Is police adopting double standards?', *The Tribune*, 19 July 1995.
103. Ibid.
104. 'Bandhu denies favouring Pahalwan', *The Indian Express*, 18 July 1995.
105. 'Congress rivals blame each other', *The Statesman*, 6 July 1995.
106. 'Is police adopting double standards?', *The Tribune*, 19 July 1995.
107. 'Sushil met Solanki on murder night', *The Pioneer*, 19 July 1995.
108. V.R. Mani, 'Sushil had fled Delhi by road', *The Times of India*, 18 July 1995.
109. 'When Sushil Sharma "wept like a child"', *The Hindu*, 16 July 1995.
110. 'Sushil breaks down at mortuary, admits "mistake"', *The Pioneer*, 16 July 1995.

111. 'Sushil in judicial remand – "I'm innocent, Bitta is not"', *The Pioneer*, 27 July 1995.
112. Vijay Jung Thapa and Archana Jahagirdar, 'Act of barbarism –Scandal and speculation follow former Youth Congress (I) leader Sushil Sharma's arrest in the tandoor murder case', *India Today*, 31 July 1995.
113. 'Confidential DNA report handed over to police', *The Indian Express*, 24 July 1995.
114. 'Head removed, being sent to Punjab labs', *Delhi Midday*, 20 July 1995.
115. 'Who will perform the last rites?' *The Pioneer*, 15 July 1995.
116. 'Women's groups offer to cremate Naina Sahni', *The Pioneer*, 18 July 1995.
117. 'Second post-mortem confirms police doubts', *The Hindu*, 15 July 1995.
118. 'Head removed, being sent to Punjab labs', *Delhi Midday*, 20 July 1995.
119. 'Women bodies come forward to do Naina's last rites', *The Patriot*, 18 July 1995.
120. 'Parents perform Naina's last rites', *The National Herald*, 3 August 1995.
121. *The Times of India*, 3 August 1995. Photographs of Naina with Rajiv Gandhi had earlier appeared in many newspapers, including *The Times of India* and *The Indian Express*.
122. 'Naina's "True Story"', *The Times of India*, 2 August 1995.
123. 'Sushil, Naina had strained relations', *The Times of India*, 6 July 1995.
124. 'Sushil was "obsessed" with Naina's "affairs": Police', *The Patriot*, 29 July 1995.
    'Naina's cremation likely today', *The Times of India*, 28 July 1995.
125. Matloob Karim's statement, FIR 486/95, 302/201/212/34, IPC, which was sworn before Metropolitan Magistrate T.S. Kashyap on 27 July 1995.
126. Archana Jahagirdar, 'Courting Disaster: Deceit and violence instrumental to ill-fated relationship of Sushil Sharma and Naina Sahni', *India Today*, 31 July 1995, also made mention of how Sushil helped Naina's aunt in a land dispute in an effort to woo her.
127. 'Massive manhunt for murder accused', *The Hindu*, 6 July 1995.
    'Sushil Sharma Still at Large', *The Patriot*, 7 July 1995.

128. Matloob Karim's statement, FIR 486/95, 302/201/212/34, IPC, which was sworn before Metropolitan Magistrate T.S. Kashyap on 27 July 1995.
129. 'Massive manhunt for murder accused', *The Hindu*, 6 July 1995.
    'Fear, shock leave the neighbours tight lipped', *Hindustan Times*, 6 July 1995.
    'Hunt on for Sushil Sharma – Ex-Delhi Youth Congress chief possible had second paramour', *The Indian Express* 7 July 1995.
    'Stern action against culprits demanded – Conman to a Congman', *Hindustan Times*, 6 July 1995.
    Archana Jahagirdar, 'Courting Disaster: Deceit and violence instrumental to ill-fated relationship of Sushil Sharma and Naina Sahni', *India Today*, 31 July 1995.
130. Ibid.
    'Stern action against culprits demanded – Conman to a Congman', *Hindustan Times*, 6 July 1995.
131. 'Sushil allegedly admits murder, says Naina was dating two VIPs', *The Times of India*, 13 July 1995.
    'I will be out on bail in two months: Sushil – Naina case almost solved: Police', *The Pioneer*, 15 July 1995.
132. Naina's family's circular, 'The True Story', stated that Naina was in 'close contact ... with the then Prime Minister Rajiv Gandhi ...'
133. Ibid. The same circular stated that 'Rajiv Gandhi had assured her funds from the NSUI to train for a commercial pilot'.
134. Sumit Mitra, 'Tandoor love and care – The gruesome murder in Delhi should compel the Congress to cleanse itself', *The Telegraph*, 13 July 1995.
135. Matloob Karim's statement, FIR 486/95, 302/201/212/34, IPC, which was sworn before Metropolitan Magistrate T.S. Kashyap on 27 July 1995.
136. Give evidence on behalf of the prosecution in exchange for a reduced sentence or pardon. In the US, the equivalent expression is to 'turn state's evidence'.
137. 'Keshav sent to judicial remand', *The Times of India*, 14 July 1995.
138. D.K. Rao was ostensibly ousted from the IAS, after a tumultuous career and much on-and-off disciplinary action, nearly two decades later. Ref.: 'High-profile bureaucrat Devarapalli Kishore Rao

"unceremoniously" dumped, say babus', *DNA*, 20 May 2011, www.dna.com, accessed on 30 May 2017.

'YSR Congress nominates Gujarat IAS Devarapalli Kishore Rao from Bapatla in Seemandhra', www.babusofindia.com, 17April 2014, accessed 19 May 2017.

139. 'D.K. Rao holds the key in tandoor case', *The Pioneer*, 17 July 1995.
140. 'Police questioning IAS officer', *The Statesman*, 15 July 1995.
141. 'D.K. Rao holds the key in tandoor case', *The Pioneer*, 17 July 1995.
142. 'Why did not Rao inform the Police himself?', *The Indian Express*, 1 August 1995.
143. A link magistrate is a relieving magistrate.
144. 'Is police adopting double standards,' *The Tribune*, 19 July 1995.
145. 'BJP for suspension of Gujarat IAS officer', *The Indian Express*, 15 July 1995.
146. 'IAS officer, witness in Naina Sahni case, gets promotion', *The Sunday Times*, 18 August 1995.
147. Sanjiv Sinha, 'I'm just a scapegoat: D.K. Rao', *The Indian Express*, 18 July 1995.
148. 'Sushil's IAS friend is controversial', *Hindustan Times*, 16 July 1995.
149. Ibid; Aditya Sinha, 'Tytler sat over charge sheet against D.K. Rao for a year', *The Pioneer*, 19 July 1995.
150. 'Tytler says Sushil a psychopath; police say psycho tests not needed', *Delhi Midday*, 18 July 1995.
151. Public Interest Litigation: Criminal Writ no. 417/95.
152. *Sushil Sharma vs The State (Delhi Administration)*, 1996 CriLJ 3944, Delhi High Court, U. Mehra, 1 May 1996.
153. Ibid.
154. Ibid.
155. Julio Ribiero, 'Stray thoughts on the tandoor murder – 'Heat and sound over man's inhumanity', *Afternoon Despatch and Courier*, Bombay, 25 July 1995.
156. Sanjay Kaw, 'Prosecutor shown door for leaking information', *The Times of India*, 16 July 1995.
157. Sreerupa Mitra Chaudhury, 'Desperate Sushil engages battery of lawyers', *The Times of India*, 28 July 1995.
158. *The Times of India*, 28 July 1995.
159. 'Sushil threatens Matloob', *The Times of India*, 27 July 1995.

160. 'Ballistic experts join probe', *Hindustan Times*, 17 July 1995.
161. 'Sushil being tortured: Counsel', *The National Herald*, 18 July 1995.
162. 'Sushil's remand extended by 4 days', *The Times of India*, 23 July 1995.
163. 'Sushil gives clean chit to Keshav', *The Indian Express*, 10 August 1995.
164. In CRMP 5519/95.
165. 'DCP threatening me in jail: Sushil', *The Indian Express*, 9 November 1995.
166. 'Sushil alleges police tried to eliminate him on way to Tihar', *The Times of India*, 14 December 1995.
167. Since the year 2010, the sanctioned strength of Delhi Police is 84,536.
168. Girja Shankar Kaura, 'Tandoor murder case hogged the limelight', *Hindustan Times*, 22 December 1995.
169. 'Sushil alleges police tried to eliminate him on way to Tihar', *The Times of India*, 14 December 1995.
170. 'Naina is alive, says Sharma', *The Times of India*, 3 January 1995.
171. Ibid.
172. 'Efforts on to make Sushil insane, says counsel', *The Times of India*, 12 January 1996.
173. Sushil's imagination working overtime', *The Times of India*, 19 January 1996.
174. Admiral Sardarilal Mathradas Nanda, PVSM, AVSM, famously known as the 'Bomber of Karachi', was a four-star admiral of the Indian Navy. He served as the eighth chief of the naval staff from 1 March 1970 until 28 February 1973. In spite of his stellar military reputation, his post-retirement business dealings became mired in controversy, with persistent allegations of cronyism and kickbacks.
175. 'Who accompanied Sushil?' *The Times of India*, 6 February 1996.
176. There is a trial court lock-up at each court complex in Delhi to hold prisoners brought from Tihar till they are returned after the court appearance.
177. This was indeed correct, insofar as Naina's family was concerned.
178. Sanjay Kaw, 'Defence says Naina Sahni committed suicide', *The Times of India*, 19 April 1996.
179. Ibid.
180. Amicus curiae in Latin literally means 'a friend of the court' – a bystander who suggests or states some matter of law for the assistance

of a court. In India, though, it is also used by the courts to refer to an advocate provided to an alleged offender as defence counsel at state expense.
181. As recorded by the judge in the order sheet.
182. Court clerk.
183. Nitish K.Singh, 'Say thank you to Constable Kunju – the cop who assured slayers get convicted', *Today*, 4 November 2003.
184. 'Team effort got Sharma convicted', *The Times of India*, 5 November 2003.
185. '4 of Babloo Shrivastava gang nabbed, kidnapped jeweller rescued', *Business Standard*, http://www.business-standard.com/article/pti-stories/4-of-babloo-shrivastava-gang-nabbed-kidnapped-jeweller-rescued-115090801273_1.html, 8 September 2015, accessed 17 May 2017.
186. 'Order on Keshav bail plea reserved', *The Pioneer*, 3 August 1995.
187. 'Court extends Keshav custody', *The Indian Express*, 11 July 1995.
188. Under Section 446 of the Criminal Procedure Code.
189. Yogesh Kumar, 'Vegetable vendor recalls the threat', *The Statesman*, 5 November 2003.
190. 'Jamaica doctor deposes in tandoor murder case', *The Times of India*, 18 November 2002, https://timesofindia.indiatimes.com/india/Jamaica-doctor-deposes-in-Tandoor-murder-case/articleshow/28683133.cms, accessed 29 May 2017.
191. *Woolmington v. DPP* [1935] UKHL 1, House of Lords, 23 May 1935.
192. *State (through CBI) vs Santosh Kumar Singh,* Crl. Appeal no. 233 of 2000, 17 October 2006.
193. *Santosh Kumar Singh vs State Th. Cbi,* 6 October 2010, Supreme Court of India, Crl. Appeal no. 87of 2007.
194. As if to emphasise Sharma's guilt, Judge Thareja omitted the operative word 'reasonable' when pronouncing his judgement.
195. *State vs Sushil Sharma, 19 February 2007,* High Court of Delhi, Crl. Appeal827/2003.
196. 'People for Breakfast: Abdul Nazeer Kunju', *The Pioneer*, 5 November 2003.
197. This refers to a landmark Supreme Court ruling in *Bachan Singh v. State of Punjab*, AIR 1980 SC 898: 1982 (1) SCALE 713: (1980) 2 SCC 684: (1983) 1 SCR 145. The court held that the 'imposition of [the]

death sentence should only be in [the] rarest of rare cases.' Aside from a mention of 'extreme depravity', the ruling did not define what constituted such a case, and this has been the subject of much debate since.
198. *Sushil Sharma v. State (NCT of Delhi)*, Criminal Appeal no. 693 of 2007, 8 October 2013.
199. Ibid.
200. *Behind Bars – Prison Tales of India's Most Famous*, Sunetra Choudhury, Roli Books, 2017.
201. Prawesh Lama and Soumya Pillai, '1 second cost me 20 years: Tandoor murder convict Sushil Sharma', *Hindustan Times*, 23 September 2015.
202. Vohra, N. N., Chapter 3.4, p.3, The Vohra Committee Report, October 1993.

Acknowledgements

There are many to thank.

First, David Davidar and Krishan Chopra, then of Penguin India, who first prevailed on me to write about the tandoor saga, and whose belief in me I could not honour twenty years ago because I could not, and would not, submit my manuscript as long as the trial remained unfinished.

My thanks are also due to the countless crime reporters and columnists all over, whose enthusiasm and hard work was of immense help to me in compiling this reportage-driven account.

Next in line, my own personal staff, and especially my then staff officer Harsh Mitter, who first put together for me the skeletal data that eventually grew into this book.

My gratitude, too, to my early readers, Monica Dutta of Sai Krishna Associates and philanthropists Veronica and Rina Kamath, who took time off to read and review the manuscript, and offered suggestions and corrections.

Also to my friends Namami Ghosh, who helped me edit the initial work and Carl Harte, who helped transform the manuscript from a policeman's report into a gripping story.

And, of course, I am grateful to Karthika V.K. of Westland and her team for making this book a reality.

www.ingramcontent.com/pod-product-compliance
Lightning Source LLC
LaVergne TN
LVHW010310070526
838199LV00065B/5512